OUR BABIES HAVE DIED

Stories of Miscarriage, Stillbirth and Neonatal Death

OUR BABIES HAVE DIED

Stories of Miscarriage, Stillbirth and Neonatal Death

Compiled by
Annette Spence, Natalina Scapin,
Anne Bowers, Sabina Nyssen

SANDS (Vic)
Stillbirth and Neonatal Death Support (Inc)

First published in Australia 2008
by Michelle Anderson Publishing Pty Ltd
PO Box 6032 Chapel Street North
South Yarra 3141, Melbourne, Australia
Email: mapubl@bigpond.net.au
www.michelleandersonpublishing.com
tel: 03 9826 9028   Fax: 03 9826 8552

Cover illustration: Meredith Forster
Typeset by Midland Typesetters, Australia
Printed by Griffin Press, Adelaide

National Library cataloguing-in-publication entry

Title: Our babies have died : stories of miscarriage, stillbirth and neonatal
    death / compiled by Annette Spence and SANDS (Vic).

ISBN: 9780855723873 (pbk.)

Subjects: SANDS (Vic)
        Infants—Death.
        Parent and child.
        Stillbirth—Psychological aspects.
        Infants—Death—Psychological aspects.
        Bereavement.

Other Authors/Contributors: Spence, Annette
                        SANDS (Vic).

Dewey Number: 306.9

Our Babies Have Died is a joint effort. The order of authorship
does not imply order of seniority or contribution.

Dedication

❧

A life conceived
A life remembered
A life mourned
In loving memory

Acknowledgements

❧

Our Babies Have Died would not exist without the initial concept, subsequent drive and direction from Annette Spence. Her idea to publish a book such as this, and her tireless work to bring the final product to fruition, is something to which the word thank you does not suffice. Our gratitude is also extended to her husband Michael for his patience and support throughout the two years it has taken for this book to become a reality.

Annette had a committee who worked alongside her on this project, and we acknowledge the time and commitment of Natalina Scapin, Anne Bowers and Sabina Nyssen in their role as members of this committee.

SANDS (Vic) owes a huge debt of gratitude to Michelle Anderson Publishing for her belief in this book and its concept. She has enabled our idea of creating a book of experiences of bereavement to become a reality.

Thank you to SANDS (Vic) Committee of Management for its ongoing support throughout this project, Don Coulson for his expert advice, Meredith Forster for her beautiful sketch on the front cover, and Professor Paul Monagle for his kind words of introduction.

And most importantly, we would like to express our heartfelt thanks and admiration to everyone who submitted their story for their courage and generosity in sharing their very personal thoughts, deep emotions and the lives of their babies. Without these stories, this book would not exist.

Contents

❦

Introduction

❦

I feel very privileged to have been asked to write an introduction for this book, "Our Babies Have Died: Stories of Miscarriage, Stillbirth and Neonatal Death" compiled by Annette Spence, Natalina Scapin, Anne Bowers and Sabina Nyssen on behalf of SANDS (Victoria).

I first became involved with SANDS in 2000 when I was asked on behalf of The Royal Children's Hospital to manage issues that arose out of the 'organ retention after autopsy' scenario. I was struck at that time by the honesty and generosity of spirit of the people involved with this organisation, hence it came as no surprise to me that so many people have been willing to contribute and share their stories in this book. I congratulate them and thank them for their honesty and ability to share their private thoughts around their experiences after the death of their baby.

The death of a child is a personal tragedy for any family, no matter what the circumstances. For those of us who have never experienced it first hand, and even for those of us who are professionals working in this field, it is hard to understand exactly what it means for each family. Over the years I have learned that the concept that 'people get over it' is false. The grief related to the death of a child remains with parents always. Parents will be functional, move on and continue with careers and family and all the things one does in life, however that grief is always there, just below the surface and at times will resurface, sometimes when least expected. One of the underlying features of the death of a child is that death does not break the bond between a parent and their child. The love and care parents have for their children while they are living, remains with them even after death.

The stories contained within this book demonstrate this depth of emotion but perhaps more importantly, they demonstrate that there is no typecast for how one should feel after the death of a baby. Everyone is different and everyone's reaction, response and ability to deal with different scenarios will be different. I think this is the value of this book for bereaved parents, families, friends and health care professionals who work within this field. My hope for people reading this book is not that they will find a story similar to their own because that would be unlikely but that instead, they will understand that their story is their own and that they can be encouraged and supported to find their own path, knowing that there are others who can support and help them through organisations such as SANDS.

I hope that in reading this book, people will realise they are not alone in their journey, however long that journey takes and wherever it may take them.

Professor Paul Monagle
Department of Paediatrics
The Royal Children's Hospital
Parkville Victoria

My Prize

❧

I knew what was coming. I couldn't see properly, I could barely speak, but I could hear, and I understood.

'Have you told her yet?' I heard a voice ask.

Instinctively knowing what that meant, I managed through the pain, the haze, and the absolute dread of what was to come to utter the words.

'You've got something to tell me, haven't you?'

Then the sentence was delivered. The one that would change my life instantly, and will stay with me forever.

'We had a little girl . . . and we lost her.'

Alarms went off, both the real one in the room in the form of the monitor on my heart, and the one inside me telling me that my child had died. The shock of that sentence hit me over and over, until finally the external alarms I kept on triggering were turned off, leaving only the deafening internal hell that couldn't be silenced.

'What do you want to call her?' I was asked.

'If it was a girl, her name was always going to be Jessica,' I said. 'Just because she's dead doesn't mean she doesn't deserve that name.' So Jessica it was, and Jessica it is. Jessica – my first-child.

My prize awaits

Up until that moment I was so naive about so many things – pregnancy included. It had taken me sixteen months to fall pregnant. I thought it was never going to happen. Then, when

I was told that I would have to be referred to a specialist the next month, I fell pregnant instead.

My pregnancy progressed normally until twenty weeks, at which time I contracted a flu or a bug or whatever was going around at the time. I also, at this same time, began experiencing stomach pains and vaginal discharge. I attempted to see my specialist regarding this, but was informed I wouldn't be seen as he didn't want to catch my bug. I took myself to a GP – not my own (she wasn't available) – and was told not to worry about the pain and discharge. These two problems continued and increased in intensity long after my bug had disappeared. I went to my own GP, so concerned I embarrassingly took samples of this increasingly coloured discharge, and was told not to worry. I brought these concerns up again at my next specialist appointment and, once again, was told not to worry. Apparently, you see, I was a first-time expectant mother and was over-anxious. So the pain and discharge continued as did my ignored worries. It must be all right, I kept telling myself over and over again. Everyone says it is. But my instincts kept telling me it wasn't.

At thirty-six weeks, still with continued and increasing pain and discharge, I had an ultrasound that concluded my baby was 'small for dates'. At my next specialist appointment at thirty-seven weeks of pregnancy I was told this was nothing to worry about. I was also told at this appointment, which took place on a Thursday, that my blood pressure was slightly elevated and to go home and rest. I was to return to the specialist on Monday. If my blood pressure was still elevated I would be admitted to hospital. So I went home, walked in the front door, and haemorrhaged.

I can still clearly remember, at the obstetrician's instructions, sitting in the car being driven to hospital after watching my own blood stream down my legs and over my floor. I was still so naive.

I'm going to hospital to have my first baby, I can remember saying to myself. My last hours of naivety lay ahead.

I arrived at hospital at midday and felt rather special to be taken in a wheelchair because, as I would be told many times in the next few hours, 'You've had a bit of a bleed.'

My specialist performed a very painful internal examination, and told me that he couldn't determine where the bleeding had come from, not to worry, and that those of us who bleed in this manner usually proceed into labour as a natural course of action and deliver. He then informed me he would be away for the weekend, would have someone else take care of me, and that I'd be 'all done' by the time he returned on Monday. And I certainly was.

The rest of that day and evening I could explain in methodical detail, but to do so would not alter the outcome, so instead I will outline this time as briefly as possible. I lay in a room in the hospital's labour ward for hours, with increasing lower back pain that became so severe I could not roll myself from side to side in an attempt at some pain relief. Instead I had to be pushed from one side to the other intermittently by someone else. I also had more bleeding. In the evening my baby's heartbeat was monitored and found satisfactory and I was sent to a ward for the night, as it was decided it was too late in the day for inducement. I asked for a private room. I had private health insurance. I was placed in a six-bed room. I was finally allowed to eat something, for the first time since the morning, and I was so hungry I happily ate two hospital meals.

Late in the evening, with the back pain I had experienced all day still present, I got out of bed for the first time since my midday arrival. Nature called urgently. I needed assistance just to get to the toilets and back, and shortly after this felt an urgent need to return, still with very bad back pain. Upon arrival my membranes ruptured. The pain I began to experience then was indescribable. I can still remember thinking, if this is labour, it really, really hurts. I told the nurse my water had broken. I then began to shake involuntarily. She found a wheelchair and took me back to the labour ward. She said she didn't think my water had broken or that I was in labour. She said the reason she was taking me back to the delivery room was that she thought I might keep the other patients on the ward awake.

At the labour ward I somehow got myself and my attached drip up and onto the delivery table. By this stage my legs were shaking so much I was holding onto them, one at a time with both hands, to try to stop them moving so much. The midwife in attendance then attached a monitor around my stomach to determine the baby's heart rate. Figures varied from low nineties to mid two-hundreds. She decided after some more observations, with me in agony and shaking, it was time to call the obstetrician.

The obstetrician arrived quickly. He told me he would have to place a monitor directly onto the baby's head to determine if foetal stress was occurring. He also told me my water had probably not broken, but my bladder had released. Upon placing the monitor on the baby's head the same result as the previous observations ensued. The baby's heartbeat was wildly erratic. And – yes – my water had broken. The obstetrician then told me he would be getting the baby out of me the quickest way possible – by emergency caesarean.

People then began arriving quickly: a paediatrician, others whose roles I didn't know, and an anaesthetist who I informed, because it really worried me, that I'd just eaten two meals. His answer was, 'Well, at this stage anything's a risk.' I knew the baby and I were in trouble.

My baby still had a very weak heartbeat as I was taken into

theatre. I remember thinking, where there's life there's hope, but also knowing instinctively that she would not survive. I also knew instinctively the baby was a girl. As someone prepared to anaesthetise me they asked, 'Are you right?' and I firmly and calmly replied, 'Yes,' knowing, as I had for some time, that panic would accomplish nothing.

And then I woke up – to be told the baby, a girl, had died. No details, but she had died.

The next hours were a blur. Blood tests, more blood tests, moving from recovery into a private room (finally got that private room!). Blood, then plasma, given to me. More blood tests. Bleeding. Shock. More bleeding. More shock.

No prize

Then the faces began to appear, always briefly, as if they were in a terrible rush to be somewhere else, anywhere else. I remember having no control over who saw me, and who saw my baby.

I vaguely remember looking at Jessica, through the drugs and haze, but only vaguely. I was not offered the opportunity to bath her or dress her. It never occurred to me to ask. I'd never lost a baby. I asked if there was anyone I could speak to and was sent someone who, in her own words, didn't 'really deal with this type of thing.' She left her card. I was told someone would phone me after I had gone home. Nobody did.

'What happened?' everyone asked, including me.

I was told I had a placental abruption. The placenta had torn off my uterus wall before birth, instead of naturally contracting off after delivery as it should have, depriving my baby of the oxygen she needed to live inside me. I was told there is no medical explanation for this occurrence. It's just a random piece of bad luck that should never happen again, therefore I should go home, 'get over it', and just have another baby. I was also told I had a further complication to do with placental abruption resulting in my sustaining considerable blood loss, to the point where my blood was becoming too thin to circulate throughout my body, requiring both blood and plasma transfusions.

So I went home, to an empty house. The bassinet was there, waiting for her. Her clothes were there, waiting for her. I was there, waiting for her. But she wasn't there. I went home to all the what-ifs. What if she was here? What would she look like? What would I be doing? Would I be coping with a newborn baby? What if I had eaten something when I was pregnant that caused this to occur? Or worked too much, or not enough, or did this, or didn't do that? The what-ifs lasted, progressively less, for years.

Her funeral was a week after she was born. I can remember going to it barely able to walk. My specialist told me it would take me longer to recover from my caesarean than it did for others because, as he said, 'You didn't get your prize.' In other words, I had no baby for my pain, only my pain. Apparently, I was told, a graveside service was sufficient for a stillborn baby. I'd never had a child, let alone buried one, so I just went along with what I was told. I was seated next to her grave, with everyone facing me. At her funeral I was told to 'stop that crying now'. I remember thinking, if I can't cry at my own child's funeral, where can I cry?

Meeting 'new' people & the polarity of reaction

The polarity of responses I received to the death of my baby, I assume, reflected the polarity of attitudes and understanding towards the death of any baby. One side seemed to say, 'This is so bad I can't speak about it'; the other, 'What's the big deal, what need is there to acknowledge someone who didn't exist?'

I had to learn how to deal with this, and I had to learn fast. I soon identified different types or groups of people. There were those who didn't want to know me, those who wanted to know everything that had happened to me, and the few who just knew I needed acknowledgment of what had occurred and to be treated as the human being I still was. From within my new-found 'groups' of people emerged more specific identities. The information brokers who wanted to know everything so they could pass it on to others. The attention seekers (often also information brokers) who couldn't seem to bear someone else being the centre of attention besides themselves (I found they persisted through the next pregnancy too). And the compar-ers. 'Oh, I know exactly how you feel,' when they had never been through anything similar. I even had one friend compare the death of her dog to the death of my baby!

Someone even asked, 'So you had, like, a whole funeral for her and everything?' I felt like saying, No, it was bin night Tuesday night. So we wrapped her up and put her out. What do you think? 'Well dear, now you have a little angel in heaven, so isn't that lovely really?' No it isn't, I'd rather have Satan herself on earth. 'Well, it's better she died at birth, and, you know, didn't live for a while or anything, so you didn't get too attached to her.' No comment required. Or even worse, my second 'favourite': 'You know,' always in a soft, knowledgeable voice 'by the time they got her out, if she'd lived, she would have been a (even softer voice) vegetable, (now a whisper) you know. So she really is better off where she is.' Thank you for that, Einstein.

And the most popular, my personal favourite: 'Oh, you'll be right, love, you can always have another one.' Yep, that'll fix everything.

My *usually* inward sarcasm at people's comments became not only my way of coping but my own personal source of amusement at others' naivety. Without it I sometimes wonder where I would be today, and I make no apologies for it. At the time I was too timid to attempt to counter most of the comments I received or, more importantly, to at least try to educate these people regarding how I did feel and what does happen when a baby dies. Fortunately, I have evolved somewhat since then – from internal sarcasm to external constructive verbalism.

My new horns

I went back to work; what else can you do? This meant standing at a counter, with all my work 'mates' terrified of me as if I had some exotic, and perhaps even contagious, disease, and all the familiar customers coming in, smiles on their faces.

'Oh, you've had the baby, dear, what did you have?' Always in a loud voice because, I discovered, people thinking they are going to hear good news speak in louder voices. Or the more accusing, 'Gee, you're back at work quick, you must like a dollar.' And me feeling the stares in the back of my head from every person who worked there, waiting for me to deliver my now much-practised 'speech'. *We had a little girl, and we lost her at birth. It's all right though, we're fine. It's okay, if no-one told you about it, then you just didn't know. It's okay.* And thinking at the same time I was delivering my speech, which I felt like writing in huge black letters on a piece of cardboard and positioning above my head, because I was so tired of going through it, *Why the hell am I counselling* you, *this happened to me?*

Sometimes I felt scared or too guilty to laugh or smile, and others, undoubtedly without meaning to, made me feel the same way for the same things. Everyone allowed me approximately one month's grace after Jessica died, then it was supposed to be 'over'. Not mentioned again, no 'How are you?' and things were supposed to be back to normal. But my 'normal' was gone.

I felt that I had grown retractable horns that everyone knew were there but I could only let them out at home, by myself. That said I was the mother of a baby whose name I could only say when the horns were out.

My only solace was other people I found who also had horns, who had lost a baby or a child, or someone close.

I am now a mother

I wanted so desperately for people to acknowledge what had happened: that I had had a baby, that she existed, and that I was now a mother. Medically, and legally, no-one would consider disputing I had had one pregnancy, one caesarean and one child, but society, it seemed, was determined to deny these things.

I did a drawing of Jessica. I think I was trying to prove she existed. It took me about two years to finish it. I think I stretched it out that long deliberately, though perhaps not consciously, as I feared finishing it would be a little like losing her again, and it was. I wrote a poem, and some years later I wrote about her. All these things were very therapeutic. I had photos of her in the bedroom, but nowhere else in the house. Anyone who saw them in the bedroom obviously felt uncomfortable at seeing her, so I thought their heads may actually explode if they saw a photo of her in, say, the lounge room. So I kept her in the bedroom. I was now a mother, but a mother without a child, without any living children, and I felt very isolated. Mother's Day was hell.

More prizes

Six months later I was pregnant again. We were told to physically wait six months, but emotionally to wait twelve. 'But you people never listen,' I can remember being told. And we didn't. It took me twelve years to fully understand why I was told to wait twelve months. The first year really is difficult. The first Christmas, Easter, your own birthday, and then theirs. After experiencing this myself and then watching so many others I have met experience the same things, I finally understand the philosophy of what I call the twelve-month waiting period. Would knowing this, as I do now, have prevented me from becoming pregnant again six months after Jessica's death? Probably not.

I found revisiting the same hospital where Jessica was born very upsetting. Someone at the hospital said they felt I needed to talk to someone, and that someone would call me. Nobody did. The next pregnancy went very smoothly, but it was hell. I was paranoid I would haemorrhage at any moment, and that the baby would die of something else if not another placental abruption. I constantly feared I would die too. Everyone kept saying they didn't understand why I wanted another caesarean when I had been told another placental abruption was unlikely. My instincts told me otherwise. Fortunately the obstetrician I chose for this pregnancy understood to some extent my paranoia and complied. I had my second daughter taken out ten days early. Marissa was fine, perfect, and alive. I finally had my prize! Several years later I realised that I had not bled normally when I came home from hospital with her, but had in fact haemorrhaged for about a week. I just didn't know differently after Jessica. It took at least six months after she was born before I stopped expecting Marissa to die too.

We moved interstate. After having Jessica, and Marissa, in a smallish country town, I did like the anonymity of a new and larger environment.

Just over twelve months later I was pregnant again. This pregnancy did not go well. I felt awful. I was far too small, just by looking at me, for each stage of the pregnancy, but was constantly told everything was fine. Again my instincts told me something was not right. The day I was booked in for this delivery, lying in hospital waiting to go to theatre for my third caesarean at thirty-seven weeks, my water broke. I demanded the baby be taken out immediately. I was made to lie in bed until delivery, not allowed to get out. Contractions did not commence. 'Why are you so stressed?' I was asked. 'Because last time my water broke, the placenta had torn off,' I responded. But nobody understood.

Justine, another prize, was born several hours later, slightly ahead of the time I was actually booked into theatre. She was small, scrawny, and had difficulty breathing. She went to intensive care. But she was tough, and she was fine. After the caesarean I haemorrhaged for what felt like an eternity. Eventually, after over two hours in recovery, the bleeding was controlled.

Three years later the girls and I moved; I divorced. Several years later I ran into a long-time friend I hadn't seen for years. We married and, after much thought, decided to try for a baby of our own. I was so concerned after what had happened to Jessica, and my suspicions regarding Justine's pregnancy, I went to my GP to ask if there was some chance I may have some type of placental problem. My instincts told me I did. Again I was told no, to just go ahead and try to get pregnant if that was what we wanted to do. And we did. Within weeks I was pregnant for the fourth time. I insisted on seeing an obstetrician who specialised in high-risk pregnancies and, after having to reaffirm this desire, received an appropriate referral. Within ten minutes of meeting my latest, and last, obstetrician, I was informed that it was likely I have an uncommon blood-clotting disorder that causes clots to form in the placental join to the uterus wall, resulting in undersized babies and placental abruption in labour as the placenta is too weak to withstand contractions. A blood test confirmed this, and my own thoughts, fears and instincts. There was a medical reason for Jessica's death, and Justine is very lucky to be here. I had my fourth and last caesarean at thirty-seven weeks of pregnancy, and my fourth daughter, the third I got to take home. My final prize – Holly.

Constant catch-up

I never fully understood what I lost when I had Jessica until I had a live child to bring home and witness grow and evolve. As Jessica was my firstborn I feel I am playing constant catch-up regarding the loss of her entire life. There are the events, things that would normally be taken for granted, the full impact of their loss only realised as her sisters live them. The first tooth, the first steps, the first tumble, the first Christmas they understand, and birthday, and Easter. The trip to the zoo, the beach, and countless other places. The fights with the much-despised, and at the same time much-adored, siblings. The little, red, tear-streaked face immediately seeking your own and then running to you with outstretched arms at the first, second, and every major and minor injury. And, of course, the first day of school. The day you are supposed to begin to lose your baby, the day they are supposed to begin their long journey into the world beyond the one you first made for them.

I didn't know what it was like to have a newborn baby, and the countless milestones and more trivial life experiences that so many take for granted they will watch their child do and have. While I have come to accept that these experiences are forever ongoing as Jessica's sisters grow and mature, the realisation as each new one occurs never ceases to affect me, reminding me sadly of her loss and proudly of her existence.

To look back

As I write this, Jessica's death was fifteen years ago. Is it now over, a thing of the past, or does it have ongoing repercussions that will stay with me for the rest of my life? Does this experience have an afterlife of its own? Of course it will stay with me forever; your children always stay with you, no matter where they are, or where you hope they are. Some things in life are never over, even though it is expected that you believe, or are expected to believe or pretend, that they are. Hopefully you learn to live with them, and get on with it as best you can. At least that's my own philosophy. Some events in life never become things of the past, because you carry them with you every day, and because they are not meant to. Some of life's experiences develop an afterlife of their own, as you might hope those who leave you do. To 'get over' something, to me, means to have no long-term repercussions, to leave no permanent scars, whether these scars take the form of memories, warning signals, grief, or anything else. So you never 'get over' losing your baby, do you?

Many things haunt me. Some are expected, some have taken me completely off guard. To this day I can suddenly be taken back to Jessica's birth and death by some trigger. It may be something someone says or doesn't say, a smell, a noise, passing the hospital she was born in or the funeral director's where I last saw her – many different situations and scenarios.

To carry her, this perfect baby, for almost nine months, this growing, kicking, living baby. To feel her strength every evening, as she kicked the same place on my right side so hard I thought she would kick herself clean through. To still feel that same kicking after she was gone, with the mind and body so utterly confused about what had been, what should be, and what was. To feel her grow larger week by week, as the space I had to carry her in grew tighter and tighter. Then to have that space empty, as if nothing had ever been there, no trace remaining, not a bulge, nothing. To look like you haven't just had a child when you are holding one is desirable; to look like you haven't just had a child when there is no child to see is inexplicable. To have waited so long for her, and to have wanted her so much, and then, in the last few moments, to have her taken, so unnecessarily, so avoidably. The sheer waste of her existence will stay with me forever.

The event itself, hour by hour, then minute by minute, then second by second, the months then days leading up to it, and the days then months after it – every detail haunted my mind. First constantly, then frequently, now occasionally. But each recollection still with the same intensity, leaving me sleepless for the night, from one more exhausting total recall. With each total recall followed the unanswered questions, over and over again. Why did this happen? What did she do wrong? What did I do wrong? Why wouldn't anyone listen to me? Sometimes the most awful thing about thinking you are right about something is to prove it. The only fortunate thing I have now is that some of the years of unanswered questions are now answered.

There is the missing child, her reflection present in the

three sisters she will never see, the endless ache of looking at three girls that should number four. The awkward, innocent questions, from the unknowing: 'How many children do you have?' It took a while to nut that one out, but eventually a satisfactory answer became another well-practised line if I don't simply, and usually flatly, say 'four'. 'Oh, I have three girls at home.' My response is true. It saves me from telling someone who doesn't need to know, or whom I don't want to tell, something about me that I don't want to share. While not denying her existence, which I cannot and do not want to do, I am simply not revealing it.

There are the irreparable relationships. Memory has a cruel way of embedding every detail of such an event into your very soul, and every detail of the actions and words of those who surrounded you also. Perhaps, I sometimes wonder, the mind does this for a reason. Perhaps it is a self-protection mechanism: one trying to shield oneself from such trauma again. But perhaps it is just me, unable to forgive those who, my mind knows, didn't know any better, who I know were doing the best they could in a situation that came with no rule book, no guidance, and no answers, but, my heart says, should have and could have done more and known better. Perhaps these relationships are not really irreparable; perhaps it is me who has simply deemed them so.

So too is my changed relationship with both the medical and counselling professions. Once any trust is broken, repair is difficult.

Pregnancies and births are an ongoing issue. I have now managed to get through three more after my 'disaster', as one doctor put it. It is still sinking in that I will not have to suffer eight and a half months of sheer hell ever again. But my own relief, and guilt, does not extend to others. Every pregnant woman I know, even strangers I see in the street, I worry for. Each newborn baby I cast my eyes upon brings tears. Every birth on television brings sobs. And to each female that accomplishes this one task assigned them, in the manner designed them, I feel utter inferiority, an inferiority, that I fear, no matter what else I strive and struggle so desperately to perfect, will never fade.

You can't win

I feel now, much as I did when Jessica was born, that most people couldn't, and still can't, win with what they say or do regarding her death. If you mention her, after not doing so for so many years, I'll wonder why. If you don't, I'll be angry and hurt and wonder if you're ever going to. If you acknowledge her anniversary one year, and not others, I'll wonder why? Why this time? If you don't, I'll be angry and hurt. If you talk about something that happened when you know I was pregnant with her or at the time she died and was born, I'll be angry and hurt. You see, you can't win. It probably doesn't matter what you did or do, I'll find fault, it will upset me. I'm not trying to explain why; I'm just telling you this so you may have some understanding of the mindset of the bereaved parent of a baby that has died.

I can't win either

Complementary to you not being able to win is that I can't win either. If I mention her, I feel self-conscious because you haven't. If I don't, I'm pretending she didn't exist either just like you do, and I can't do that. If I acknowledge her birth or death day in some way I feel I have to do it secretly, because you might think I'm mad, haven't coped with her death, or can't let go. If I say I've had four children, I feel like others think I'm saying something I shouldn't, because a 'failed' pregnancy doesn't count.

I find it perplexing that it seems to be more socially acceptable to cry in a cinema full of strangers over people you've never met playing parts you'll never be, than cry at the death of your own baby. Or at your sporting team winning, or a princess you never knew dying, or people being killed in large buildings you've never been to by other people you don't know. It's also accepted and expected that we acknowledge the anniversary of mass death or what some deem the tragic death of people we've never met, but not to acknowledge your baby's death, or at least not after the first twelve months. No-one acknowledges my baby's death now. No-one has for years. Yet every year on her birth/death day I think of the gifts I should be buying, the party I should be planning, and the maturing girl I should be wishing happy birthday. Right now I'm supposed to be arguing with a teenage girl. Instead the most I can do is take flowers to a cemetery. I'd give anything for that argumentative teenager.

I wish I could say her name

I feel I also can't win because I can't freely say Jessica's name in daily conversation. There are two reasons I have come up with for this. Firstly, I can't bring up what happened because my story is real, not some storyline in a play or a television drama series. Secondly, my pregnancy story wasn't a near-miss. It doesn't have a happy ending I can dine out on at lunch with other mothers with all their near-miss stories. Mine had the unthinkable ending, making it the unspeakable story and Jessica the unmentionable child.

17

I do forgive your ignorance

Not everything to do with Jessica's death is negative. Some aspects are educational. To all those people who crossed the street to avoid me, deliberately ignored me, didn't acknowledge the existence of my child or my pain, do I forgive you? Well, yes I do on one level. What I don't forgive, after years of pondering this, is that while you may have been, and probably still are, uneducated in how to deal with such people as me and such events as mine and Jessica's, your primary motivation for ignoring me was fear. You were afraid of what might happen, and therefore you put your feelings first. And I have trouble in dealing with that, because I was the one who was hurting. Not you. My child died. Not yours. My world fell apart. Not yours. I was ignored. Not you. I do forgive your ignorance. Your self-ishness I'm working on.

I am grateful

Although I wish that instead of writing this I was living with a fifteen year old, had four living daughters, and was still naïve of the experiences of a parent whose baby has died, there are many things I am grateful for regarding, and as a result of, Jessica's death.

I am grateful not to be as naïve as I was – this, as far as I can ascertain, can only be a positive thing. I am grateful for the education I have received from and about other people's experiences. From what I have learnt from other bereaved parents sharing their stories with me, I am grateful that I saw Jessica, and that I have any photos of her at all. I am grateful that Jessica has a gravesite, and that I can visit it. I am also grateful that I am able to write about her – to share both her existence with other people and her story.

I am grateful for Jessica's three sisters.

I am grateful for the ways in which the experience of her life and death has changed me. I no longer fuss or stress about trivial things as I used to, or things that cannot be changed. I have a greater acceptance of the fact of illness and death. I no longer fear asking questions in order to clarify or comprehend – anything. I never simply take good health for granted, or think anything 'will only happen to someone else'.

I am grateful for all the wonderful people I have met whom I would otherwise have not known if Jessica had lived although, as fond as I am of them, I would trade their places in my life for hers without hesitation (as I'd expect they would for their own lost children too).

I am grateful I am now able to listen to other people and, perhaps, understand a little of what they may be going through. More importantly, I am grateful that if I am unable to understand what they are going through I am able to admit that and simply offer support and space.

I am grateful that I have found things to be grateful for.

A different view

I do now feel I have the beginnings of a better understanding of the pain others experience at a loss, whether that loss be a grandparent, parent, sibling, spouse, friend, or especially a child. By child I now refer to, which I didn't before and am embarrassed to admit, a child of any age from conception onwards. Miscarriage is not something I understood before in the manner I now do. I now understand that the loss of a child during pregnancy, from one week to forty, means the loss of that child – that baby won't be born on approximately X date, that baby won't come home, won't grow up, won't grow old, won't bury you. Loss at any stage of pregnancy is loss and results in grief – your baby has died.

I never say, 'Oh yes, I know how you feel,' because I don't, regarding anything, even if someone tells me they have lost a baby. I will likely have similar experiences and feelings, but every loss is unique to particular circumstances, and everyone's reactions to their losses or experiences should be respected as individual and valid.

I do believe, after the experience of the loss of my baby, that there is a general and widespread lack of education in our society regarding death in general and the death of children and babies in particular. How will anyone suffering bereavement attain from others the acknowledgment of their loss and grief so vital in the grieving process if the reinforcement of ignoring their loss and grief continues?

Some final thoughts

After years of 'hiding' my baby that died I have finally brought Jessica out into the lounge room. I discovered that many other parents in similar circumstances proudly display photos of their babies for all to see, and don't worry about what other people think. So I've finally done the same, and feel much better for it. I have a right to remember her, and am exercising that in this simple act. Talking to other bereaved parents was the best thing I eventually did and I would encourage anyone else to do the same.

If you know someone whose baby has died, don't be scared to say the baby's name, to talk about the pregnancy, to acknowledge their grief. I understand and accept that life isn't fair. I don't think any life is a waste. Jessica produced this piece of writing and her life is affecting you as you read it. I'm not angry about her death but permanently saddened by the loss of her life. I know no-one meant her death to occur but unfortunately at the end of the day it did. I've written this in the hope that anything you learn from reading this is better than nothing and maybe will leave you knowing a little more than you did before. Hopefully the next time someone you know suffers a loss you might think a little about their needs before yours and offer acknowledgment, space and support. That is my hope.

Annette Spence

Memories of Bradley Leonard

*Written in 1999 – eight years following his death at
sixteen weeks' gestation*

*Bradley's life ended through miscarriage at
sixteen weeks on 13 February 1991
His body (in a container of formalin) was buried in
the front garden of our home 17 February 1991
His due date was 2 August 1991
Exhumed from garden 2 August 1998
Remains cremated at the Necropolis,
Springvale 24 August 1999
Memorial service 30 August 1999*

In the early hours of 13 February 1991, my fourth child, Bradley, died at sixteen weeks' gestation. It was the very day I had been booked in to have an ultrasound, the first time I would have seen his form on the screen. I discovered his sex when we viewed his tiny body in the kidney dish at the emergency department of my local hospital. I was then admitted to have a D and C later that afternoon.

As I lay in the hospital bed in the morning darkness, stifling sobs of utter shock and grief, I was becoming slowly aware that my 'miscarriage' was not going to be regarded as the death of someone very special to me. I was told, 'Don't worry, you can always have another one.' And, 'You already have three children.' The worst was when my son was referred to as 'products of conception'. Regardless of these attitudes, when the day dawned I requested that I be able to bring his tiny body home. When I told the nursing staff of my wishes I felt as though I was morbid as it wasn't 'the done thing'. I didn't care. I didn't want my son chucked away as though he was just nothing. On my discharge that afternoon I was politely told to come back in two days when I could collect my son, or 'products of conception', as he was still referred to by the pathology department.

In those hours of loneliness following Bradley's death, I decided my son needed an identity and a name. I decided to call him Bradley. By 5.00 pm that afternoon I was home. What do I do now? I'm confused, feeling empty, lost and disappointed with the way I was treated by the hospital. They had been kind and friendly, but didn't they realise that I had experienced a death!

Two days later I presented to the pathology department and meekly asked if I could collect my son. He was handed to me across the counter in front of other patients in a white plastic ice-cream container!

Once home again I tried to occupy my eighteen month old son as I was lost as to what to do next and wanted to spend time alone quietly with Bradley. Deciding to be strong, I had a look at my son. He had been placed in a transparent container like when you get takeaway. This had then been placed in the ice-cream container.

I *cried*. I looked at his feet with such tiny well-formed toes and his tiny hands. He was obviously a little boy. In the foetal position I could not obtain a good look at his face. The umbilical cord was still attached, very thin. Years later I feel so much regret that I didn't open the container and hold Bradley in my hands and take a photo. I sobbed as I thought, I shouldn't be looking at you like this, you should not be out here, you should be in my womb growing and living.

I carefully arranged a large old wooden jewellery box with a clean nappy and some flowers, placed the container holding Bradley in it and sprinkled some baby powder. Then placing my son's 'coffin' in a towel, I closed my eyes and cradled it in my arms, imagining I was holding a little baby boy near my heart. The next day Martin (my husband) and I gently placed 'our baby' in our front garden and planted a beautiful camellia in his memory. That's all we have of Bradley; there are no photos or memories and yet he feels such a part of our lives. Although upset by our most unexpected loss, I felt a feeling of warmth and love envelop me.

At the time of the miscarriage no support from the hospital was offered, not even a mention of a support group. In the deep recesses of my mind I recalled hearing something on the radio a couple of months or years earlier about an organisation that supported parents bereaved through miscarriage or stillbirth. I searched through the telephone book. I called and hey, I found someone was really listening to me! She acknowledged my feelings and I cried tears of appreciation. I was not going crazy after all. My loss and grief was finally being recognised and validated.

Through my involvement with SANDS and personal endless searching for information, I began to learn about the concept of 'disenfranchised mourning' and was able to articulate the importance and special meaning of this lost relationship. This I partly achieved through becoming a parent supporter and being there for others who experienced the death of their baby before, during or shortly after birth.

Besides my involvement with SANDS and journal writing I also found support from reading, and still continue adding to my collection of bereavement-related books. Music, walks in the forest and time alone with my thoughts helped, although with three young sons this was often difficult. I became a newsletter junkie and still subscribe to as many bereavement-related newsletters as I can. I particularly enjoy poetry and keep my favourite pieces in a special folder. A bereavement can create an increased awareness of the fragility of life, that each and every day is an absolute gift and so very precious. I have a continuing need and desire to learn more about loss and grief issues, which is helping me to learn so much about life and living.

I wrote letters to anyone who had connections with the pre-born, even to the famous photographer of the pre-born, Lennart Nilsson in Switzerland, who wrote me a personally signed reply. Letters were sent to my local hospital along with photocopies of recommended practices for patients who had experienced a miscarriage from books I had read. The director of nursing responded positively by inviting me in to talk with her.

A few years after my miscarriage my local hospital introduced 'angel boxes'. Parents who experience the death of their pre-twenty-week unborn baby are now invited by the hospital's social worker to take their baby home. Not all parents want to do this, some preferring the hospital to take care of things. Other changes for the better have also taken place within the healthcare industry, due to such a caring organisation as SANDS and to individuals who advocate for better practice and recognition of the value of these short, but totally loved, lives.

One of the complications of disenfranchised grief is the exclusion or lack of ritual. This had remained a huge issue for me over the past eight years as Bradley's body lay in the earth still submerged in a container of formalin. How undignified. On reflection, eight years after Bradley's death I felt there were basically two reasons why there was no ritual for Bradley's spirit.

Firstly, due to my disenfranchised grief within my family and friends, I felt they wouldn't understand my need to give meaning to his short sixteen weeks of life through a ritual. Secondly, I became so heavily involved within the SANDS network that my own needs were overlooked.

On the seventh anniversary of Bradley's due date (2 August 1998) I literally attacked the front garden with a spade, searching for Bradley under the camellia bush. About forty-five minutes later, with a huge hole in the broken earth, he was finally found. Photos of the process were taken, photos of his container were taken. Some may think this morbid, but I needed to create what little memories I could. The wooden jewelley box had rotted a fair bit, but his tiny form was still clearly visible in the intact formalin in that takeaway food container. I brought him inside the house, unsure of why I had really exhumed him and unsure again as to what to do now. I looked through the container as I had seven years earlier, his body still clearly to be seen, but still I was afraid to open the container and hold my son in my palm.

Due to the impact of Bradley's sixteen weeks of growing under my heart and the continuing impact of his short life on mine in 1999, I undertook a year-long course on Loss and Grief. In March of that year one evening, we did an exercise where we were asked to write something from our hearts to someone dear to us who had died; I wrote to Bradley.

This simple exercise led to his memorial service held on 30 August 1999, albeit eight years following his death.

Joanne Switserloot

Why?

❧

A cold early June morning, thirty years ago, eighteen years old and facing a pile of post-holiday washing. Tired, heavy with babe and six weeks to go. Must get on with it!

Babe felt 'tight' last night. Probably aftermath of jolts and bumps on rough dirt track leading to my pregnant cousin's home. She's due a month after me, so we exchange thoughts and feelings about our forthcoming births and babies.

The visit was great. Photos, big bellies and big smiles. Home now.

'Oh, my God!' Blood! More blood . . . soaking thick stockings, slippers. Clean up. No phone. Telephone exchange a hundred metres up the road. Girls doing early day shift. Knock at door. Blood again. Hot, soaking, down legs.

'Oh my God!' Ring her husband, ring hospital . . . country hospital.

Bells ringing, wheeling beds, curtains pulled. Nurses, sisters, quick, quick, hush. The pains begin. 'Where's her husband? Where's doctor?' Together, for a quiet chat. Vomiting, diarrhoea, pain comes again. Husband gone a hundred kilometres to get blood for transfusion.

Needles, drip, messed bed, pain, worried. Too much happening. Too much pain, crying. Need my mother. Not here. Don't know what's wrong. Don't care any more. Anaesthetic. See what is happening. Maybe a caesarean. Chaos.

'Jenny, Jenny! Wake up! We are sorry, Jenny. We had to do a caesarean. We are so sorry, Jenny. Your baby passed away. It was a girl. Only lived for a little while. Breathing abnormalities.'

Hazy, drugged, not true, enormous weight on my chest, go away, cold, shivering. Lonely. Oh so lonely!

'What did she look like? Can I see her?'

'No, it's best if you don't.'

'Why, was she deformed?'

'No, she was a lovely little baby. Hush, Jenny, be a good girl. It will be okay.'

Husband gone to get a coffin, white, I think. A hundred kilometres away.

Change dressings, drip out, tight bandage around breasts to stop the milk.

'IT' has to be named, registered and a 'real' burial performed. Do it while she is still in hospital. Fourteen days all up. Can't remember visitors. Hushed talk, sideways glances.

'Everything's going great. You can go home. Don't worry, you will be able to have other children and next time you won't feel guilty because you will already be married. Won't you, dear?' Pat, pat.

I'm frying chops and boiling vegies again. Who am I? No-one talks about 'IT'. Am I a mother? The crib is ready. Still. The mosquito net with the lace trim is still draped over the pretty white bassinet. I'm cold in this old rented flat. My husband is at work or he is out riding one of his horses somewhere.

I go into the 'spare' room and feel the little singlets and the little booties that the nana-to-be knitted, and the little coloured bunny rugs that I bought on special. I guess I will put it all away soon. Soon.

Life goes on. My scar is healing. I go shopping, aware of the stares, muffled whispers, and people I know trying to avoid me. Did I do something wrong?

I go into the 'spare' room because I heard my baby cry. I lift the lacy mosquito net and look into the crib. I'm sure I heard

'IT' cry. Am I going mad? I must not tell anyone about this. Now is the time to put it all away.

I feel lonely, scared and hollow. But in the back of my mind I can hear people saying, 'She's a strong girl, she's a survivor.' 'Put it all behind you.' 'Get on with life.'

Now, thirty years later, I realise how wrong they were. I didn't survive, nor was I strong. I just lived my life with unresolved grief.

My husband and I divorced after ten years of marriage, nearly costing me my lovely daughter and two handsome sons. I have since been blessed with a marriage to a wonderful, caring, gentle man for twelve years.

It is only in this year some thirty years later that I have faced my unresolved grief and its consequences, now realising the profound ripple effect of the past is still affecting myself, my second husband and my adult children.

With courage, love, patience, support and education, I am going to smooth out and stop the ripples.

By the way, *her* name was *Dionne Rachel*.

Jenny Bricknell

Dads DO Cry Too

✎

Oscar Bradley Ryan
Born sleeping 14 February 2007

It has been fifty-nine days since we had our hello and our sad goodbye. My lovely wife, whom I adore, and for whom I now have an even stronger sense of admiration for her strength and courage, has been through hell and has not come back yet, but they do say time heals. I would like to have a chat with 'they' as I am sure we will never heal and in some ways I do not want to heal.

My wife Joni had a difficult pregnancy with our first son Jack William, with a constant bout of morning sickness and heartburn right up until the day of Jack's arrival. Jack did not come about too easily. Joni was suffering from high blood pressure at thirty-eight weeks. The doctors looked further into things and found our firstborn Jack was breech and Joni would need an emergency caesarean. This was done the very next morning. Joni suffered a disastrous procedure in which they cut her bladder and she had to endure over a week in hospital with multiple blood transfusions. This was a time of very mixed emotions, as we had our baby but Joni was unable to do any of the normal mum things like bath him, feed him or change him. She was stuck in bed with lines and drugs being pumped into every part of her tired body. We thought at the time that this was the worst thing that would ever happen in our lives. How wrong we were.

Our second pregnancy was a lot different. We were excited

about the fact Joni was pregnant again and I was about to become a dad for the second time. We are both very family-orientated people and just adore the fact of being able to bring a new life to this world and see it grow, just as our parents have done with the both of us. Joni and I would have loved to have a girl, to give us the classic pair of a boy and a girl, but as all parents do we just wished for a healthy baby with ten fingers and ten toes. We did not find out the sex of our baby as we wanted it to be a surprise just as we had done with Jack. My wife was not as big with the pregnancy this time but was still very sick again. Everyone, including myself, kept telling her that second pregnancies are different. This, however, did not wash with Joni as she kept saying, 'This baby does not move around as much,' and that it felt smaller than Jack. I was not too concerned, as this time we had private health insurance and were seeing a top doctor who would allow Joni to plan a natural birth.

How wrong could I and everyone else have been. At our thirty-five-week check-up, the only one I had been to this time, we had the real shock of our lives. The doctor had now heeded Joni's concerns about the baby's size and would organise an ultrasound. I felt he was just doing this to keep her happy. While he was talking he said he just wanted to check the heartbeat. This he did for some minutes without a single hint of sound from the machine. It may have only been thirty seconds but it felt as though he was looking forever. There was *no* sound. How could this be? We had great health cover, the top doctor, Joni is healthy, does not smoke, rarely has a drink of alcohol and has not had a single drop whilst she has been pregnant. The doctor booked us in to go to the hospital to get an ultrasound straightaway.

On the way to the hospital I don't think we spoke. All I kept thinking was that his machine must be stuffed or that maybe the baby is sick and that's why it has not grown and maybe, just maybe, there is a very, very, very faint heartbeat and they can do another caesarean and our baby will be born early. Hey, I see stories on the news just about every second night about the miracle baby who was born weeks earlier than our baby would be, so everything would be just fine. Again how wrong I was. The nurse at the hospital spent a long time checking and finally the words came out that will always ring in my ears: 'Your baby has died.'

We made our way back to the doctor's, past all the pregnant people at the hospital, all excited about getting their ultrasound so they can keep the little photos or watch the video when they get home. I hated these people right now. When we arrived at the doctor's we discovered that our baby was another breech baby. However, the doctor would allow a natural birth for two reasons. Firstly, it was what Joni had wanted all along, and secondly, the healing time would be a lot quicker as opposed to major surgery with a caesarean.

That night when we arrived home we spoke to Jack and tried to talk to him like an adult – he is only three! He just did not understand what we meant but he could tell we were upset and gave us lots of special Jack-hugs.

That night I got very drunk and all but passed out. I look back now and see how selfish it was leaving my wife to cry all night and not sleep a second for two reasons: she had just lost her baby, and now she was going to give birth to a dead baby.

On the way to the hospital all I could think was: How the hell are we going to do this? and What is the baby going to look like? When we arrived at the hospital I again saw those people. I hated sitting there with their big bellies getting ready to have their babies. We were taken away to a birthing room and Joni was induced to give birth. It was eight horrible long hours for Joni; she was doing it tough without an epidural. Then the pains of the labour and the pain of giving birth to a baby that was not alive were too hard. There was no real reason to go though all this horrible torture for a baby that would not cry, so Joni did to my relief have an epidural.

When the baby came out it was limp and covered in the entire normal baby gunk and looked kind of scary as they all but dumped it on Joni's stomach, but after half a second I could see my baby, my second child and as it turned out, a boy! I was sad but also excited. I now had two sons, Jack and Oscar. We looked into each other's eyes and could smile, for Oscar looked just like his big brother Jack and had Daddy's nose and Mum's beautiful long fingers, and his feet were huge! We were very lucky at the hospital as the nurses were just fantastic and helped us do little hand- and footprints of Oscar and bath him, then to dress him and wrap him in a blanket. He was so peaceful just lying there fast asleep. Joni and I chose to have a room away from the midwifery as we could not bear to hear the sounds of other babies crying or mums going through labour. We had our own room, tucked away from everyone and everything.

It was as though Oscar were alive. We had family everywhere in the room with us. They all kept asking, 'Are you okay?'

I felt like shouting at them, 'What the hell do you think, that's my dead son lying over there,' but I know they, like us, just did not know what to say or what to do. They just wanted to be there for us, and for that I will always thank them and hold an extra bit of respect for our families as now we are closer than ever before.

Joni and I spent hours in bed together holding Oscar and talking to him and holding his hands, and letting him know how proud we were of him and that he would have grown up to be a great man and one day a dad too. We wanted Jack to be with us for this special time and he came into the room with us and cuddled his little brother and gave him kisses.

'He's all cold, Daddy. Why is he cold, Daddy? I want to see his feet, Daddy.'

I was as proud as could be. I was sitting on a chair with my sons: one whom I would be able to kick the footy with, the other just to have this moment with. I look at all the photos we took and boy, did I take a stack of them! There is one that both makes me proud and also extremely sad at the same moment, and it is of Jack up on the bed with Oscar, giving his little brother a cuddle, and Jack just has this glint of joy in his eyes, sitting there holding Oscar all on his own. That was and will always be one of the proudest moments in my life and I am so happy I have a photo of that special moment.

Later that night Oscar was not looking as well as the colour he had in his face slowly faded away and we wanted to let him rest as it had been a big day for him too. We said our goodbyes to Oscar and both just watched in disbelief as he was taken out of our room, away to that cold place they called the morgue – such a terrible word. Joni and I just held each other tight and cried for hours, for our son was gone and we had nothing left with us except each other.

The next day we awoke to try and take on our first day without our son Oscar. I started to read the information the nurses had gathered for us to read about the death of our baby. I *had* to be the strong one and help my wife through this, and tried to cram as much information into my head as quickly as I could so as to help Joni. I think one of the worst things a parent can ever do is to pick a coffin for their child, and make decisions like burial versus cremation and what would you like to say at the funeral. Somehow we did this together and saw ourselves through this very hard day. We had to do this for

Oscar's sake and somewhat for ourselves as well, and with the help of each other we did get through those days and it hurt, it hurt a lot.

We had a funeral for Oscar and only allowed our family and a few of our very close friends to attend and share that special time. Joni and I got to see Oscar one last time. Joni and I had made one of the toughest trips ever to the shops, as we had to buy an outfit to bury our son in and we wanted to put some mementos in his coffin for him, to help him remember his mum and dad and with these we placed a photo in a frame of Mummy, Daddy, Jack and little baby Oscar all together, the only family photo we will ever have. I as a dad had to buy some Matchbox cars for him to play with, and Mummy had to get him a cute, fluffy teddy bear. Jack drew him some pictures. He looked so at peace surrounded by all the things we had put together for him. Joni and I did the service ourselves at the funeral; we could not have someone talk about our feelings and our son. How could they do that, when we barely had a chance to know him? It was as nice as a funeral could be for a child. We lit candles, had some music and read a poem. Joni and I found a book at the shops that we read out loud to Oscar and everyone there, as we had not had a chance to read him a story and never would again and nor would our family and friends, so we felt it special to be able to share this moment with Oscar. At the cemetery we all let go yellow balloons into the sky and sprinkled fairy dust over Oscar's coffin, sad but special moments we will always treasure.

We are now somehow getting through the days. Joni has been doing it hard as I have had to go back to work. Not only is it hard mentally and physically but also financially. With my work – I am a director of a real estate agency – I find it hard just about every day, though the team at my office are great.

Some of them too are parents and feel for Joni, Jack and me and have been great in keeping their distance at times but being there when they know I need them. I am having past clients/friends whom I have made over the years call me and drop by saying, 'Hey, what did you have – a boy or a girl?' They all knew we were having another baby. I had told everyone, as all dads do. On some of these days when they ask me 'the hard question' I do find it hard, but it does feel better to talk to them and let them know what Oscar looked like and how beautiful our son was – I am so proud of him. However, it's going out to meet new people who don't know me or what has happened that I find the hardest. They are happy families and are moving because they are having another child or have just had one. It's hard being around these people every day and not being able to express my feelings and tell them what we have experienced and just how lucky they really are.

It is these days when I'm away from Joni that scare me the most, leaving her alone with too much time to think about what she could have done differently and what went wrong and looking for someone or something to blame. I feel we are now only starting to accept what has happened to poor baby Oscar.

Joni and I get some comfort from going to the cemetery to talk to Oscar and to sit there at his grave and cry and talk about what has been happening and what his big brother has been up to. It has been these visits to the cemetery that have made us realise we are not alone, as there are so many little children all around our Oscar who have had their time cut short, and there are too many other parents who are about to, who are experiencing and who have experienced what we are going through right now. I decided to write a small poem for my son and have it as a special gift for my wife, to show her one way of dealing with my emotions: it's hard as a dad. We have now printed the poem and Joni has made up a picture frame for it. It's good for both of us to do something and I know while I am at work she can keep herself busy doing something for Oscar.

Joni asked me to put my thoughts down on paper for others to read. The good people at SANDS who have been there for Joni said not many dads do this. This I can understand, as it has been hard to write these words but also comforting in the fact that another dad or dads who may have just experienced what we have been through can see that as far as the first two months go you can do it. I know my little baby Oscar would be proud of his dad doing this and that his death is not in vain as I might be able to help someone else go through the pain, now having had a snapshot of mine. Yes, there have been tears with just about every word I have written, and I have found a way to get through the pain. The tears do hurt, but hey, 'they' say you will get through this.

You will always be with me, Oscar.

Love you always.

Daddy.

Brad Ryan

Not the Birthday Present I Wanted

❦

We were pregnant with our second baby, happy and excited to be having our second child. The pregnancy was a hard one. It was much like my first, 24/7 sickness and heartburn, but this time it seemed a lot worse and was much harder to cope with. I put this down to the fact that I had a three year old son to run after and worked three days a week.

We noticed as time went on that this baby was not as active as my first baby, but it still let me know it was there. Nor did I seem to get as big as I did with my first. At my 33-week doctor's appointment I questioned the size of my tummy, because by then I felt I was too small. I also felt that the baby's movements had slowed. But the doctor assured me everything was fine. The baby was the right size and there was a heartbeat. There was no need to worry about anything.

Leading up to my 35-week appointment, I was concerned again about the baby's movements. I felt the baby had been quiet, but it was still letting me know it was there. Previous to this appointment there was concern that the baby was breech; this was the one thing I was worried about. Our first baby had been breech but was not diagnosed until thirty-eight weeks, when I was about to be induced due to my high blood pressure, and they had to deliver the baby by caesarean. They cut my bladder and the recovery was long and hard, so this time round I was determined to have a natural birth.

The doctor could not work out where this baby was laying and said we should have an ultrasound. He then checked the heartbeat. As the seconds and minutes passed, I went cold and sheer terror set in. We went to hospital immediately. At the ultrasound I knew straightaway the baby had died because it was taking too long for the nurse to say anything. When she finally said she could not get a heartbeat I felt like my stomach had dropped out. I kept thinking that maybe they were wrong and the baby was still alive. Back at the doctor's office, I was booked in to be induced the next day.

I did not sleep a wink that night. My husband did, but he had a great deal of help from Jack Daniels. I was also still feeling the baby move, although more flutters than kicks. Even though I knew the baby had died, I held out some hope.

When we left the next morning for the hospital I had never been so scared in all my life, partly because I had no idea what labour would be like. One part of me kept thinking everything was normal and we were just like any other normal couple going off to the hospital to have their baby induced. The other part of me knew it was not true and that this was anything but normal. Labour started slowly but surely. I had an epidural after the pain got too much; the midwife said I would need my strength for what was to come and there was no point going through all that pain for a baby we knew was not alive. Eight hours later our second son was born: Oscar Bradley Ryan, born 14 February 2007. He only weighed 4.12 pounds and was 33.3 centimetres long, so he was small for a 35-week baby. The doctor examined the placenta, saying it looked as though there was a tear in it, otherwise known as placental abruption. No other cause was found but we did not have an autopsy performed on our Oscar; we could not bear the thought of it.

They passed him to me straightaway. We looked to see whether we had a boy or a girl; we had a boy's name and a girl's name picked, so we named him straightaway. The night before we had decided that if it was a boy we would give him my husband's name as his middle name.

He was beautiful, our son. After our first look at him we both said he looked like his big brother Jack. (When people look at the photos they say that I look like I am in shock and that my husband looks sad beyond belief.) We held him and cuddled him, kissed him, bathed him, dressed him, took his hand- and footprints and a lock of his hair. We told him how much we loved him and how we wished he didn't have to go. We told him how much we would miss him.

It was then time for his big brother to come and meet him. We had explained to Jack the night before that the baby in Mummy's tummy had died, but he didn't really understand. So when his nana brought him in, Jack just thought the baby was sleeping. It was very easy for me to pretend that the baby was sleeping and that he would wake up and cry at any time, but of course he never did. He looked so peaceful all wrapped up in his blue blanket. It all seemed so normal, with both sets of grandparents coming in to see the baby. The only difference was that everybody was crying and the baby wasn't moving.

At about midnight we said our goodbyes and my tears came then. It hurt so much to let him go. I felt like my heart had been ripped out and was going out the door with him, but it still didn't feel real somehow. That night, I don't know how but we managed some sleep. I think it was a case of crying ourselves to sleep and the fact that we had been up for about thirty-six hours. We went home the next day, dazed and shocked. Our family and friends rallied around us. Sometimes it helped to have them there or on the phone, but at other times it was the last thing we wanted. Jack kept asking us to go back to the hospital and bring Oscar home. That was really hard to deal with.

We then had to organise a funeral for our baby. How we managed that, I don't know. Going shopping to pick an outfit to bury my baby in was a horrible, surreal experience. Again, it didn't feel real. When we went to the funeral home to see him one last time, before the funeral, and I saw him in the outfit we had bought for him, I was so proud of my baby. He looked so beautiful in the jumpsuit and hat we had picked for him. But I also realised that I would never get to see him look that beautiful again. It was agony leaving him for what we knew to be the last time; the last time we would ever see our baby.

After the funeral Jack seemed to accept a little more that Oscar could not come home. He would say to us and anybody else who would listen, 'That baby Oscar is in a white box in the big hole and has to stay at the cemetery forever.' And he would say that Mummy, Daddy and Jack wanted Oscar to come home but he couldn't because he had died. People would say to me, 'Does it upset you and make you cry when he says that?' It doesn't. I think it's Jack's way of coping with it. We had spent the last six months telling him about this baby and preparing him for a little brother or sister, and then all of a sudden it didn't happen. In his own way Jack has been sad and grieved for the little brother he didn't get to know or see grow up. So I am happy that he can express his feelings like that. We also told him that we can see Oscar up in the sky at night-time when we look at the stars. So now, most nights before Jack goes to bed, we go outside to look at the brightest star and Jack talks to Oscar and tells him what's been going on.

In the days and weeks that followed I seemed to move as though in a fog. It was hard to keep going and to keep being a parent to Jack when all I wanted to do was stay in bed all day and cry. After a couple of weeks I got a little better and getting out of bed was not so hard, but the days seemed endless, especially when my husband went back to work. Jack and I would go out and stick to the routine of kinder and swimming. Coming home was the worst. We would walk through the front door and I would instantly be aware of an emptiness in the house. Even though I was home with Jack, I was aware that Oscar should have been with us. At times I would catch myself looking to where I would have put his rocker, just in case he was there. I should have both my boys with me at home.

As my due date approached, I became restless and anxious. I was hoping that after that day had passed I would be able to let go a little bit. The opposite happened. I felt like I was going through it all over again. I thought I should definitely have my baby now. And that was when I got angry. The due date was the day before my birthday and the joke had been that I wasn't getting any presents because I was getting a baby and that was the best present I could have. Well, I didn't get the baby and so I got angry instead. But I realise that you have to go through the anger. After it, I felt a kind of release from some of the emotion.

At the time of writing this story, it's only been two months since the loss. I don't remember how I got through those two months. I don't really remember how I got through the days and weeks to get to this point. The pain still seems endless; the longing and wanting for my baby does not go away. I am impatient to get to a point where it won't hurt so much. They say that time heals, and it probably does, but time has a habit of going so slow when you want this sort of intense hurt and pain to go away, or at least soften. I was not prepared for the intensity of the feelings and emotions; it seems to hit so hard that it becomes a physical pain. I felt as though I had something stuck in my chest and couldn't get it to go away.

I started doing some things to help me get through. A very good friend of mine is mad on scrapbooking and she suggested I do an album for Oscar. I wasn't sure at first, as I'm the least creative person there is. But when she turned up with an album and everything I would need to get started, I couldn't let her down. So off I went into the land of scrapbooking and I've never looked back. It's still a work in progress, but I love doing it because I'm creating a beautiful memory of Oscar. I have also painted an old picture frame and framed the reading we had at the funeral on the same paper as the service books. We have had a memory box made and I bought letters to put on top that say *Oscar's Box*. I've painted them all different colours.

I started writing in a journal, thanks to another friend, and I write in it at least once a week. My parents bought me a gold locket in which I have put a photo of Oscar and another of his hand around my husband's finger. I also go to the cemetery at least once a week; I feel close to Oscar when I'm there, and calm, like I can face things more easily after I've been there and spoken to him. Making memories of my beautiful Oscar has made it a little easier to cope.

We have decided we would like to try and have another baby, but I don't know how I could go through an entire pregnancy thinking that this baby will die too. I don't know how I won't be terrified the whole time just waiting for it to happen again. We have decided to wait six months and see how we're going then. If it was to happen again, how would we all cope? How would it affect Jack? I don't think waiting any longer would help. It wouldn't matter if it was six years later, I would still be terrified. I also want Oscar to have *his* time, to have his mummy and daddy to himself for a while. I want to feel like I have given Oscar's death the respect it deserves. I don't want to feel like I'm moving on too quickly, but I do know I want to try again. I want to try again, not only for myself and my husband but also for Jack. I don't want him to be an only child. He was so proud to be a big brother. I want him to have a brother or sister, to know what it's like to have a sibling that is living. I know having another baby won't replace Oscar because he will always be our second-born son and nothing will ever change that, no matter how many more children we may or may not have.

We have also decided to change doctors. I cannot help but wonder whether, if the doctor had taken my concerns a little more seriously, my baby might still be alive. But we cannot live our lives on what-ifs and maybes; we have to learn to live with the reality that our baby did die and we cannot change that.

I grieve not only for the baby we did not get to bring home, but also for the man Oscar will never grow to be. I grieve for the things his big brother will never get to show him and teach him. I grieve for the smile on his face I will never get to see, and the tears I will never get to wipe away. The comfort I will never get to give him when he's upset or scared. The joy I will never get to feel at seeing him accomplish babyhood through to manhood. We will never forget Oscar. He will always be with us and be a part of our family, our second-born son. We will always love him, miss him and cherish his memory. I hope in the years to come we can look back and see how far we have come through our grief. And look back with happiness that we got to meet him at all.

I know that bright star up in the night sky is Oscar looking down on us and looking after us, telling us not to be sad, that he is happy now and he will make sure we are going to be okay.

Oscar, you will always be in my heart and mind.

Love always, Mummy.

Joni Ryan

Our Love for Maddy . . .

I look out my living room window into the backyard. The breeze is gentle as it sways the bushes and branches under a cloud-filled sky. The sun tries to break through but can only release patches of light. Desperate in its mission, it continues to try to radiate its light out in shards across the green grass. My eyes catch the swing set, and I notice the empty baby swing rocking to and fro, gently, empty.

Maddison would be nearly five. Nearly five years since we held her in our arms. The empty swing, such a stark reminder of our lives. Always a piece of us missing, an empty feeling, which just can't seem to ever be filled. We try to shine through with our strength, love and happiness, just like the sun, yet our deep longing and sadness always seem a part of us. Like the clouds filling the sky, our grief fills our hearts; it seems a constant battle to shine through. The gentle breeze is a reminder of our family, loved ones and friends, that they are always here to sooth our pain – to listen, to place a hand on our shoulder, to smile with us and to cry with us.

Maddison lived in my uterus for thirty-six and a half weeks. She was conceived out of love on 25 April 2002, Anzac Day, and she was born into this world on 22 December 2002 at 3.29 pm after an emergency caesarean. She only took four breaths of air on this earth, not even consecutive breaths, just four separate breaths of our air before she returned to the angels in heaven.

It was then that our lives, our selves changed forever. We are not the same people we were before she entered our hearts.

Sometimes I miss the old us, but most times I just miss the innocence we once had. I think back to a time when becoming pregnant seemed my only obstacle. Even that for me was not a great obstacle: I just wanted it so badly and immediately. We had planned our lives around the 'correct' time, working hard, saving, and trying to set ourselves up for when we could introduce children into our lives. I was a lucky one, falling pregnant almost immediately after 'trying'. I always knew there could be difficulties in getting pregnant. Maybe it wouldn't happen immediately, but it would happen . . . I knew miscarriage was possible, but not to me . . . and the thought of a baby dying at birth or close to term was just not conceivable in this day and age.

Our luck ran out after falling pregnant easily. We first became pregnant in October 2001. At thirteen weeks we went for our first, very exciting, very-long-awaited ultrasound, where we were going to meet our baby for the first time on screen, January 2002. Instead we were left in a dark, quiet, lonely room with an empty screen and a box of tissues. Our baby was classified as a 'missed miscarriage', a trite term for our dreams shattered. I had a curette the following day. The miscarriage introduced us to what could happen, and the fact that it could happen to us. A little piece of us gone, just like that . . . We tried again immediately and four months later we were pregnant again.

I took the pregnancy test on Mother's Day 2002 and there she was . . . two very pink, dark lines . . . We were ecstatic. Although very eager to get past the first thirteen weeks, we couldn't help but think, we'd had our turn with bad luck and we would be okay. We went to the first ultrasound with our hearts in our mouths. It was here that we first met Maddison: a healthy baby bouncing on the screen, with her stumps for legs and arms and her very big head, as all good twelve week old foetuses look. To us she was perfect already, and we were past the 'danger' period. It was all good from here . . . we thought.

I had the easiest pregnancy, just like the books tell it . . . I was buzzing around, glowing, just waiting for the due date so I could have the perfect birth and the perfect baby. All the check-ups were okay, everything was in order. I wrote my labour plan only a week before having her, and I look back on it now and cannot believe my naivety. When I wrote that plan I never would have contemplated a caesarean birth, let alone an unplanned emergency caesarean birth three days before Christmas that would end in such a horror story.

Mum and I were baking for Christmas Eve and Christmas Day and I told her that I had not felt the baby move as much today as usual. We both reassured each other that all was okay, because after all I had only been for my check-up with the obstetrician three days before, and it is written in all the baby manuals/books that the baby's movements do slow after thirty-six weeks as there isn't as much room left in there.

That night we went to a friend's house. We watched a movie and the boys had a quiet beer. We went home late and climbed into bed. I was still really worried about the kicks I had not felt but told myself that it must be okay because I had felt flutters in my lower pelvis, which I figured were the arms and hands moving. In hindsight, I should have known something was wrong then, when I realised that the baby's feet hadn't given me a big kick for a little while. But I told myself that she was okay, I had felt movement, so the baby was alive and okay, she was probably just tired from trying to move in such a small space and after all, I had been really busy with Christmas coming up. We were all maybe just a little tired. I am ashamed to say that I slept well that night . . . It is something I have thought about with great regret. How could I sleep well while my baby fought for her life inside me? I woke in the night and went for my regular toilet trip. I hugged my stomach back to sleep after I felt another flutter, and once again I told myself that it was okay.

In the morning we had pancakes. We had a lazy morning, relaxing and reading the paper; all the while I worried for our baby. While I was in bed, Craig brought me a glass of ice water and an ice pack. We thought that this might wake the little one up. I drank the ice water and placed the ice pack on my tummy. Nothing, no wild movements I had experienced a week ago, no kicks to the ribs. The baby seemed to flutter in my lower pelvis again, so I assured myself that it was okay.

While Craig read the paper I decided to ring the hospital maternity ward for advice. I explained to them that I was experiencing lack of movement and that I was sure I was being silly but that I was concerned. They invited me to come into the ward where they could test with a heart monitor and put us all at ease. The nurse explained to me not to hurry, to take my time and come in and the baby would probably move on the way to the hospital.

I immediately had a shower and got ready while I assured Craig that this was just to check things were okay. We laughed about how we were probably being paranoid parents and we would probably be sent home happy knowing all was okay in a few hours.

The hospital was fantastic. We arrived and were shown to the labour ward waiting lounge area. We were there only a few minutes when we met our midwife for the first time. She showed us into a room where I was hooked up to a baby heart monitor machine. This was the first time that I had this machine used on me so it was all unfamiliar and I wasn't sure how it was going to work or what it should show. The midwife placed the straps around my big stomach and turned on the machine. She fiddled with it calmly as she pressed different buttons and moved the straps on my stomach trying to get the heartbeat to show up properly and print out. I was sitting in a chair, so she moved me onto the bed to see if a different position would help. My heart started racing; it was the beginning of the proof that was going to confirm my gut feeling, my greatest fear.

Another nurse was called in and they decided to change the machine, as they hadn't seen it do this before, so maybe it was faulty. Another machine came in and the same thing happened. Then they tried different leads and plug, all to no avail – the machine wasn't broken, it was Maddison's heart, and most certainly mine which was breaking.

The midwife tried to count the heartbeat of our baby manually as the machine wasn't doing it; she counted it at give or take 300 beats a minute, way too fast . . . The panic in my heart was unbearable. I wanted them to get the baby out, to help it, to make it better, but on the other hand I wanted it to stay inside me, just to stay there and be safe like it had been for eight months.

By the time the obstetrician had come in, which was only about ten minutes, it had already been decided that I was to have an emergency caesarean. My regular obstetrician was unavailable so her emergency double was called. We met with her for a few short moments before being rushed off to theatre. She quickly explained that the baby's heartbeat was irregular and that we needed to have this baby immediately. We asked if Craig could attend the birth, but she explained that I needed to be put under an anaesthetic, as an epidural would take too long to prepare, so Craig could not attend. Like a flash she was going to prep and I was being made ready at the same time.

It was all happening so quickly yet I felt like I was in a slow-moving bubble. For a few moments Craig and I found ourselves alone in the room while the nurses all rushed around preparing and calling anaesthetists, pediatricians and the like. I will never forget that moment. We looked at each other, holding hands tighter than ever before. I cried to Craig that something was wrong, something was wrong with our baby, and I will never forget those words back.

'Today we are having a baby. Me and you are having a baby today . . .'

The excitement in Craig's eyes for that split second and that smile will stay with me forever. That last split second when we allowed ourselves one more self-indulgence of innocence. *We're having a baby.* I often think back to that moment, even as short as it was, that was the last time I can associate any feeling of absolute happiness. The last moments of our innocence. Helpless, yet still hopeful. After all, it couldn't happen . . . not to us . . .

Craig then had to go off with the nurse to register me in the hospital. I was panicking that they were going to have to take me away before Craig could get back to us, but then he was there. He gave me a kiss and I was wheeled quickly to theatre.

I cannot imagine what it must have felt like for Craig. He was left alone, pacing, waiting. I asked him to call my mum and dad and his mum, which he did, but he was alone the whole time I was in theatre. It must have seemed like an eternity to him. He could see into the area through the swinging doors and he could see nurses and doctors literally running around but he could only wait to know if we were all right or not.

The white walls rushed past me as I lay on the bed, and I

tried desperately to keep calm. I prayed, God please keep my baby safe, please keep my baby safe, over and over again in my head.

They transferred me this time onto the operating table. There seemed to be so many people in there, all racing about, all talking to me calmly. I started to get the shakes, and shudders: I was terrified.

The anaesthetist explained to me that because this was an emergency procedure he needed to give me as little anaesthetic as possible. There was a possibility that while I would not feel pain I might be completely aware of what was happening around me but be unable to communicate. I quickly signed the necessary consent form, as all I wanted was to save my sick baby.

My eyes fluttered and I could hear movement. I couldn't open my eyes yet; I was waking to the nightmare.

'What did I have?' I asked and a woman's voice answered back, 'A girl, you've had a baby girl'. I closed my eyes to the nothingness again. I fought it and asked, 'Is she okay?' and a woman's voice answered back, 'They're working on her.'

The next thing I remember is another woman's voice, the doctor's voice, saying, 'I'm sorry . . .'

I opened my eyes to see Craig walking towards me holding a bundle of baby blankets and inside, my beautiful daughter. I looked at his face and knew immediately. I remember turning my head away to the side, thinking if I didn't look it would all go away. I remember saying 'no' over and over again. I don't really remember taking her from Craig or looking at her for the first time. I just remember holding her, smelling her, squeezing her tight, willing her to come back, loving her back to life. I remember wondering if I was in a dream. I remember telling myself I was already awake . . .

For me it is a moment in time that seems to last forever, yet it also ends so abruptly in my drugged mind's state. I can't remember everything, and I hate that. I would give the world to remember exactly what went on in those moments, to remember seeing her for the first time, everything, every second. I want to remember it all, but the drugs and my ability to protect myself protect me from my memory. My life had changed. My future, my relationships, myself, changed in an instant.

We named her Maddison Michelle and she was the most beautiful baby girl, our baby girl. She had a head full of hair, literally long enough to brush to the side out of her eyes, the cutest nose, and the softest skin. She was perfect: 8 pounds 3 ounces, 57 centimetres long, all her fingers and all her toes. She just looked like she was sleeping. We cuddled her, nursed her, and handed her around to family and close friends to hold. She stayed in our room with her mummy and daddy.

It was so quiet. While the visitors were around we could muffle the silence. But it screamed at us like a siren. No baby cries, no gurgling, no rubbing of a fist to her mouth to suck, no sucking noise, no feeds, no nappy change, no tests, no needles, no weight check, no breastfeeding, no after-baby exercise program, no bath time, no vomits, no changing singlets . . . Nothing, just deafening silence. The room filled with flowers, but no *Congratulations!* cards, no *It's a girl!* cards, no balloons to acknowledge the new arrival, just that deafening silence.

We decided to sign the paperwork to allow an autopsy. We wanted to know what had happened. We wanted answers. What on earth could make a perfect pregnancy, a perfect baby die at thirty-six and a half weeks? No warning, no signs prior to lack of movement, no reason, no abuse of alcohol, no drugs, no smoking, no listeria foods. There was no reason for it . . . Passing her over that day was so difficult and being without her for the day even harder. But we hoped for answers, answers to the reasons for this pain. They were not to come. It turned out that there were no answers to any of our questions. Maddison was the perfect baby she looked. She wasn't sick or missing any parts. No reason for any of it, just speculation about what might have been.

This was difficult news. But I sometimes wonder if an answer would have been difficult to bear also. After all, I like that she was perfect. I like that she was all okay for her time in my uterus. She wasn't sick, she wasn't in pain. I am glad that they didn't find something wrong that I had caused. They say not to blame yourself, and I try not to. One side of me, the rational side, knows I did everything I could to protect my unborn baby. But there is another side that just can't help but wonder: if something was done differently, would it have made a difference?

After the autopsy we were allowed to bath her for the first time. We asked the midwife to help us. Obviously Maddison had been cut from the autopsy and the scars were difficult to handle and we were afraid we might hurt her. Our midwife was tender and made our experience as nice as it could have been. As much as I would have liked to do this on our own, we needed help and I am glad that she was there to take over and let us experience what we felt we had to do in the most respectful manner. The water washed over her head and the midwife talked to her as she shampooed her hair, her beautiful hair that already had curls like Daddy's. We dressed her in our clothes and wrapped her in our blankets, the same ones she should have been wearing in such different circumstances.

It was Christmas Eve and we had decided previously to hand her to the morgue on this night. After all, we had to let go. But

Christmas Eve came and we couldn't do it. Instead we chose to have her with us just one more night. She lay in her hospital cot, the only one she ever knew, beside our bed. We kept picking her up, stroking her, loving her, all the while knowing that the end of our time together was coming near. Soon we wouldn't be able to look at her, smell her, touch her. Soon she would be gone completely. Soon we must give her body over as well.

We spent Christmas Day 2002 in our hospital room with Maddison and our family and friends. There was a room full of people, yet it was so lonely. Our hearts were empty, our souls ripped out. I am glad we spent a Christmas Day with her. I'm glad she had a Christmas full of love, family and friends.

On Christmas night we asked the priest to come and give her a blessing. Not long after, they came to take her body away from us. She left us Christmas night at 9.30 pm in a navy material bassinette basket, which they zipped up over her head after they left our room. Our hearts broke again.

The hospital room had become our safe territory. I had never ventured out. It actually never entered my head to. I knew there was a world outside these four walls but I wasn't ready to face it. My new world, our hospital room, was the only place Maddison had been with us. There was no other world, well, no other that I wanted to be a part of. But the time came to leave and go home. Home, what was that? Maddison had never been there. Going home was so difficult. Seeing the world keep on going. I wanted to scream out the window that they all should stop. Wear black, do something to honour my baby's death, acknowledge our pain . . . but the world kept spinning and we were expected to spin right along with it.

Together we came through. I don't know how. There was heaps of love, heaps of tears, family support, support from

friends, crying, sobbing, laughing, loneliness, silence, screaming, stories, remembrance, acceptance, questions, some answers
and just plain time. We will never be over this . . . it's a part of
us. She is in our family, she is our daughter, our firstborn baby
girl. She will forever be talked about, forever remembered,
forever in our hearts. She is a piece of us and she has taken a
piece of us with her.

Every day she enters our thoughts, our life, in different ways.
Sometimes it's a familiar smell, a baby cry, a thought of what
should have been. Sometimes it's in her sister's eyes, sometimes
her daddy's, but she's always there.

Five months after Maddison passed over to the angels my
own father joined her. And another month after that we were
pregnant again. This pregnancy was far from innocent. It was
the longest pregnancy in history, or so it seemed, and there
was now no word in our dictionary for 'innocent'. This pregnancy was a blessing every day. Every day we thought ourselves
lucky to have her one more day.

Mia Grace was born by planned caesarean on 19 February
2004, at thirty-four weeks' gestation. We took no chances this
time and she was out at the glimpse of a problem. It was
probably a little early for her to come out in hindsight but we
just couldn't bear it anymore. Mia was a healthy 4 pounds
11 ounces and came home from Special Care Nursery two
weeks later.

Mia showed us what we had missed out on with Maddison:
a crying baby, dirty nappies, bath time, cuddles against a warm
cheek, her first smiles, rolling over, crawling, walking and those
eyes so full of love right back at you. We are so lucky to have
Mia. We were so lucky to have Maddison. Even if only for a
short while, we had her and we would never trade that.

Two years and four months after Mia was born we had our

third daughter, Monique Allana. Monique was born by planned caesarean on 3 July 2006 at thirty-seven weeks' gestation. Our fourth pregnancy, our third daughter, our second daughter at home with us. We are blessed to have three beautiful girls. Mia and Monique will grow up knowing they have a sister in heaven. A sister who is older than them, another sister who is as much a part of the family as they are.

Although the swing rocks empty, gently, in the breeze, I know it will not be long before Mia and Monique hop on for a ride. They cannot, and never will, replace their sister Maddison, but they show us what she would and should be doing. They help fill the void in our hearts. Not replacing, just filling extra parts. Slowly but surely the sun comes through. It's persistent against the clouds, just like we are in life. We still need the breeze, our family and friends rocking us at bad times, a hand on our shoulder, but together we are breaking through.

We are different people today, and we like these people . . . we understand absolute love, we are more caring, more understanding and we are parents. We love all our children equally, although we joke that Maddison will always be the good daughter who did nothing wrong!

Michelle Comodromos

Loving Madeline and Ashleigh

❦

My name is Kathy and I am the mother of twins. Madeline Kate and Ashleigh Brooke are my twin girls. They were born on different days: Madeline on the 26 August and Ashleigh on the 27 August 2002. I was twenty weeks into my pregnancy when my precious angels entered this world silently.

I won't go into the details of my labour and the birth of my twins. I'll focus on my feelings regarding being the mother of twin girls who are no longer with us in this world.

To those who have lost singletons, please don't think I value your loss any less by what I write, because I certainly don't. What I write is simply an account of my feelings and they are not meant to cause harm or distress to any other person. So please don't think I mean you any more sadness than you already have to bear.

I feel so cheated after the loss of my girls. Having twins is a unique and a marvellous miracle. To think of carrying, giving birth to and raising twins is something amazing, and I've been cheated out of that. I feel so hurt that I lost my girls and still don't understand why. Is it that I did something so bad that I don't warrant having twins? Or did God think I couldn't cope?

Having twins is also a bit of a novelty with others. It's special, and while I was pregnant I felt so special and so lucky. Selfishly, yes, I loved the attention I received from family and friends. No-one in my family had twins and only one of my friends had twins. I felt like I was so important, I guess. Now that's gone too.

I walk down the street and seem to see nothing but twins. Twin strollers, twin babies, twin toddlers, twins, twins, twins. On the anniversary of our babies' death I went down the street and wouldn't you know it, every person in our small town who has twins was in the shop at the same time as me!

I have this almighty urge to run up to people I see with twins and say, 'I've got twin girls too!' But of course I don't. I just cry inside and try to smile pleasantly as I pass by. My heart breaks. Each time I see twins I relive my loss all over again. Every time I see babies I relive this loss but it seems worse when I see twins.

I try to associate myself with others I know who have twins by asking questions and talking about my twins. But it's not the same. Sometimes I feel like an idiot. What would I know about raising twins; mine are dead!

At times I feel like wearing a big sign saying *I am the mother of twin girls* just to make me feel special again. I want strangers to know. I don't know why I feel like this but I just want people to know. I don't want pity or anything like that. I just want others to know I have twins.

I feel so unbelievably cheated. We have really struggled to have children, requiring treatment in the form of IVF, so to lose both our babies in one go just seems so cruel.

In all my pain and anguish over losing my girls one thing happened that has touched my heart. A friend who is pregnant with twins came to see me to ask for my advice regarding being pregnant with and raising twins. The fact that she acknowledged me as the mother of twins, and was so innocently genuine with her wanting my advice, was so precious and meant so much to me. Of course I couldn't really offer her any practical advice and I didn't want to worry her, because what could I tell her? My experience with my twins has not been a positive one to say the least.

Since losing Madeline and Ashleigh we have given birth to two more babies (singletons), a girl, Alex May and a boy, Jonty Francis. They are beautiful and the love of our lives. I feel guilty now at times because I don't want them to feel any less important than their sisters, either because the twins died or are twins. Because we have had such a hard time to get them, Alex and Jonty are true gifts from God, real little people to be loved and treasured for themselves.

So not only am I the mother of twins, I am the mother of three beautiful girls and one beautiful boy. How special and how blessed am I!

Kathy Hoffmann

Remembering Harrison

With a seventeen month old daughter already, Peter and I were eagerly awaiting the arrival of our second child. At the twenty-week ultrasound we were told that we were going to have a son and we decided upon the name Harrison. When I told my sister-in-law about our son, she said, 'Now you have the perfect family.' These words neither she nor I have ever forgotten.

At thirty-seven weeks I had a standard appointment and I heard Harrison's heart beating loud and strong. We had been a little concerned about Harrison as at about thirty-two weeks he had turned into the breech position but had now corrected himself and was head down, ready to go. Two days after my check-up, I noticed that Harrison had not moved all day. As he had been so active throughout the pregnancy I was a little worried. In the pregnancy books it always says: *If you do not feel movement for twenty-four hours then go see your doctor . . .* but the books never say what may happen next.

After an anxious night Peter and I decided that I should see my doctor in the morning. On my way to the appointment I kept reassuring myself that we were worrying too much and that everything was all right. We weren't even sure what it was that we were worried about. My doctor was away that morning so I had to see another doctor. He was unable to detect a heart-beat and so arranged for an ultrasound. I asked, 'What happens if the ultrasound does not find a heartbeat?' but he tried to assure me that I should not worry and to wait and see. I still couldn't name what it was that was frightening me – it was impossible to think that my healthy, active baby boy had died.

There was just a sick feeling of not knowing and waiting for time to pass until we could go to our appointment.

The staff in the radiology department did not read the instructions on the referral which clearly said, *Thirty-seven weeks no foetal heartbeat* and they were chatty and friendly, asking if we were coming to the same hospital to have our baby. Peter and I nearly gagged trying to answer. It was almost a relief to go into the quiet room and hopefully get an answer to what was going on. The ultrasound operator was also chatty and friendly (he didn't read the referral either!) but as soon as he started the ultrasound he became very quiet. We could see our baby was not moving and there was no sign of a beating heart. The operator went to get a doctor, who came in and they engaged in some technical chat. Finally Peter said, 'We expect the worst, please tell us what's happening.' The doctor said, 'I don't know how to tell you this, but your baby has died.'

The next few hours are a blur. I remember being taken into another room to wait for my doctor. We were given a SANDS book which I flicked through, and I managed to read that I should bring some clothes to the hospital to dress the baby once he was born. I also remember reading some of the things people may say like, 'Don't worry, you can have another one.' And I clearly remember thinking, No-one I know would say anything silly like that. Oh, yes they would!

My doctor arrived and I will never forget the look of utter shock on his face. The last time I had seen him we were listening to my son's heartbeat. He talked through our options and somehow Peter and I managed to make a decision about what we would do. We decided to go home and get our daughter organised to go with my parents, who had been minding her while we were at the hospital, and then we would return to the hospital later that day to begin inducing our baby. We had to stop on the way back to buy an outfit for Harrison because I did not have any clothes small enough to fit him. I cannot remember having any conversation with my parents but we must have done. What could we possibly have said at that time? We probably talked mostly about my daughter and made sure she had everything she needed. When we returned to the hospital the waiting began.

The support we received from my doctor and the midwives at the hospital while we waited for Harrison to arrive was fantastic. We were very well prepared for how he would look and the fact that we may not find a cause of death. I still do not recall a definitive moment when it hit me that my baby had died. I do remember one time standing in the bathroom looking at my pregnant belly and heaving with sobs, imagining him dead inside me. Harrison finally arrived on Saturday, 29 March at 6.20 pm. My strongest memory of his birth was the intense anger I felt pushing him out. I was convinced he would be born alive and had told my doctor this. My doctor, very kindly, reaffirmed that Harrison had definitely died but I thought I knew better. I knew he was going to be born screaming and kicking. But there was only silence.

Harrison was born with the umbilical cord wrapped around his neck twice and also around the body. My doctor said there was bruising on the cord to indicate he had died from umbilical strangulation. The photos taken straight after Harrison's birth show both Peter and I looking dazed, but also immensely proud of our beautiful baby boy. Those joyful hormones that follow birth are not stifled if your baby has died, and I can still remember that overwhelming feeling of love. Soon afterwards our family arrived to meet Harrison.

Over the next two days we had friends and family visit. Harrison was in the room next to ours and some people chose to see him. Peter and I spent as much time with him as we could. We were not able to hold him after his birth because he was too fragile, but we sat with him and stroked his hands and feet. I sang lullabies to him when I was with him on my own and told him how much we had wanted him to be born alive and how much we would miss him. On Monday he was taken by the funeral director for his autopsy. We wanted to make sure there were no other reasons for his death that could affect our decision in the future to have more children. It was a difficult decision to make because I didn't like the thought of what would happen to him during the autopsy, but he was always shown the greatest respect by anyone who met him so I felt confident that this would continue.

The hospital staff made sure we had lots of memories to take with us – photos, hand- and footprints, and a little book with his birth statistics in it and some poems and thoughts about grief. It was difficult leaving the safety of the hospital because the outside world was terrifying. We didn't want to go home to our empty house but we desperately wanted to see our daughter and hold her. The midwife made sure there was no happy couple in the car park putting their newborn in the car when we left. The attention to the details of our emotional state was just remarkable and I cannot praise the hospital staff enough.

I cannot remember who asked, but someone did say, 'Will you have another one?' and sometime early on Peter and I started saying, 'We always said we would have two children, and we have.' No-one dared say anything after that, but fancy asking that question when we had just lost our son. All our thoughts were with him and any discussions we may have had about the future were private and personal. I know the question was asked in an attempt to be positive and look to the future, but it was very inappropriate.

We were then faced with the prospect of arranging a funeral. My father didn't want us to have one. 'Why put yourself through it?' he asked, but we were quite surprised by the response we had from our friends and felt they needed the ceremony to say goodbye as much as we did. I am glad we went ahead because I am still touched by the number of people who took time to come to Harrison's funeral, and the intensity of the grief for a baby most had never met.

Afterwards my father said to me, 'I know now why you had the funeral. I really felt like Harrison had a life we should celebrate.'

My father now attends a memorial service every year with me to remember Harrison, along with other families remembering the babies and children they have lost. Many people are confused about whether it's okay to mourn for a baby that never breathed, but for Peter and me the answer was always that Harrison was part of our family, not just for the thirty-seven weeks he lived but he will always be a part of our family. The hole where he should be will never be filled.

For those around us, the return to normality came much more quickly than it did for Peter and me. When Peter returned to work, he received a lot of support as his boss had experienced a similar loss a couple of years earlier. Peter threw himself into his work and it was like he had tunnel vision for about six months. He didn't really want to talk about Harrison as much as I needed to, but I found every day I was confronted with challenges. I was a full-time mum with a toddler, so I was always around women with babies, friends who didn't know what to say and strangers who asked, 'When's the next one coming along?' I stopped taking my daughter to playgrounds because I couldn't bear the questions.

I eventually retuned to part-time work and found it a great

refuge from my thoughts. I also saw a grief counsellor for a number of months, and was able to vent the incredible anger that had built up. I never cried a lot for Harrison but I was so angry with the world. No-one could say or do the right thing, and when they looked to me for guidance I couldn't help them because I didn't really know what it was that I wanted. It was only with time that I learnt how to explain my needs and to feel comfortable talking about Harrison and not worry about the response I would get. My need to tell his story became greater than my fear of what people would say when they heard it. I couldn't control their response anyway.

We did decide early on that we would probably try for another baby. After six months we realised that we would never wake up one day and say, 'Hooray, let's have another baby,' so we may as well stop trying not to and see what happened. Our second daughter was conceived very quickly, which surprised us, and certainly took a while to get used to. Once we started telling people, I was worried they would think I was now 'better' and 'over it', but my grief for Harrison continued as my anxiety about this new pregnancy grew as well.

My mother seemed to spend the pregnancy chanting, 'It won't happen again,' until I said to her, 'I am back in the same statistical pool as everyone else – it could happen again'.

I kept trying to stop myself imagining the new baby dying but our experience with Harrison was still so raw in my mind. So one day I sat down and thought, What will I do if she does die? I planned her funeral in my mind, picked music and readings, and then felt much better, because at least this time I was prepared. I then stopped worrying so much and started thinking, Wouldn't it be a bonus if this one is born alive? My baby turned at thirty-eight weeks into the breech position necessitating a caesarean delivery, which made her arrival an anxious time, but our second daughter was born healthy and beautiful.

My feelings were so mixed following her birth. I was incredibly happy she was alive, but I kept reliving Harrison's birth and thinking about all we had missed out on with him. Each milestone she has achieved is a reminder of what we will never have and of how we will never know what he could have become. It is the loss of the future that continues every day. However, we do keep our memory alive. Our daughters know they had a brother and we remember his birthday every year with a trip to the beach where we scattered his ashes on his first birthday. We have mementos of his life on display in our house. We have been very upfront with friends and family and talk openly about Harrison. His death has changed Peter and me forever and we cannot pretend it didn't happen or that it didn't have this incredible effect on us as people and as a family.

There continue to be awkward comments such as, 'Are you going to try for a boy?', 'What a lovely age gap you have between your girls', or even, 'How many children do you have?' But now I know what to say, when to say it and when to keep quiet.

My story is not shared with everyone, although it is shared with most. I want to keep Harrison's memory alive for as long as I live, because although his life was short, it was meaningful, and it had an impact on the lives of many others.

Liz Lyons

Losing My Sons

❧

I was twenty-seven years old when I saw two tiny heartbeats on the ultrasound screen. I cried in shock and delight. My husband was speechless. Over the next few weeks leading up to the twelve-week scan we could not keep our news to ourselves. How excited we were, not just to be pregnant, but to be carrying two babies. Everything was fine in the twelve-week scan, and the nineteen-week scan broadcasted two very healthy babies looking like yin and yang in their top-to-toe position.

We found out they were identical, but wanted to keep the sex a secret, something to speculate on over the next four months. We nicknamed them Lefty and Righty. Lefty was a circus performer, always flopping this way and that. Righty was the chilled-out groover, just cruising along, enjoying the ride.

I was seeing a private obstetrician/gynaecologist at the time I became pregnant. He was referred to me by another doctor of mine. It did not occur to me that he may not be an appropriate choice for a 'high-risk multiple pregnancy'. He was an obstetrician, right? I'm paying him a lot of money. Don't they all know what they are doing?

At twenty weeks I asked my obstetrician about the hospital he had booked me into. Were they equipped to manage a (quite probable) early delivery? No. Did he have admitting rights at any of the three hospitals that have specialised neo-natal care? No. Did he consider that a problem? 'No, let's just make it to thirty-six weeks and then we'll be fine. I perform caesareans anyway at thirty-eight weeks, so there's nothing to worry about,' he said.

But just after twenty-two weeks I became uncomfortable. I was large anyway, but during the last couple of days I felt as though I had doubled in size and could not manage a walk around the block. I made an unscheduled visit to the obstetrician who assured me, 'There's plenty of water in there, nothing to worry about. Off you go home and why not just finish work a couple of weeks earlier if that makes you feel better?'

What I did not know about was a condition called twin-to-twin transference syndrome (TTTS). In TTTS the blood flow is unbalanced, resulting in one twin producing blood for both of them, which may lead to lack of growth in one baby and too much growth for the other. This syndrome can occur at any time during the pregnancy and is said to occur to about fifteen per cent of monochorionic twins (those sharing a placenta). Bearing that statistic in mind, most women carrying identical twins are routinely given regular ultrasounds to keep an eye on the condition developing.

Clearly my obstetrician was either unaware of the condition or was unable to recognise it.

That evening I lay in bed feeling incredibly uncomfortable. I could not sleep. When I went to the bathroom I saw a pinkish discharge. At twenty-two and a half weeks, I had not attended any antenatal hospital classes. I did not know what a 'show' was, or recognise any early sign of labour. I paged my obstetrician twice but he never made contact with me. In the end I called my hospital. They advised me to come straight in.

When my obstetrician arrived, he made no apologies for ignoring me during the night. He told me that I was in labour. If the babies were delivered they would die as they were too young to survive. I then focused on not delivering those babies of mine and somehow, miraculously, the contractions stopped later that morning.

On the advice of the head midwife I transferred myself, via ambulance, to a larger hospital with neonatal care. I had a fight with my obstetrician as he wanted me to stay in his 'care' whilst my babies died.

I was assigned to a magnificent man, an obstetrician who had a special interest in complicated deliveries. His bedside manner was confident and yet soothing. Eventually, against all my prayers and rantings and manipulations, I went back into labour the following day. To describe it as surreal is similar to suggesting that childbirth is uncomfortable. I was in a complete daze. I thought I had a sore back from lying in a bed for two days. I thought I had lost bladder control from the stress. I thought I needed to go to the toilet.

But in the end, I just needed to deliver my babies.

Righty was delivered first. He was stillborn. It was a fate befitting a baby who was so chilled out – he was at peace until the end.

Lefty stayed alive for half an hour, in mine and my husband's hands. He was so perfect and yet so tiny. He weighed 420 grams and his eyes were fused closed, too young to open.

My husband and I cried for days. The sheer physical emptiness of being enormously pregnant one day and then empty the next is indescribable. Then my milk came in, just to add insult to injury.

The pressure on me to prevail was huge. Here I was: successful, confident and capable. Surely I would bounce back and just 'try again'. I tried that, but it was no good. I fell apart about six weeks later. I had to pull over on the freeway one day because I could no longer drive through my tears on the way home from work. I called my husband and told him to call me a shrink. I had gone mad.

In the end, we all pulled through okay. I joined a wonderful support group called SANDS and ended up becoming a phone supporter to give strength to those who followed after me. I became pregnant three months later. I knew everything would be okay when we were told the due date: it was exactly a year after my boys had died.

I now have five children. Two have died, three are living. We visit the cemetery whenever any of us feels like it. Sometimes my six year old likes to picnic there. She likes to hang out occasionally with her big brothers.

Sally Stewart

'It's Gone'

❧

The doctor said, 'It's gone'.

I said, 'What do you mean it's gone?'

He simply replied, 'That's your heartbeat we can hear, not the baby's.'

That's how I remember hearing the most devastating news I've had to hear: my baby died. From that moment on, I know I've become a different person. It is amazing how your life can take a different path in just a minute. In that minute so many things were going through my brain, my heart and my body that I can still remember clearly the pain and anguish of the thoughts crowding me and the overwhelming sense of disbelief – that I had no other option but to cry, cry and cry. In fact I still can and do cry when I visit that deep emotional journey of the birth and death of my dearly treasured baby John Dean.

Although I had treatment for endometriosis, I conceived my first pregnancy relatively quickly. We were so excited that we were going to have a baby. I felt special and things were going according to plan. The pregnancy was relatively normal – no real dramas. I was the normal, anxious first-time mum worried about the impending birth and the baby.

It was the day before my due date. I went to see my doctor (my actual doctor was away on leave so I had a doctor I had only met one other time before). He decided to admit me into hospital the next day for bed rest and monitoring, as I had a little fluid and blood pressure. I remember feeling very safe in the hospital because it alleviated my previous concerns of when and where. I was kept in a maternity ward and the doctor visited me every day. Mid-Monday afternoon he gave me an internal examination as he was trying to promote the onset of labour (it was the second time he tried). He left me, confirming he would be back the next day and that if I hadn't gone into labour he would consider inducing me – by this time I was five days past my due date. I did experience pains within the hour and about three hours later the nurses asked me to gather my things and that they would bring me to the labour ward. I had a shower and my husband and I excitedly got ready to have our first baby.

I was settled into the labour ward (it was about 9.00 pm). I recall going to the toilet and I had a show of blood – the head midwife tested the sample and confirmed all was okay. I was worried and asked her to call the doctor.

I was politely dismissed with a chuckle and told 'You have a long way to go. This baby won't be born till tomorrow. You need to get some rest.'

I accepted her comment. I remember my husband being advised to go home and to also get some rest.

At about 6.00 am the following morning I was awoken by the prodding and probing of a midwife trying to check the baby's heartbeat. She was having trouble so she called another midwife; she also had trouble and left the room chanting that she'd be back. In she came again with another midwife and they left saying they were going to call the doctor. It was at that point I started to fret and I asked them whether I should call my husband. They replied it wasn't necessary and not to worry. I was left alone for what seemed forever. I can recall explicitly the doctor walking in, with such a concerned look on his face, and even though I had only met him a few times previously I think deep down I knew something was wrong.

Then he said with such a caring tone, 'Where's your husband, Natalie? Where's your husband?'

It really struck me. 'Why, why? What's wrong?' But of course no words came other than, 'At home, he was sent home.'

The doctor quietly proceeded to examine me internally. There was meconium in the waters and he advised me he was going to put a monitor internally on the baby's head. I could hear a single beat, a beat and then a beat – not the usual sloshing/swishing and fast heartbeat sound I had heard before. The doctor and midwives fumbled to lower the sound on the monitor machine. He grabbed my wrist and that's when he turned to me and said, 'It's gone.'

Thoughts flooded my brain: How could my baby die? How is that possible? What do I do? What do I do? How can I tell my family? How do I tell my husband? I was already thinking of others and I was already thinking I was a failure. How do I do this? I don't want to do this – get it out – please please just give me a caesarean. Please stop this. I can't do this. I don't want to do this.

The doctor rang my husband and told him to urgently get to the hospital. To this day I still don't know exactly what was said, but he came in very distressed and upset that he wasn't with me. He even spoke the words, 'You don't blame me because I wasn't here, do you?'

Looking back it's amazing how you can remember some things and comments so vividly and others are a blur. I remember so vividly being worried about how to tell my family. I felt like I had failed. It was distressing to believe that I was going to give birth to a dead baby. How could it be gone? Thankfully I was given an epidural and the labour pains subsided and I was then able to start giving some thought to how I was going to survive this day. I now reflect on the words:

'First we survive and then we grieve,' as quoted by Mal McKissock, a well-known grief counsellor. It was this I was doing: I was surviving (I even recall being told that I was good in hospital). It wasn't till I got home and alone in the depths of loneliness that I could or did start to grieve for the baby I didn't bring home.

I had a 'special' midwife who came to care for me during the birth. Now I know she was specially trained to help bereaved parents. She gently encouraged me through different thoughts, about seeing and holding, about creating memories, and the most challenging for me was facing my family: my mum, my dad, my very pregnant sister (she only had six weeks to go), my brother and my husband's family. I felt like everyone was waiting anxiously for the exciting news of a healthy baby and we had to ring to say the baby died. How horrible! I've failed! The question of 'why' was already racking my brain.

My husband rang my parents first. I don't know what he said but they came into hospital to see me straightaway. They were in such disbelief. There I was lying with my full pregnant body, crying and crying for my baby. Upon reflection they just wanted the hurt to go away; they were trying to protect me from the pain. Dad was trying to talk to people, trying to say, 'Come on, do something, help her have this baby and then we can move on.' He already had that attitude of 'let's solve this'. Mum was sitting with me quietly – I think in just utter despair and disbelief like me.

The doctor eventually returned and announced it was time for the baby to be born. They encouraged me to push, but I didn't really want to push – I was scared. My husband was with the doctor and saw our baby being delivered. There were gasps of, 'Wow, it's got lots of hair, it's a – a – boy! Oh wow – a boy!' He was a big boy at 9 pounds 2 ounces.

We called him John Dean. This was the original name we had ready if we had a boy. (I recall being quizzed, 'Was that the real name you had chosen?') The cause of John's death was a cord accident in uterus; his cord measured ninety-one centimetres long and had a true knot in the middle and it was wrapped around his neck, and one leg. They believe as I was having contractions during labour and my body was pushing the baby down into the birth canal, the cord would have pulled tight and he died.

John was born in the late afternoon on Tuesday, 27 August 1991. I wanted to see him; I had no hesitation. I knew I had to welcome my baby – I'd been waiting and wondering for so long. He was beautiful. I felt a sense of love and loss all at the same time. He was warm, but lifeless – he looked like a sleeping baby. We cried and cried. I wanted him so badly, I truly loved him. I was missing him already. I cuddled, I cradled, wrapped and unwrapped John, and I even remember rocking him, and my mum must have been scared, as I remember her hand on my shoulder stopping me. We took numerous photos: they look like any other photos of newborn babies but there is one photo of my husband and me and our faces with this stonecold emptiness – you can see the pain and anguish of emptiness and the question 'Why' on our faces (it brings me to tears). I love my photos. No, they are not morbid; they are my baby. They prove he existed. They prove and remind me that my feelings are real, that it wasn't just a bad dream and that I did have a son. And I grieve for my son John Dean.

We had called a priest to say prayers and name John with my parents and my husband's parents – it was special. I was being encouraged to let go: my dad was chanting in the background, 'Too much – too much – too many memories.' Little did I know that's exactly what we were trying to achieve. But how do you let go? I wanted to hold him forever. It was decided to let him go. He was wheeled into another room – and that was the last time I saw my baby.

I was moved from the labour ward to a room in the maternity ward. It was hard to hear others' babies crying. I could hear people's excited voices during visiting hours, a constant happy buzz around the ward. I never left my room during that week; I was too scared someone would ask me about my baby. I felt safe and sheltered in my room – the nurses or any visitors I had obviously knew that my baby had died. I did have an instance when a lady burst in calling out, 'Nappies!' No, sorry, no nappies for me – my baby died. I did receive flowers – they were special, because it helped me feel loved and special. I had a few visitors. I recall showing one girlfriend my photos and trying to talk to her about my baby, but she wasn't really interested. I remember thinking, Well, why did you come? People were already expecting me to move on, almost as if I had some medical condition. In hospital I was in shock. I would change from being okay to being a mess. Nights were the hardest; I was so lonely. I would just think and think, Why me, what have I done? Did I want too much? Did I do something wrong? and then feel even more lonely. I just sobbed and sobbed every night. I feel for the person who was in the next room to me – how distressing.

I was loaned (they made it clear it was the hospital's copy) a book to read: *Your Baby Has Died*. I remember just looking and looking at it. I was in awe that such a book existed and I cried even before I opened it to read the pages. I cried and cried reading that book. It was of comfort and also confronting at the same time. I was a little scared to read what was ahead. But that also softened the blow later when I did experience something the book may have touched on. My sister-in-law bought me a copy when I left the hospital. It was good to have reassurance that I was okay and not losing my mind. I wish I was able to keep that hospital copy: that book had my tears, my tears for John, splattered all over the pages.

I remember being in hospital and having aching arms (just like in that book – it was very uncanny). They just ached and ached with a heaviness of wanting to hold my baby. I actually asked a nurse if I could hold a baby to get rid of this heaviness, though of course I wasn't able to, so I just cried and cried with the knowledge that the baby was not going to be mine and in fact, mine was gone.

I was discharged from hospital early on Monday morning (the day after Father's Day) after being quizzed with, 'Where are you off to so early in the morning?' We just didn't answer. I don't think the nurse would have liked our response: 'To our son's burial.' It was only my husband and me with the funeral director and the cemetery representative. It was very lonely. I recall and still feel a sense of deep sadness and failure when sitting in the car in the car park with my husband, thinking that instead of a pram for our son, I bought a coffin for our son, and that we were going home without our baby. Without our John. I remember leaving the cemetery with my husband and saying, 'Oh well, that's that.' Even though that was very difficult and lonely I'm glad we went to the burial because now when I visit I feel a sense of closure, that yes, I really saw my baby being buried there and that is where his little body lies to rest, whilst I know his love is in my heart.

We arrived home, and there it was – the new mat with *Welcome* in green writing on it which my father-in-law had bought. We had just finished a large extension just in time before the baby was due. The mat was there waiting for us. It was meant to be an exciting time. I just broke down into tears and couldn't even walk through the door. I so desperately wanted my baby. I knew then everything was different and that there were some really tough times ahead. I think that's when I also started to think: I don't want to do this. I can't do this. What's the point?

The large house was empty – I had no job – I felt like I had nothing – I felt I was nothing – I was empty – there was nothing really to live for – nothing was of any interest to me. I was so desperately lonely and afraid of what was happening to me. My husband would come home and worry for me. He could see I did nothing all day but cry and cry. I was getting pressure to pack away the baby things that were out ready for John's arrival at home. I recall eventually doing that one day whilst listening to 'The Rose' (the song we had at his funeral). It made everyone else feel better, but not me. I still felt lonely and had no interest in doing anything. I remember going to the city and meeting with a close work colleague: it was so hard just putting the fake mask on, that everything was okay when it wasn't really. In the city everyone was going along merrily in the hustle and bustle. All I wanted to do was scream at the top of my lungs, 'My baby has just died!' I wanted everyone to stop. I wanted them to know the pain I was feeling.

I started to learn very quickly how sincere people were when they asked 'How are you?' and I would respond accordingly. There would be times when I knew I could be honest and truthful and they would accept and listen to me. Then there were times when I would just reply the standard answer I knew they wanted. But really I was protecting them, not myself. Although having said that, maybe I was protecting myself because I didn't want to hear their negative and condescending comments, which are very damaging to someone recently bereaved. It takes a lot of work to accept that they perhaps had good intentions but just didn't know what to say. Comments like, 'How's the woman of leisure going? . . . Oh. Well, if you were ready for that baby you're ready for another one.' 'At least you know you can get pregnant.' 'It's not like you knew him.' 'You were too big, you got very big and the baby was too big.' 'He was a big boy, why didn't you have a caesarean?' Or, 'Who was your doctor, my doctor is fantastic, and you should've gone to him.' Or even, 'Yes! It was a lot on your plate – your career, the extension and pregnancy and all.'

Slowly, slowly by talking and talking, taking time to think and reflect (I would read all types of books about grief and healing) and more importantly, taking time to share with others who truly empathise and listen, I was able to sort out some of the feelings and thoughts – of guilt – of failure – 'if only' and 'what if' – the anger – the blaming and – why me.

I found a few supportive people in my life who luckily are still in my life – namely my sister. She had a baby girl just six weeks later after John had died, and although difficult at the time, I was able to bond with and be an aunt to my dear little niece. There were even times I would just hold her and wonder and feel comforted by her. She always accepts me to talk and talk about my son, and understands it's part of who I am.

I had made contact with SANDS (this was encouraged before I left the hospital) and I was linked with a group in my local area. That listening ear and the nod of acknowledgement of my thoughts was so reassuring, that I was okay and that I was normal and that I was grieving. I was able to share stories and thoughts and I realised that 'It's not just me'. I clearly remember going to my first support meeting and feeling that deep urge to ask the leader about her story (I hadn't met or didn't know anyone else who had experienced the death of a baby). It was profound to acknowledge and see that she was okay. She was surviving this tragedy, and that life didn't end.

Life went on because there I was, still counting the weeks, days, hours and minutes since John's death, whilst she had to stop and think and remember how long it was since her baby died. It gave me hope that yes, I too can grow and help others and learn from this experience.

I did actually visit a therapist and quickly discovered that my emotions and issues with regard to difficulty in coping were not really related to the death of my baby but normal issues relating to family and self-esteem.

I found myself desperately wanting another baby. All I wanted was a baby. I had stopped work to have a baby. I was planning to bring a baby home – and I thought I needed a baby to keep going on. I found myself pregnant within five months and discovered I was due thirteen months after John had died. I was happy, although quickly realised that everyone just wanted me to have another baby as well and I resented that this subsequent pregnancy meant not many people wanted to hear about John: they wanted me to focus on the happiness of the new pregnancy (not that they asked too much about that pregnancy for fear of getting me anxious). This subsequent pregnancy was very confusing at times. I found it difficult to bond, because I was still very much mourning and grieving for my son, yet I had to try and enjoy and welcome and prepare for this new baby. I kept regular appointments with my doctor as I desperately needed reassurance all the time. I was scared something would happen to this baby as well. We discovered the sex of the baby at about twenty weeks (a girl) and this really helped my thoughts to planning and preparing for her safe arrival: we were already privately calling her April Maree. I had an elective caesarean ten days before my due date, as I was truly terrified and emotional that something would happen to her. It was exactly fifty-four weeks later to the day after John's death we welcomed April Maree – a healthy 10 pounds 11 ounces – and it was wonderful because when she was born, I felt that connection, that same love I felt for my son, and I kept chanting, 'April is here, April is here.'

Starting to care for a baby made me happy. I found purpose to my life and it alleviated that deep yearning for a baby. But it also brought it home exactly what I was missing without John and what he missed out on. April was an ideal baby. She was very calm and blissful, which certainly made it easy to care for and love her.

As the months passed and slowly the year ticked over again, I was still thinking of my dear son – perhaps not every minute or every hour, but the fond thoughts and remembering were there. I was able to sort through the anger, the guilt, the blame and the never-ending questions, which could or couldn't be answered. I'd discovered with time I was able to heal slowly.

I was able to think about another pregnancy three years later and we tried again for another baby. This time it took a little longer to get pregnant. I was able to enjoy the pregnancy with all its doubts and concerns. I discovered at twenty weeks I was having a girl. I again chose to have an elective caesarean and Lily Rose arrived safely nine days before her due date. Lily was a healthy 9 pounds 3 ounces and all was good. We loved her deeply from the moment she was born. She looked like her brother and sister and we could enjoy April celebrating the arrival of her little sister.

John would be sixteen now. I think about what he would be like. I see my nieces and nephews and friends' children and wonder how he would be. I wonder what he would look like. I find comfort in growing old with him in my mind. I like remembering him; it makes it real that I had a son. I feel I honour his memory. He is part of our lives as a family. My daughters accept and appreciate that they have an older brother who died.

I have some regrets, like not taking charge and listening to my inner instincts and insisting the head midwife call the doctor. I wonder if something could have been done to avoid his death. I regret not being able to bath my baby. I was given the opportunity, but I was scared. I had never bathed a baby before, let alone a dead one. How could I do that? I had to watch the midwife do it. What a shame. I couldn't feel his body in warm water; it would have been special. I regret not looking at the colour of his eyes. I regret not having more time with John; I would like more memories. I regret not having the opportunity to share my son with the rest of my family and my husband's.

I also have feelings of thankfulness. I'm thankful the cause of death is known. I'm thankful to accept that this was just a freak-of-nature thing and no one could have predicted this scenario by means of testing. I'm thankful I held, saw and spent time with John. I'm thankful for my photos. I'm thankful we had a little church service with prayers and music for him in the hospital chapel. I'm thankful we were able to attend his burial.

I accept the regrets, as I accept the thankfulness. I try to appreciate that everyone was trying to do their best in the worst situation, and although hindsight is a wonderful thing, you don't have that at the time. We need to acknowledge what was real at the time.

I'm thankful to accept that. Unfortunately those thoughts of 'what if?' don't really help, other than to help me accept reality. The reality for me is that life can change in a minute, that shit happens, and that bad things happen to good people.

Each year as the month of John's birthday/anniversary

approaches I think of my dear son. I think about the difference it would have made if he had lived and was with us in this world. My family would be different. My life and my thoughts would be different. I know I can visit that place of remembering John and it is still as raw as it was the day he died; I can still shed tears of grief. Or I can silently reflect on how special his gift of life was to me and my family. We celebrate his birthday/anniversary with a family dinner and then go to the cemetery. I love it when family or friends remember it's John's special day. I love it that they care enough to remember. (Mind you, they can still say distressing things, but I just look beyond that and accept that they are trying.) It's special that they remember these dates and let us know that they care and are thinking of us.

My son is gone and also gone is a little piece of me that will be forever John's; a part of me died. Also gone are my innocence and my naivety, but what I've got is a heart capable of love, compassion, empathy and understanding.

On his sixteenth birthday, I wrote a poem in remembrance.

16 CANDLES

*I think about you, every day, sometimes fleetingly and
sometimes deeply.
I think about you, and how my love for you never fades.
I think about you, and my heart hurts with pain to feel the
sadness of your death.
I think about you, and my eyes well with tears of missing you.
I think about you, and how special you are to me.
I think about you, and the difference you would have
made to our family.
I think about you, and the difference you have made
to our family.*

Our Babies Have Died

I think about you and how much you have changed my life.
I think about you, and the different people you have
brought to my life.
I think about you, and wonder what it would be like
to have a son.
I think about you, and I'm grateful for my two daughters.
I think about you, and wish I could share the special
occasions with you.
I think about you, and I remember you.
I think about you, and I miss you.
I think about you.

Natalina Scapin

If My Brother Were Here Today

❦

As I think about my brother John I think about the difference in my life if he were here with me today. Would I still act the way I do? Would we be really close and share all our secrets? Or would we hate each other and want to be as far away from each other as possible? I always wanted an older brother to be close with. But if John were here today we would probably be like all the other families – annoying each other – and I wouldn't have this unanswered question.

When I think about John I think about my mother, how she must have coped. It must have been very hard for her and everyone else. I can't imagine how I would cope. But with the help of SANDS my mother has made it through. I've always admired my mother for being so loyal to SANDS for all these years. I'm proud of her – after all that she's done she's still got time to help people in their rough time of their lives.

John has always been my brother and always will be, and he will be with me and my family in the good times and the bad. He belongs in all our hearts and will remain there forever.

MY BROTHER
Would we get along as well as I think?
Would you take me out for my first drink?
Would we fight all day long?
Would we like the same songs?
Would you help me with my homework?

Our Babies Have Died

All these things I wonder each day,
With no way of finding out,
What would happen if you were with us,
My mind is but a doubt.

April Scapin

To Have and to Hold

❧

In memory of Jeremy Leslie 31/3/2001

At 11.05 pm a baby was born. A boy.

But there was no cry; there was no sound.

The room was dark, dimly lit to provide comfort and shed no bright light on a tragedy that had enacted its final scene. The room was not busied with midwives and doctors. There was no laughter or joy, only two stunned and disbelieving parents who had just witnessed the birth and death of their legacy, their miracle baby. By their side, two very quiet midwives who knew the job that they had to do and did it with respectfulness and compassion.

'Is the baby alive?' I remember asking, ever so quietly, still in a daze and fog from the delivery.

'No,' was the sad and tearful response from my husband.

'Oh.' I sighed, somehow not fully understanding the enormity of what he had just said. I felt numb. 'Is it a boy or a girl?'

Trying to gain some composure and with the little strength that he had, my husband got the words out, ' It's a boy, we have a son.'

It was then that he brought Jeremy over to me cradled in his arms, naked; he put him on my chest. Part of me found it difficult to look at him. I was scared, but with encouragement from my husband, I saw the fullness of him. His body was limp, his leg had been broken in the delivery. He was warm and pink. He had hair, blond, and the most beautiful face. He was perfect.

He had the tiniest hands and feet, but I could clearly see his eyelashes and I opened his mouth to see his tongue.

'I knew it would be a boy,' I said. Jeremy Leslie.

Warren called our parents. Tonight we were proud parents of a baby boy.

Love between a man and a woman is the most beautiful of things, but for a child to come from that love is truly wondrous. Our love could not make a child naturally; we had fertility issues. After three years of trying to conceive naturally, we realised that with my endometriosis not resolved after a couple of laparoscopies we were not going to be blessed with a child. In 2000 we decided to take the path of IVF. A brave move, one that was not taken lightly, but it seemed to be our only hope. After an unsuccessful first cycle with the loss of two embryos and no viable ones in the freezer, we gained the strength to have another attempt. We repeated all the drugs, injections, blood tests and scans. I started bleeding heavily at four weeks and realised that again we were losing our embryos. But a miracle happened: at five weeks I had confirmation that in fact I may still have one viable embryo with me.

At six weeks, we were officially pregnant. This truly was our miracle baby. Could this be? Was it our turn now? Had our prayers finally been answered?

I was monitored by the IVF clinic up to ten weeks, and after that I began allowing myself to enjoy this wondrous life and experience. We had a scan at week twelve and all was good, then another at sixteen. The doctor had concerns that the baby was a little small and perhaps the dates were wrong. But after some discussion he put our minds at rest and said he thought everything would be okay.

At about the same time, I took myself off into a children's shop and indulged in one gift, a baby blanket for the cot. I bought this with some hesitation, as I felt that if I bought something too soon I might jinx it. I pushed those thoughts aside and proudly and excitedly walked out of the shop with my first baby's blanket.

At nineteen weeks, we treated ourselves to a holiday. My belly was swollen, I looked pregnant, wow , I was so happy. I watched what I ate, I took walks on the beach and we would daydream together on how our future holidays would be. Three of us.

A few weeks later we went for another routine scan. My mother was so excited as she had never been to an ultrasound before, and I was so happy that she could be there with us to see her grandchild for the first time and share our joy. Both sets of parents had been the most wonderful of supporters throughout our long journey to have a child, and for us to finally get pregnant was overwhelming, a dream come true for them.

The technician delayed in speaking to us and pondered over our scan for a long time, and we had difficulty seeing the baby. I knew something was wrong. She asked me to empty my bladder in case the baby was not clearly seen due to the positioning, but again I knew: our baby was in trouble. The reason given for the baby not being seen clearly was that there was little amniotic fluid. Amniotic fluid is the baby's urine and it seemed evident that our baby had not developed his kidneys or bladder, and as a consequence he was terminal outside of me. How could this be, this is not correct, our baby is fine . . . A call was placed to our obstetrician and we were told that it was possible that our baby could have potters syndrome (see note). To be sure, we were sent to another hospital straightaway for a second opinion. My poor mother, in shock and tearful disbelief, drove home. For mum to be there with us to get the news was cruel, but to have her there also provided the enormous support that we needed.

The second scan proved to be conclusive, but I could not watch. The pain of knowing that we were going to lose this child to something we knew nothing about and that could not be beaten, was too great. We were numb, we were in shock, and we were in denial.

That night my husband and I lay in bed cuddling each other, knowing that this may be the last time we lay as a family together, three of us.

The next morning on the way to the doctor's, we suddenly realised that it was important for us to get a camera to take photos of our baby once he or she arrived. We were glad to have done that as we now have the most precious of photos, of the one day of his time on earth, to remind us of his and our struggle with his life and death.

The doctor cleared his rooms of other patients, for which we were grateful as I don't think we could have sat in a room with largely pregnant women innocently oblivious to our unfolding tragedy.

He expertly and gently explained to us that Jeremy would not survive birth. The syndrome he had was incompatible with life and if we continued with the pregnancy (which would still result in his death), he would be in constant and increasing pain, growing disfigured in an environment where there was no fluid, with the additional potential danger to me if my uterus ruptured. We had no choice. His fate was sealed: induce me and let him die with dignity.

This was the most difficult decision we have ever made. How do you reconcile yourself to ending a pregnancy, and bringing into the world a beloved child without life? A life that should have been so full, a child that is needed, wanted and loved, who had a whole life ahead of him. A soul, a spirit.

To commence labour, tablets had to be inserted. After the first tablet was inserted into me, we left the clinic, and I remember my husband and I falling to our knees in the car park together, realising the fate of our child and the road we were all now on. The feeling of utter helplessness was overwhelming.

We spent the next six days in hospital in the maternity ward, waiting for the arrival of Jeremy. I was haemorrhaging very badly throughout these six days – blood loss was going to be a problem for me. By Friday, I had had over twenty tablets inserted, but still no movement.

It was my birthday . . . I was thirty-three. It was a solemn day. Unlike any other birthday, it was cruel. All I knew was that I did not want to have Jeremy's birthday and anniversary on this day. My family came to see us and help support us. I was really not even aware of anything that was going on around me. I can't even remember if we had cake. Warren and I were simply marking the time. Happy birthdays were no longer. During that week I talked to Jeremy during the quiet times in hospital, asking him to forgive us, telling him that we would never forget him and that he did not deserve to die. We were given a book called *Your Baby Has Died* and we both read it in disbelief. It did provide us with information that allowed us to put into plan things like funerals, photos and creating memories.

By Saturday afternoon, I no longer wanted visitors or to take phone calls. I was beginning to feel that this day was going to be it, that our baby was going to be born. I threw up and the constant bleeding and clotting had become stronger. I felt weakened by the blood loss, and more anxious of what was finally going to happen. I went into labour at 8 pm and by 11 pm, Jeremy was born. He was still.

As a result of the six days in hospital and the massive blood loss and trauma, my blood pressure was 50/40. Now I was in trouble. I was rushed out of the room past my husband, with Jeremy in his arms, to emergency theatre to have the placenta removed and receive two blood transfusions. My husband sat with Jeremy in the room alone, a dead baby in his arms – numb and alone.

At 2.45 am I awoke in the recovery room, remembering that I had had a son; he felt alive to me. I wanted to be with him. Had I been with him in my sleep? Did he and I have some time together while I was under anaesthetic? Why did I feel that he was alive? I was taken up to another room, a new one in the maternity ward, and there in a crib he lay, perfect little angel. The three of us were again all together. Neither of us could sleep.

The next morning, with our family present, we had a small baptism service, carried out by a wonderful nurse who used to be a nun. It was dignified; it was beautiful. Like any father, Warren wanted to show his boy the world, so he took him in a little basket outside to the hospital playground, showed him the sun and the sky, let him listen to the sounds of nature and quietly told him about us and who his family was. This was a very special and precious time for Warren. He had spent a harrowing night the previous night with Jeremy on his own, not knowing if he was also going to lose his wife as well. He often tells me how lonely and isolated he had felt. From 11 pm to 3 am he never put Jeremy down.

By 6 pm Sunday night, it was time to let Jeremy go. We had taken pictures, but there was never enough time. I talked to him as much as I could, but I still feel guilty that I did not talk to him or hold him more during this one day, but because I was sick and weakened from the week we had just endured, I felt I was in another place. Letting him go to the morgue to have his autopsy was extremely difficult. We were comforted by a nurse telling us that Jeremy was not on his own; he was with some other babies. Somehow that made me feel a tiny bit better but very sad knowing that there were other bereaved parents like us somewhere else, living this nightmare.

The day before the funeral, we spent two precious hours with him. He was dressed in a beautiful smock and I had bought a medallion of Mary and Jesus, which had been blessed by the priest. We put this around his neck. We placed him in his white coffin, and our family gave us things to send him on his way – a Richmond scarf, a blanket, a wedding photo, some booties and a bonnet along with a letter we wrote him. His funeral was beautiful; it was a perfect, sunny day and over seventy people attended. He was eulogised by us and he was introduced to our friends and family. He lies in a cemetery with all the other babies that have gone to God. It is a beautiful and safe place.

The following days, weeks and months were dark, very dark. Life had changed; it had gone from us. The sun was no longer seen by us, the sky was always grey and the colour was no longer in the trees.

We were broken people. So much of us had died with him. Waking up was hard, sleeping was very difficult and most nights at 3 am we were sobbing, howling into his blanket. Trying to exist was all we were doing. Our grief was all-consuming. I cried every day for twelve months. I left my job. How could I work when I was meant to be a mum at home looking after a child? One day was the same as the next. Friends had babies, family had babies. We were happy for them, but so sad for ourselves and the life that Jeremy lost.

Nine months later we somehow managed to survive another full cycle on IVF. Against hope we found ourselves pregnant. In cautionary disbelief, we found ourselves hoping that things would be different. Unfortunately at eight weeks I was taken to hospital after experiencing abdominal pain – the pregnancy was ectopic. We found ourselves asking again, 'How can this be?' 'How can you have an ectopic pregnancy (pregnancy in the fallopian tube) on IVF?' The only option that we had was to end this pregnancy.

We did manage to have five more attempts on IVF but only to lose all our embryos. We have now closed the door on IVF. We do however continue to try and conceive naturally even today, twelve years since we started this journey, but we have given up any hope of ever having any more children.

It has been seven years since Jeremy died and we still cannot believe what happened to him and how we have managed to survive. I put our survival down to a few things: having the courage to grieve, honestly and openly; having a partner that allows you to 'just be'; acknowledging Jeremy's life and what he continues to mean to us; the support of our wonderful parents, brothers and sisters and the old and new friends (some from SANDS) that have been with us every step of the way. And of course SANDS. If it had not been for SANDS, I don't know how I would have coped.

The loss of a child does change you. You say goodbye to the old you, and try and understand the new you. The pain of loss is a physical pain that you carry with you every day and some days it still catches you out. The added burden of infertility compounds that loss.

We would give anything to have Jeremy here today, a beautiful seven year old with blond hair and blue eyes. But he is not. We have not been blessed with any other babies, but we know we have our baby boy, our son. He is in our hearts and minds and it is his strength we draw off every day. We also recognise the loss of all our other IVF babies and our ectopic.

We celebrate our baby Jeremy; he has shown us much about love, loss and compassion. We are his parents, and I am a proud mother as Warren is a proud father. As hard as this is to accept, we know he has a greater purpose than to be with us on earth. We look forward to the day that we can wrap our arms around him, as he welcomes us to his home.

Note

POTTER'S SYNDROME:

Potter's syndrome is one of several serious or fatal kidney abnormalities. In Potter's (or Potter) syndrome the baby's kidneys do not develop in the first few weeks of life in the womb. The baby's kidneys are essential for the production of amniotic fluid in the womb. If there are no kidneys, there is little or no amniotic fluid (this is known as oligohydramnios) to expand the womb around the baby and to allow the baby to grow and move. The womb remains small, and in its confined space the baby's lungs cannot develop properly. Many babies with Potter's syndrome are stillborn. In those who are born alive, the immediate cause of death is failure to breathe (respiratory failure) due to underdeveloped (hypoplastic) lungs, usually one or two days after delivery. Even if this problem is treated the baby cannot survive without kidneys. (Potter's syndrome is also known as renal agenesis, which simply means that the kidneys did not develop). Males are more commonly affected than females.

Letter written and read for Jeremy at his funeral —
read by his mum
Eulogy — Jeremy Leslie
Born and died 31 March 2001

Dear Jeremy,

You were conceived on our second attempt on IVF, after being unsuccessful for four years, and your family and friends here today knew of you as our 'little miracle'.

We first met you when you were seven weeks old with an ultrasound scan showing us a 'flicker' on the screen, which we learnt was your heart. Our lives as a family had begun.

We watched you develop and grow through further scans, with each one revealing a hand, or foot, your bones and the reassuring sound of the strong beating of your heart.

It was with delight that we saw how you changed your mummy's shape and she relished in the new clothes she had to buy to keep you in fashion. You were kissed goodnight by Daddy and welcomed into every new day.

You made your presence felt at nineteen weeks just before a seafood banquet in the hinterland at Noosa, when Mummy felt little butterflies and she knew that you were saying hello from the inside.

A few weeks later our world was shattered, our hopes and dreams for you torn away from us. Life for us would never be the same.

When you were born, we did not hear a cry or see your eyes open. However, we could not believe how perfect and how beautiful you were, which made it so easy for us to fall in love with you. The nineteen hours we spent together as a family were the happiest of our lives and will live on with us for eternity.

During this time we relished and rejoiced in touching you, kissing you and admiring you, our miracle boy, realising too that our first child, our only child, was gone, along with all our hopes and dreams.

Our hearts and bodies ache for you, our empty arms yearn to hold you and your mother's breast wants to nurture you, but you have fulfilled us in a way we could never have imagined and created in us a love that can never die.

Jeremy, you are our first child, our son and you can never be replaced. Your memory will sustain us through our darkest days and inspire us to go on and make you proud that you chose us as your parents.

We cannot yet understand why you have been taken from us in this way and not be given a life that is whole, to ride your bike, jump out of trees, play with your dogs and drive your mum and dad mad. We do take great comfort in knowing you have been welcomed into God's loving family and care, and somewhere in time we will be reunited with you.

Rest in peace, our son, may your soul and spirit be free and thank you for opening our hearts to a new kind of love, that is both innocent and everlasting.

We will miss you every day!!

God bless you Jeremy,

Love, Mum and Dad.

PS A copy of this letter is with you for when you are old enough to read.

Veronica Steinicke

Our Precious Ones

❧

Many people list material assets and careers as their greatest achievements in life, but I've never been a very career-oriented person: all I ever wanted was to be a wife and mother. Yes, I am both of these and oh so proud of it. My husband and I have been married thirteen years, and have suffered a lifetime of heartbreak in those thirteen short years. We are the very proud parents of nine children, three living and six whom we have to carry in our hearts, as they are together in heaven with their gran.

Our first pregnancy was an ectopic. We found out I was about eight weeks pregnant and possibly losing the baby all in one day. Thankfully and gratefully there was no physical damage internally, and no major medical intervention needed.

Next came Daniel on 5 April 1997; he is a very healthy eleven year old boy. This pregnancy was relatively easy. Daniel was a big baby at 9 pounds 8 ounces and about 53 centimetres long and was a forceps delivery after a very long induction.

The next pregnancy was a miscarriage at twelve to thirteen weeks and ended up being delivered at home on my own. Later I had a dilation and curettage (D and C) in our local regional hospital and everyone involved was wonderful.

My doctors told me that our losses were just unlucky and nature's way. I was always determined that I didn't want an only child if we could physically help it, but I was beginning to wonder.

Benjamin Robert was our fourth child. He was stillborn at forty weeks and two days on Wednesday, 27 October 1999. He died in labour two hours before I delivered him, but he did give a final goodbye kick. Benjamin was 8 pounds 10 ounces and absolutely perfect. The only thing wrong was that he wasn't breathing. We delivered Benjamin naturally with the help of an epidural (which alerted us to the passing of our son). As awful as it sounds, it was a day of many mixed feelings. It was one of the worst days of our lives but on the other hand it was a very wonderful and special time. My husband and I were fortunate because unlike many bereaved parents we received an answer: it was strep B (the common sore throat virus), but how he contracted it will always remain unanswered and a mystery.

Six months later we found out I was pregnant again. It wasn't easy, but my doctor saw me every two weeks and every precaution that could be taken was taken. Everyone was wonderful. Almost a year and one month after Benjamin I had a caesarean and delivered a beautiful healthy little girl named Rebecca. Oh, the relief for everyone. We got to take her home.

November 2002 Rebecca turned two and a few days later we were moving for my husband's job. It was strange leaving home after seven years, leaving our friends, our home, our security net, the birthplace of all our children.

A surprise package came our way in 2003, in the form of another pregnancy, but alas I miscarried another precious baby at eight and a bit weeks. Of all my losses, for some strange reason this was the hardest. Strange I know, but I can't even begin to try and explain what I mean. But the medical profession could start to listen to bereaved parents.

In 2004 another pregnancy came our way but alas, just as before we miscarried at about ten weeks. If only they would listen and understand.

On 15 May 2005 – my thirty-sixth birthday – I found out

I was pregnant again. Oh what a birthday present! This time I was determined; this pregnancy meant more than anything else. Everything was going smoothly. We got over all the hurdles until Tuesday, 16 August, when I went for a routine check-up and there was no hearbeat at seventeen weeks. I could not believe it. Neither could anyone else for that matter. I delivered Adam at 6.05 pm Thursday, 18 August 2005, he was 16 centimetres long and weighed approximately 80 grams and was a perfect little boy. I was induced and it was a very long day, but still an incredible day.

Sunday, 9 April 2006 we were blessed once again with the surprise of yet another pregnancy.

There are so many mixed emotions coursing through our bodies at present, we are happy, and unbelievably scared of that roller-coaster ride again, but as I write this I am fifteen weeks pregnant and all is well so far. So we just pray that we get to late November/early December and we get to meet this little bundle of joy face to face!

Well, as time has now passed Joshua Gordon was delivered by caesarean section on 28 November 2006, a handsome and healthy boy.

As only other beareaved parents will know and understand, we miss and love them all dearly and wonder for what may have been. One thing that does help keep me somewhat sane is the thought that my precious little ones are with my mum. A regret of Mum's when she died was that she wouldn't get to meet any of my children. Now she has six of them to love and care for and spoil as only a gran knows how. After all my husband and I have been through, I still don't feel complete or finished even now after having had Joshua, but I have come to the realisation, those feelings will never go away because of the precious ones we have lost. But I don't think our families or our family can take anymore heartache. A lot of people say be grateful for what you have. Yes, we are lucky and are very blessed, but that does not fill the void and I'm not sure I can ignore that feeling deep within, but it certainly inspires me with my voluntary work as a parent supporter, just listening to and understanding others, whom unfortunately are on that same long, hard, never-ending journey.

This is only a brief summary, but it's still our story of love, hope and loss that I've dedicated in loving memory of all our precious ones.

Fiona & Jeff Sly

Friday's Child

✥

On 2 February 1996 I woke up with labour pains and I had never felt happier. The day was clear and beautiful and I was going to have the baby we had all been so looking forward to. We didn't think life could get any better.

I was thirty-seven weeks pregnant when I went into labour with our third child. My husband came home and took our daughter Mischa to our neighbour. Our son Lachlan had started prep excitedly the previous day and was safely at school. As we drove to the hospital we were both filled with excitement and happiness. Everything had fallen into place with this baby; we had our own house, we were doing well at work, and to top things off we were going to have our very-longed-for baby. I will never forget how blissfully unaware we were of how our lives were about to change.

When we got to the hospital, my contractions were two minutes apart; a midwife examined me and said she couldn't find a heartbeat. When she told us that, my heart sank, and I knew in my heart that the baby had died. The midwife contacted my doctor, while giving me oxygen to try and save the baby if it was still alive. It was a small hospital, so a paediatrician prepared me for possible surgery.

By the time the obstetrician came, I had a feeling of increasing disaster and absolute terror. We went for an ultrasound. All I could say to him was, 'Get the baby out! Help me!'

We had to be pushed through a public area of the hospital and it was so humiliating, feeling like a trapped animal and being watched like a sideshow. Once we got to the ultrasound room, David was distraught to see the monitor with the words 'no pulse' written across it. They waited till we were back in delivery to tell me the truth.

My obstetrician said, 'Sophie, I think you know what I'm going to tell you. For reasons we don't know yet, your baby has died.'

David was crying and I denied to everyone that it was true – but I knew that our happy dream was shattered.

I delivered my daughter a couple of minutes later, at 2.22 pm. The birth was silent; no sound of a baby crying and no urgency. After she was born, I kept asking if it were true – had the baby died?

The doctor replied, 'I'm sorry, Sophie, but it is true.'

We asked if we could hold her, and she was beautiful. We named her Somerset Rose. There was no obvious cause of death, and our obstetrician recommended we did not need an autopsy, as he thought the placenta had just stopped working for a minute, and in that minute she had died. He called it acute placental insufficiency. We were both relieved that she didn't have to have an autopsy.

We spent two very special days and nights with her in our delivery suite. Somerset slept between us and to us she was alive in this time. David was by far the more distraught; I woke up at night and he was just sitting in our bed holding her and sobbing. I was so shocked about losing her I just couldn't think and didn't want to think – it was all too awful. I couldn't bear the idea of having to give her up and leave her behind, so I was in a very scary place – I thought I would and probably could die from sadness. But part of being a grown-up is protecting other people and we both tried very hard not to let other people see just how desolate we were. We needed to be strong, particularly for Lachie and Mischa when they came in to meet

Somerset, and it was just the worst thing in the world to see them try to wake her up. They said if they talked really loud it might wake her up. They both also said, if they were very good she would come back to life, but they cuddled her and kissed her and weren't afraid of her; they were just extremely interested in her. But it broke our hearts to see their sadness and loss.

It was wonderful that our families all dropped everything to come and see Somerset.

We had wonderful midwives and a good obstetrician. Our midwives guided us step by step as to what happened next. They gave us the SANDS book *Your Baby has Died*, and worked their way through that.

We had her baptised by a lovely priest. Even though I'm not christened, it was important for me to have a special ceremony as she would never get married or christen her own children.

When we left the hospital, I carried Somerset to our car. We were lucky to be allowed to, as a midwife told us we had to leave by a back entrance. But we were adamant that we were going to walk out those hospital doors with our baby and with pride. And we did. Somerset had her pretty baby rug over her and we had dressed her in her beautiful delicately made nightie that my mum had raced to finish before I had her. It was beautifully embroidered. And Somerset was the prettiest girl you ever did see.

We drove Somerset to the funeral home, and held her as we drove. We were finally alone with our daughter. And we both just wanted to run away with her and hide and never give her up. We did give her up to the funeral director and they prepared our little girl so gently and thoughtfully that we could never repay them enough.

Her funeral was a terrible blur to David and me. We had a very well organised funeral celebrant who spoke appropriately about our little girl and our family. However, David was the most wonderful father and stood up and spoke about how proud we were to have Somerset as our daughter. He also spoke about how much we had longed for her and how we loved her. The reason he could stand up and speak was, as he said, the only thing he could do for her as her father now. The celebrant said some lovely, lovely things and then it was over. It was time to take Somerset to her private cremation. Just David and me and our special little girl. Our families took our other children to our house where we were to have a small lunch after her cremation. Before we had Somerset, we had joked that we wouldn't get any flowers this time, being our third child. But now, sadly, every surface of our house was covered with flowers. David stayed for a few minutes at the funeral and thanked everyone for coming. We were so fortunate that everyone who attended had only the kindest of words and actions. Again we can't thank them enough for honoring Somerset's life.

We drove Somerset past our house on the way to the cemetery to show her where she would have lived. Never have we felt so empty and filled with despair. Once we were at the cemetery we went into the chapel with her to say our true goodbyes. As we went in the sun was shining. How could it be such a beautiful day when we had to let our daughter go? All our feelings were so intense, it was as though we had packed her life into five days.

We said goodbye and let her go. The two people who had created her out of such love took her to her final moments on earth.

We did survive. But it was a long and very lonely journey of desolation and yearning. Having two other children and our own business forced us to get back into public life all too quickly. And in that life everyone seemed to be pregnant or have little babies. We both found it very hard to concentrate on anything and went through a period of fury at each other. We both felt alone, even when together. We had one of those fights where cups of tea go flying with lots of screaming. We got all our frustrations out about being very sad about losing Somerset and also feeling guilty about having to go on with mundane activities that made no sense after she died.

I went and still go through periods of researching why Somerset died and feel so helpless that I don't have a solid answer, just a suspicion of how she died. Although it may be seen as morbid I managed to save some of Somerset's clothes and blankets from hospital with her blood on them and have saved them and maybe one day they will be able to tell us what caused it.

My thought is that it is a maternal liver disease called obstetric cholestasis which is known to cause stillbirth mostly at the thirty-seven-week mark. However, I will never know, but I do try and let other parents know about this complication, and that they should always tell their doctor or midwife and never be put off if they are concerned – demand a blood test. This way they can save your baby by inducing it prior to thirty-seven weeks.

We decided to try for another baby quite soon; however, it took over a year to become pregnant. After a very long and stressful pregnancy, with much monitoring and late-night visits to the hospital, we had a little son who was induced at thirty-seven weeks. Oscar has been a total joy and is a very indulged and loved little boy. And in 1999 we were overjoyed to have another son, Flynn, who is a delightful and very thoughtful little boy.

Every year on Somerset's birthday, David takes the day off work and we take the children out of school and have a day dedicated to Somerset and celebrating her life. We buy the most colourful selection of roses we can find and take out a cake and a picnic to the cemetery and sit under a shady tree next to her grave and sing her 'Happy Birthday', then we have a chat and feed the ducks at the pond that is nearby. Then we head out to a family activity like taking the children to the cinema, a fun park or mini golf. It's always a fantastic day, but also so bitter-sweet; we should be a family of seven, and when we are out it still doesn't feel complete, there is always one missing.

Although we have had our wonderful subsequent children, we will both always miss Somerset forever and wonder what our lives would have been like if she had lived.

SANDS was wonderful and we both looked forward to our monthly meetings. It was a place we felt we could talk about our daughter, and people understood and never offered platitudes. We felt normal.

We are also very fortunate that some of our closest friends and my mum still send us flowers and cards on her birthday. I wonder if they ever know just how amazing they are to do that and how much we appreciate it.

Sophie Strang

It's Always There . . .

My first birth experience started fine in 1969. When I first went to the hospital the staff began the usual prep. The nursing sister came back to listen to the baby's heartbeat: she seemed nervous, anxious. I remember saying to her, 'Sister, I spent six months learning relaxation techniques and you are making me nervous.' She started pacing up and down the hallway looking out for the doctor. Then all of a sudden they rushed me into another room, the doctor arrived pulling on gloves and his white coat . . . There I am up in stirrups, and not sure what was even happening. Someone handed him the forceps, crunch . . . the baby was delivered and wrapped up. The sister gave me a quick look at the baby as she rushed past – not even stopping. Then as quickly as it started, I was stitched and washed, sat on a bedpan and told that I could not see my husband until I had 'passed water'. I sat there like a stunned mullet, until I was blue with cold and my teeth chattering. I finally got the courage to ring the bell and eventually the nurse came back . . . I told her that I was sorry, but I could not pass water. She said that it was okay and took the pan away. I heard her outside saying to another nurse, 'I forgot about her. I forgot about her.' Eventually they put me into a huge room with ten other mothers. I think that was the first time I saw my husband, but I did not see my baby.

They seemed to avoid telling me anything at all and kept passing it onto the specialist who was to be there 'the next day'. When he arrived he told me that a valve in the heart had not formed.

I said to him, 'Does that mean she will have brain damage?'

His answer was that we would have to wait for the results of the tests.

That night, while I was asleep, a young nurse came in and said to me, 'The baby was dead.' Just – like – that. I was stunned. I wanted to scream, but couldn't. I would have woken the others in the ward. I just slid under the sheets, desolate. Then the nurse came back with a sleeping tablet. The next day, a new room.

The doctor said, 'Get her out of here.'

Then I was told to 'go home and have another baby'. The doctor wrote me out a prescription for tablets to dry up the milk.

I was completely bewildered.

No-one came to visit me, no-one showed me my baby, no-one even mentioned my baby. I went home with my husband. We had no funeral.

Then the questions and self-recriminations started. Why is no-one talking to me? Maybe the doctor will ring and tell me when the next step is. How come no-one is telling me anything?

We had no funeral.

I felt guilt . . . so much guilt. How could I have left the hospital without seeing my baby?

We had no funeral.

The next week the health centre nurse came to our home to visit my baby. I remember saying to her, 'She is dead.' Then the nurse was gone.

All I can remember was the loneliness, and platitudes, keep up the stiff upper lip.

I had always expected to see my baby and to hold my baby. It never happened. I had no choice and I was given no options.

My trust in everything was broken.

I remember crying to my husband, 'How could we let our baby go without holding her and telling her that we loved her?'

My husband then said it was okay, that he had held her. Can you imagine my reaction? Why didn't they allow me also? What was wrong with me? I saw myself as a failure as a mother. I felt that it was all my fault. That self-recrimination deeply affects one's self-esteem. I cried at every television show, be it sad or happy.

Eventually we got the bill, months later, from the funeral parlour. My husband then went to find where she was buried. There was nothing there – just a paddock. It is a basic human right to be able to bury one's own and to know where they are. And for me again, it was not good enough.

We were unable to share our grief. If I expressed my grief to my husband, he would get upset as it looked like I was blaming him. Two completely different experiences. Very alienating. I learnt to shut up and lock my feelings away. No voice. Disempowered.

Somehow we learn to cope.

I look back and wonder how I got through being pregnant again. It was a nightmare. I was so nervous. I have two sons.

In 1994 an acquaintance told me about SANDS and she said I should go.

I told her, 'It was so long ago.'

She then said, 'You need to go.'

I remember that first phone call. I was a nervous wreck. The woman asked me about my experience. 'What did you have?' 'How much did she weigh?' 'What did you call her?' 'And then what happened?' Wow! In twenty-five years, no-one had ever asked me those questions. My experience was validated. I was normal. Yes, babies live and die.

When I discussed going to the meeting with my family, they

were horrified. My two sons said, 'Dad, will she start crying again?'

I went to the group meeting and listened to all their stories. All of the other parents saw and had held their babies, and some even had photos. But I felt my story was hideous in comparison to theirs.

On returning home that evening, I was asked, 'What was it like?'

My answer was, 'Great'.

'What do you mean?'

Everyone was in the same boat. I felt validated and reassured . . . and that I really was normal.

In 1996 SANDS formed an older loss group. I was one of the group of six that was in that foundation group. We had a supportive environment in which to share our stories. Validation. Normalisation. Courage to open up old wounds. Verbalisation: To be able to say my baby's name! SANDS holds a memorial service each year.

During the first one I attended I was asked to write Alina Jane's name on a card to be included in the service. Each one of us was asked to light a candle and place it on the table. It was a very emotional time for me. This was my time to claim the lost time with my baby. I do not know how I got through that day. But the group gives strength and support, for the next task . . .

To make a plaque in memory of Alina Jane. I think I nearly drove the group to distraction, with my wording and the constant re-wording of the plaque. But to me, the issues were the wording, as I had to say what happened and that it was not okay. This is what I wrote:

I did not have the chance to look into your eyes and to say you are so beautiful and to say you are mine. You were taken from me without my consent, no chance to say goodbye, you are part of our family – always remembered.

A great thing for me was when my husband said that he was proud of me and that he was glad I had done it. So healing. And we had a SANDS celebration afterwards with champagne and balloons in the cemetery!

Lynne Vago

Life on a Rollercoaster

❧

My journey has been long and varied, but it has made me the person I am today, of whom I am very proud.

We had been married about six years when we decided to try for the first of our family of four children. After a year of not getting pregnant, we were referred to a gynaecologist for tests and investigation. It was found there was a problem with antibodies in my husband's sperm which were stopping any healthy sperm from fertilising my eggs. A course of cortisone which made him blow up like the Michelin man seemed to do the trick as I became pregnant within three months. The day my pregnancy was confirmed we were ecstatic. We told everyone. I started buying things for the baby, we discussed names and I dreamed about our new life.

At ten weeks I had some bleeding, and was sent for an ultrasound and given a big envelope to take back to the doctor, and when he said, 'You've had a miscarriage,' I didn't really understand what that meant. I was told to go home and wait for a phone call to tell me when to go to the hospital. *What for?* I wanted to ask but was too scared to. I drove home in a blur of tears, realising then that our precious baby was not alive. I didn't ask nor was I told what a curette was, but when the call came I dutifully went to the hospital like I was told and had surgery about an hour later. After a short time in recovery, I was sent home – no explanations, no words of sympathy, nothing.

I felt so sad and empty, but after being patted on the hand and told, 'Never mind, there was obviously something wrong with the baby,' I felt silly for crying, so I pushed down all the grief feelings. I felt quite alone; no-one explained that I might feel like this.

We tried for a baby quite soon after the miscarriage as we were quite confident I would fall pregnant quickly. When nothing happened for twelve months, we went back to the doctor. We were referred to an IVF clinic and went on the waiting list. Almost eighteen months later, we were told it was our turn. To my huge disappointment, the first cycle was cancelled as I had only produced one medium-size egg follicle.

For the next cycle, the hormone doses were adjusted from the beginning to the maximum, but still no joy this time either. Then the doubts started to creep in. What was wrong with me? Why was this happening? Will I ever get pregnant?

After a series of blood tests I went to see the doctor, and the words he spoke still ring in my ears: 'I'm sorry, there's nothing more we can do for you.'

I don't know how I made it out of the doctor's office when I realised what those few words meant. We would never have our family of four children, not even one child. I had never imagined a future without children. I was gutted and held back my tears all the way home. I collapsed inside the front door, inconsolable and not able to see past that moment. For days I stayed home grieving for my future without children.

After much reflection and processing of my thoughts, I was able to move through my grief, and started to accept my new future. Several months later, by chance, I was reading an article in a magazine about some new IVF technology that may be able to help us. I immediately looked up the number of the clinic and had my doctor write me a referral. My first visit gave me some hope and for the first time in a long time, I started to feel like it was possible to achieve my dream.

We patiently waited two years before our name came to the top of this list. The first transfer was nerve-wracking as I got used to the daily hormone injections needed to 'kick-start' and then sustain a pregnancy. The two weeks between the embryo transfer and the blood test to tell us if we were pregnant were very long. The call finally came – we were not pregnant. Again disappointment, but we had not given up.

The next transfer gave us the result we had been waiting for. We were finally pregnant six years after the first time. We celebrated, but we were still cautious. An ultrasound at six weeks showed a small blood sac next to the baby, but we saw a heartbeat and started to be hopeful that everything would be okay this time. However, a follow-up ultrasound at eight weeks showed a smaller than average baby and no heartbeat. Another failure. What sort of woman am I? I can't get pregnant, and I can't carry a baby past the first few weeks.

This time I didn't have a dilation and curettage (D and C), and one afternoon had severe cramping that came in waves. I now know this was like labour and giving birth, only not on the full-blown scale! The next day at work the sac and baby appeared when I went to the toilet. I stared at it for a while, then panicked and flushed it down the toilet. That still haunts me to this day, that I just flushed my baby away. For months the last thing I saw before I eventually fell asleep was my baby. As we hadn't told anyone we were pregnant this time, I kept quiet about the miscarriage. I felt more alone than before. At least people were there for support last time as they had known about the pregnancy.

Several further transfers failed and we were still not pregnant. We had reached the end of an emotional journey, and so faced a future without children, again. We decided we would have one more try, and regardless of the outcome, this would be the end of our IVF rollercoaster ride. The daily injections and the long two-week wait were worth it when we heard the words, 'Congratulations, you're pregnant!'

We dared to hope that this pregnancy would be the one. I continued with the injections and had weekly blood tests to check my hormone levels. Each week when the results were rung through, we held our breath, but each week they were fine. We crept past the eight-week mark, then the ten, and by week thirteen I was able to stop the injections. With rising excitement, we had our nineteen-week ultrasound and everything was perfect. I remember the words of the sonographer and listened to them over and over on the tape: 'That's a happy, healthy baby you have on board.' We soared out of the ultrasound rooms.

I started to buy things for the baby and felt fantastic. The most magic day for me was when I felt the first kick at around twenty-three weeks. I couldn't get enough of my growing tummy and the prods and pushes from our little miracle. Each appointment with my obstetrician was one week closer to meeting our baby. My check-up at thirty-seven and a half weeks was no different to the rest: good strong heartbeat, head down, good size. Only three weeks to go . . .

The next night my baby was *very* active, like it was an acrobat in the circus. I watched for an hour as the little feet and hands moved across my stomach, revelling in every movement. The following day I didn't feel much movement but wasn't too worried as my baby Bible said that babies may slow down their movements in the last few weeks. By the next day I was having some slight cramping pains and thought I may have been in early labour. The lack of movement started to concern me so we headed off to the hospital. On the trip there my fear levels were rising.

After several attempts to find the heartbeat were unsuccessful, the doctor finally arrived with an ultrasound machine and her words are imprinted on my brain: 'I'm sorry, your baby has died.'

The worst moment of my life – my heart shattered into a million pieces. Why? How? What went wrong? Why are we being punished like this? My poor baby. What happens now? My head was spinning with all these thoughts while I was sobbing, not just crying, but deep painful sobs. I don't remember what happened next, but we managed to drive to my mum's place and tell her, then somehow we got home and collapsed. I don't think I slept that night but one thing I remember is rubbing my tummy and talking to my baby, willing it to move, hoping the doctor was wrong, and determined to make a miracle happen.

The next morning we packed a few things and went back to the hospital to be induced. Two lots of gel and not much progress. I was exhausted physically and emotionally, and halfway through the night had an epidural to relieve some of the pain so I could get some sleep. The following morning my waters broke and things started to move along. At 10.14 am on 18 July 1995 my baby was born feet first and was put straight into my arms. I stared for what seemed like the longest time at my beautiful baby, the one I'd been waiting thirty-eight weeks to meet. How could we create something so beautiful, so perfect? Then the doctor asked if we had looked whether it was a boy or a girl. I lifted the baby up to see we had a daughter. Instantly I spoke her name. 'Stephanie.' I fell in love in that first second. Please open your eyes, please breathe, please cry. I was pleading with her silently. Prove those doctors wrong and please be alive. I took in every detail of her gorgeous face, not wanting to forget anything.

When I finally realised that what the doctor had told me

was true, the tears began to fall. They wouldn't stop, and I just kept staring at my beautiful daughter. How did this happen? Why did she die? Why did this happen to us after all the years of trying to have a baby? Was this our only chance of being parents? So many thoughts going round and round in my head, and all the while I couldn't stop looking at my little girl. I held her for what seemed like just a second, and then passed her to the midwife, who dressed her in a nightie and nappy, then wrapped her in a bunny rug. It was her dad's time for a hold. The look on his face was a mixture of sadness and pride.

My mum was next for a cuddle and my everlasting image is of her rocking Stephanie and patting her gently on her nappy, like everyone does when they are cuddling a baby. A close friend who had also been there for the birth gave her a cuddle as well. Stephanie had so much love around her and I know she felt this. I was sad she had died, but in those early moments I was also sad that she would not be here to share our lives, for us to see her grow up and become a beautiful young woman.

I wanted to bath her before my family came to see her, but as I had had an epidural, I was not able to get out of bed. The midwife brought in a crib filled with water, so I could wash her from my bed, but I was not able to move to the edge of the bed. I watched as the midwife gently bathed her, treating her with respect and talking to her as she splashed water over her. I regret that I had not waited and done this later, so I could be the one talking to her, splashing her and gently bathing her. The midwife then passed her to me on a towel and I carefully dried her, taking in all the details of her body – her long fingers, her big feet, her lanky legs and of course her beautiful face. I dressed her in a fresh nightie and wrapped her in a hand-knitted shawl made by my auntie, her great-auntie. She was now ready for her visitors.

My sister, brother and sister-in-law all came in to see her, but a lot of the afternoon is a complete blur. I remember the midwives giving me a little book with some hand- and foot-prints, some photos and a lock of hair. I still treasure these memories of my little girl. We took what seemed like a heap of photos, but when I got the film developed, there were only ten. I wish someone had told me to take lots more – to take two or three or four rolls of film. I didn't realise at the time that these would be the only ones I would have – forever.

After all the visitors had gone we spent some time with our daughter as a family and gave her kisses, hugs, told her we loved her over and over, and tried to fit in a lifetime of loving into a few hours. We called the midwife to take her about 5.00 pm, which was one of the hardest things we've ever done – letting her go, never to see her again, being taken away from us. I felt like part of me left the room with her and I have never felt so empty in my life. We both sat and stared at the door for ages after she left, not knowing what to say, not wanting to talk for fear of crying again. The silence in the room was deafening and closing in around me. I wanted to scream 'It's not fair' but kept quiet in case I upset any of the other patients.

With no visible indications as to why she had died, we agreed to have an autopsy done to determine the cause of death. We were told that there may be no reason found, but we decided to have it done in case there was a genetic problem that may impact future pregnancies.

I was moved from the delivery suite to a small room away from the new babies for which I was very grateful. My husband went home and I was finally on my own. I had a shower and cried for what seemed like hours. I was aching to see my baby, and finally fell asleep. I wish I had asked to have her with me that night – just Stephanie and me sleeping together for a whole night. I was too scared to say I had changed my mind about having more time with her. I didn't want to be any trouble for the staff so I kept quiet. Another regret.

The next morning I was allowed to go home. The walk out of the hospital without my baby was so hard. I was leaving her behind, going home without her. My heart shattered into more pieces as we drove away from the hospital. Silence again in the car as we drove along, each in our own thoughts. Not wanting to voice what we felt because then it seemed more real.

The house felt unbearably empty and silent. No baby cried to break the quiet. The nursery door was closed and I wasn't able to open it. Streams of flowers arrived and the phone was ringing. I didn't answer it, and only returned calls when I felt strong enough to speak to people. My house was my safety zone. I was able to let in who I wanted to and keep out who I didn't want to see. The days leading up to Stephanie's birth and the birth itself replayed over and over in my head. I wanted to stop the tape and turn it off but I couldn't. I kept thinking about the what-ifs and punishing myself for letting her die. It must have been my fault because I am her mother and mothers protect their children. She died inside me – what sort of mother am I?

I hardly slept for those first few nights and I was exhausted mentally and physically. My mind would not stop – a constant whirl of thoughts from which I only got a break when I finally fell asleep. I felt my thoughts were irrational and that I was hanging onto sanity by my fingertips.

My husband returned to work the following week and I was living in a fog. Time stood still and I couldn't remember what had happened five minutes ago. He would ask me what I had eaten for breakfast and I couldn't remember. He would ask me what I watched on television and I couldn't remember. He would ask me if I had had a shower and I couldn't remember.

120

My world had stopped and I couldn't understand why everyone else was carrying on as though nothing had happened. It was then I realised that 'life goes on'.

The funeral was held two weeks after Stephanie's death. We had been given the option of a hospital-arranged funeral, and because it was the easy option, we took it. It was held in the chapel at the hospital, and there were eleven other babies being buried that day along with her. We were only allowed to have five other people there and the service, while it was very touching, was not personal. The names of the babies were read out at the end of the service. We didn't attend the burial at the cemetery. A few months later we were notified that the plaque had been laid, and we visited for the first time. The plaque had each baby's surname and date of birth. I was very sad we had not chosen to arrange her funeral. We could have had all our friends and family there to say goodbye, we could have chosen the cemetery where she was buried, we could have chosen the readings and the music that was played, and most importantly, her name would have been on the plaque. This is my biggest regret. It was the one thing we could have done as her parents, and we didn't do it. I still punish myself for not being strong enough to arrange her funeral.

Six weeks after Stephanie's death, I visited my obstetrician for my check-up and to get the results of the autopsy. He took a lot of time to read through and explain all the medical terminology in the report, with the end result being that there was no apparent reason for her death. All her organs were normal, tests for infection were normal, in fact the word 'normal' was repeated over and over in the report. I felt quite sad that there was no cause for her death, and then had to look elsewhere to find someone or something to blame. I, of course, turned that blame inwards and thought, in the absence of any other reason, that I must have caused her death. I knew this wasn't the case but that didn't stop me thinking it. The only possible explanation was that she had turned around (from head down to feet down) and in the process compressed the umbilical cord with her foot, or her head, or her arm, long enough to cut off her oxygen supply, but not enough to damage the cord itself.

My family, especially my mother, and my close friends were fantastic support to us in those early weeks, listening every time I wanted to talk, bringing dinner, doing washing and just being there. But I needed more – to talk to someone who had experienced the death of a baby so I could find out if my thoughts and feelings were normal or if I really were crazy. I dug out the book that I was given in hospital from SANDS and after reading it, nervously rang the number and spoke with a lady whose baby had died a couple of years earlier. We chatted for a while and it was such a huge relief to feel that my thoughts were normal and that one day I would start to feel better, that I would start to heal and be able to look to the future positively. I could cope with the fluctuating emotions knowing that I would one day move forward and not be in this place forever. I needed reassurance that I would one day be able to think about Stephanie without the intense sadness and pain I felt in those early weeks and months.

I attended a support meeting the following week and to walk into a room of people who knew how I felt was so comforting. I was not ashamed to cry in this room and I identified with others when they were talking about their experience. I wanted to shout at the top of my lungs on the way home, 'I'm normal!' I continued attending meetings over the next few months and after each one could feel myself moving forward in tiny steps.

Three months after Stephanie was born I went back to work. The journey there was terrifying; my stomach was in knots, anticipating how my work colleagues would treat me and react to me. Would they talk to me? Would they ask me about Stephanie? Would they not mention her at all? Would they pretend nothing has happened? My head was spinning. I walked to my desk and the first thing I did was to put her photo on my desk. Over the course of the morning, more and more people came over and spoke to me, some even asked if I had any photos. I gladly pulled out my album and showed off my beautiful girl. By the end of the day, I felt really good and had even remembered my computer password!

Slowly over the next couple of months, I rejoined the world. I was able to go to the shops and not feel terrified of every pregnant woman and every pram. I was able to talk to people and tell them what had happened. Christmas was very hard. We went to the cemetery in the morning and then to my sister's place for lunch. After handing out the presents and quickly eating lunch, we left and spent the rest of the day at home, thinking about what might have been – that Stephanie should be here joining in the Christmas fun – her first Christmas.

Two days later we packed up and went on a two-week holiday. We had booked the holiday when I was pregnant, so it was bittersweet being away. It was fantastic to be in a place where we were just another couple of tourists and nobody knew us or what had happened to us, but sad that Stephanie was not here with us to share the holiday. It was the best thing for us, and we came back renewed in our energy to restart our quest for a baby.

I had one last thing to do before we returned to the IVF clinic. I visited Stephanie at the cemetery and told her what we were about to do. I explained to her that it didn't mean we didn't love her any more, or that we loved her any less and were trying to replace her. We just wanted a child that was here to love and nurture and watch grow up. After I had explained all this to her, I was ready to move forward with our baby plans.

Seven months after Stephanie's birth we had another IVF transfer – three embryos. After a very long two weeks, I made the nervous phone call for the blood test results. I nearly dropped the phone when the voice on the other end said, 'You're pregnant.' I was happy and scared at the same time. I continued with the daily injections and the weekly blood tests. My hormone levels were rising normally, and we dared to hope. When I was almost six weeks pregnant, I got up out of bed one morning and felt something fall out. I looked on the floor to see a huge clot and blood running down my legs. I rang my husband and told him we'd lost the baby. I rang the clinic and they said to come for an ultrasound in two days' time. We spent those two days grieving for another baby, and feeling like we had had our last chance at a family.

The day of the ultrasound was for me a formality, a confirmation of what I already knew. I was going along just to see if I needed a curette. Imagine my utter shock when the sonographer found two heartbeats! We were having twins, and I had miscarried a third baby. I couldn't contain my delight. I had gone from utter despair to happiness in the space of a few minutes.

I waited a week for the bleeding to settle, then told everyone we were having twins. As the weeks crept along, I expected to miscarry the other babies. Every time I went to the toilet I expected to find bleeding, every little twinge made me think the babies were gone, and I tried to hope that this would be okay. Because I had only known failure, why would this pregnancy be any different? Slowly the time passed, and I had another ultrasound at thirteen weeks.

The sonographer turned on the machine, looked at my file

and said, 'The baby's heartbeat is good and the baby looks fine.'

I excitedly asked about the other baby and he just shrugged me off and said there was only one baby. When I told him there were two, he looked closer and found the remains of the sac. He told me that the baby appeared to have died at around ten weeks and had been absorbed back into the lining of the uterus. I had had no bleeding or cramps, so had no idea that I had lost another baby.

I spent the rest of the pregnancy in a state of anxiety and nervousness. I had lost hope that I would have a live baby. I tried with all my being to be positive, but all I knew was failure and heartbreak. Each week seemed like an eternity. I had several more ultrasounds, as well as the normal glucose tolerance test, and each time I was told everything was okay. The feeling of reassurance only lasted a couple of hours, then the fear crept back. I felt I was going insane, and only my active baby kept me grounded. As long as it was kicking and moving I was fine. I prodded the baby every thirty minutes just to get a movement.

As I got bigger I talked to my obstetrician about the possibility of delivering early. Stephanie had been born at thirty-eight weeks and one day, and I felt that I would go around the bend if I got that far this time. We agreed to an elective caesarean at thirty-seven weeks and six days – one day earlier than my hoodoo number of thirty-eight!

The day finally arrived and still I was filled with apprehension and a sense of foreboding. There was still time for something to go wrong. The last hour before going to theatre dragged. I watched the second hand on the clock for the whole hour, counting down the time wishing it would go quicker, so nothing could go wrong.

Finally, after the epidural had taken effect, I was wheeled into theatre. After what seemed like a few seconds, I felt some pushing and pulling and the doctor held up a beautiful baby boy, who was crying and moving! I sobbed tears of happiness. I couldn't believe he was mine, that I had actually delivered a healthy, living, breathing, crying baby. A baby I could take home and love, and cuddle and nurture. I could finally be a mother in all senses of the word. After a brief touch, he disappeared with his father and it was another hour and a half before I was able to have a proper cuddle.

Life has been full and fantastic since Nicholas was born. While he fills a hole in my life, he certainly doesn't replace Stephanie. He helped with my healing, but I still think of her often. What she would look like? Would she and her brother be similar or very different? Would they like each other? Would she love me as much as I love her? Would she be a tomboy like I was? A bookworm, a sporty person, creative, practical, a storyteller? So many unanswered questions that I will ponder for the rest of my life. She is a part of my family, my firstborn child, and she will never be forgotten. Her life and death have changed me into the person I am today. While I still grieve for the 'old' me sometimes, I believe the 'new' me is a good person, in some ways a better person. This is from having known and loving my daughter.

While I will always think of Stephanie with sadness, it is now sadness for her not experiencing life and all its ups and downs, twists and turns. She will never grow up and fall in and out of love, be a mother, be a grandmother, have some adventures and for that I am sad. I wish she was here for me to share her journey.

I cherish my connection to Stephanie and my four other little babies, who I have named Casey, Tyler, Regan and Shannon.

Anne Bowers

Life Since

❦

I have no memory, no baby face to remember
Only the seventeenth day of the month of September
They thought it best I did not see
The child I carried was not for me
His little space was all stripped bare
More pain for me, no longer there
There is no feeling of being wronged
Just the grief for the child we longed
Nine months of hopes and dreams
Years of grief and silent screams

It was 1978. I was forty-two weeks pregnant, had been sent home twice because, 'You are not ready, dear.' My son died hours after my second discharge. I returned to be induced and after hours of labour gave birth to a healthy, good-weight, but dead baby. He was taken away and the hospital arranged the funeral, at a mass grave. When I went home with empty arms, all his little things were gone, even his bassinet. All these things were done in order to protect me but I needed and wanted all of it.

This was one of the most painful and shattering experiences of my life. In two years I had lost my first child to miscarriage, followed by my stillborn son.

Later, after giving birth to two healthy beautiful sons, I joined SANDS and from then on my life changed. I learned empathy, I met families worse off, and I found friends who became friends for life. I went back to school and I studied and I counselled others.

My life had changed forever.

I have my babies to thank for my life since. I never met them, never saw them but they had an incredibly positive impact on my life.

I am who I am because of my life experiences. Every moment, every day, the people I have loved and lost have left their mark on me, even the ones only I knew.

Deidre Diggeden

Butterfly Kisses for Our
Little Man, Rhys

On 20 September 2003 our first baby boy was born at twenty weeks. Our nightmare began four days prior to his birth when we went for our nineteen-week scan.

This day was like any other day. I went off to work as did my husband Adam, and we both agreed to hurry home that afternoon as we had to be at the clinic for the scan early in the evening.

I was very nervous about the well-being of my unborn baby right from the day I found out I was pregnant. This may have been for a couple of reasons. Firstly, I'm a nurse and worry about all things medical. Secondly I had spotting throughout my pregnancy. Due to this nervousness I didn't really enjoy going for previous scans as I was worried what they may or may not find. However up to this point I was reassured by my obstetrician that all was well and my baby was healthy. 'Don't worry,' he said.

Despite these worries I was actually excited about seeing our baby in more detail. I'd told myself they would have found something at my twelve-week scan. That was the stage where things go wrong isn't it? After twelve weeks you're out of danger, aren't you?

When I left work that afternoon I was feeling great. Everyone at work knew I was off to see my baby. They were all excited for me and asked me if we were going to find out our baby's sex. They said they would look forward to seeing me the next morning. Instead I was lying in bed wishing I were dead!

At the scan the sonographer went through our baby's growth measurements first and was telling us how normal and perfect everything was. She started with the head circumference, then the brain and down the body from there. Two arms, ten fingers, two legs, ten toes. After all limbs were accounted for, she excused herself saying she needed to catch the doctor before he went home. I immediately panicked, whereas Adam, who is always optimistic, reassured me.

The doctor walked in with a look of concern; at that point my whole world came crashing down. I knew something was horribly wrong. The doctor asked us to give him ten minutes of silence as there looked to be something wrong with (in his words) 'the foetus'. Boy, do I hate that word. How could I be silent?

I started to ask questions, 'What is wrong with our baby?' He wouldn't answer until he'd finished scanning. So I lay there clinging to Adam (who had tears running down his face), screaming inside my head, wanting to throw up all over this horrible doctor who would not speak to us for what seemed like an eternity.

After this horrific silence he told us that our baby had a severe condition called diaphragmatic hernia and went on to explain it. He suggested we have an amniocentesis to find out if it was due to any chromosomal abnormalities.

I asked if we could have a few moments alone to think about all this, not realising we would need a lifetime to comprehend this tragic news. I wanted to ring my sister, who was interstate. She couldn't make sense of what I was saying as I was hysterical, so Adam had to explain to her what we were just told. Our baby had a condition from which there was very little chance of surviving.

We left the clinic straight after the amniocentesis in absolute shock and disbelief. All our hopes and dreams for this, our first-born baby, had been taken away in the matter of minutes. I remember getting in the lift to go down to our car and my husband letting out a wail that was like nothing I've ever heard before and never ever want to hear again. I kept saying over and over again, 'What are we going to do now. What's going to happen?' whilst crying uncontrollably. Adam was not able to answer my questions.

When we got home I felt like the world had just ended or at least I wished it had. We were lost souls not knowing what to do. Unfortunately, we didn't have any family around. My parents were overseas and Adam's parents were interstate as well as the rest of the family. I rang my obstetrician; he said he would see us the next day in his rooms.

The following days were a blur. Friends called in, not knowing quite what to say. We had tracked our parents down on holidays and had to give them the horrible news over the phone. The whole time my baby was kicking away blissfully unaware of what was happening which tore my heart out.

We had a second opinion regarding our baby's condition which just confirmed the initial diagnosis. We were told pretty much the same as on the night of the scan that our baby had a very severe form of the condition and his chance of survival was less than one per cent. We were also told that if our baby were to survive he would have to be immediately operated on and be subjected to far more than a baby should endure in his first hours of life.

So although the decision to terminate was ours, we felt at the time the decision was already made, as we thought this would be the kindest thing for our baby. I now know that I was definitely not capable of making any such decisions; I was numb to my core and in shock. The funny thing was, we just accepted what the doctors told us and booked into the hospital. We didn't even think at the time to research his condition ourselves. Looking back, I don't know that we had the capacity to think. A friend later said that in a situation like ours you do what's right at the time. I don't know about that.

It was when I asked my obstetrician about termination that my fear and sadness strangled me until I couldn't breathe. Because at this point I hadn't thought about it, and just assumed I would have a general anaesthetic, wake up and no longer be pregnant! (I never did do midwifery in my years of nursing.) But no, I had to be admitted to the maternity unit and have a tablet inserted into my cervix which would bring on labour, then another in four hours' time, and continue this until I gave birth. My two sisters flew down to be with us as our parents couldn't be there.

Waiting for the day of admission was like being on death row; it was three days of hell. My baby was so active, he kicked twenty-four hours a day, I tried so hard not to think about what we were about to do. It was a strange feeling – while I felt sick to my stomach with sadness I also felt like I just wanted to get this baby out of me and this horrible nightmare to be over and done with. Initially I thought of my baby as a monster, irrationally thinking it would have no arms or legs and be incredibly disfigured. I didn't want to tell any of my friends about my baby's condition. I just wanted to tell people that we lost our baby to miscarriage. Of course this passed after we met our son.

We got to the hospital and were told to go up to the maternity unit and wait in the waiting room until a room became vacant. A midwife came in and talked through the upcoming procedures. Due to what I think was shock, I felt I was handling things reasonably well until the receptionist came and took us to my room. She took me to a four-bed room where three other women had pink-and-blue balloons bobbing around and babies in cribs next to their beds. I backed out of the room thinking this was some sick joke. My sister took the receptionist aside and not so kindly asked if she knew the reason for my admission. In reply, the receptionist said she was terribly sorry but there was no other bed available. It wasn't too long before I was sitting in a private room.

As I was having the tablet inserted, my baby was kicking around as if to say, 'Hey, Mum, what are you doing, I'm very comfortable in here.' This was so hard to bear. I thought a mother should do everything in her power to protect her children yet here I was killing mine. This was the guilt I would have to live with from this day on. After having a pethidine injection towards the end of my labour I opted for nothing more, as this made me feel out of control of the situation and I wanted to be lucid when my baby was born.

Eighteen hours after being admitted to hospital I gave birth to our firstborn son Rhys. I asked my sister and husband if it was okay for me to look at our baby as I had no idea what to expect. Adam said through tears that he was just gorgeous. I then looked down and picked our little boy up and cuddled him. This was such a special time in my life and one which I will never forget but cherish forever. Adam and I felt so much love and pride for him; he was just a perfect-looking baby, only tiny. He looked so much like Adam.

Funnily enough it wasn't a sad moment but a happy one. Adam and I felt blessed we were given the opportunity to meet our son and hold him. We had to give him a name after seeing him, as he was our baby. Whether he was dead or alive he was our little man whom we created. The hours that followed were a blur, with lots of tears and cuddles. We held our little boy for about four hours, looking at every inch of his beautiful little body and talking to him as if he were living and breathing. Thank goodness for shock as I'm sure this is the only way we got through this time. It gave me a sense of happiness but unfortunately this ended the moment we had to leave the hospital. My world again came crashing down around me. How could we leave without our baby? Somehow we did, and another cruel joke came when we got into the lift with proud new parents and their brand-new baby boy wrapped snuggly in a blue blanket. The tears flowed and they didn't stop until about a year later. They still haven't dried up completely.

We were seen by a social worker at the hospital, who gave us some numbers to ring when we felt we needed to talk to someone about our grief.

The grief Adam and I experienced took us to the end of the earth and back. We were just at a complete loss. I wanted to have died with my baby and didn't think life could or would ever be the same again. I felt that each day I got worse. Every day was a struggle for me. I cried a zillion tears. I went back to work after only two and a half weeks off and didn't cope at all. I wondered if I was ever going to be able to cope.

Friends and family, I have to say, were trying their best to be supportive but they had never been through anything like this. So I felt very alone. Everybody we knew seemed far too sure we had done the right thing. I felt the opposite: I felt (aside from devastation) guilt and regret that we had acted too quickly. My strongest feeling a week or so after having Rhys was a feeling of panic, that we were never going to see or hold our little boy ever again. This feeling was excruciating.

After about a month, friends and family stopped asking us how we were going. They stopped talking about Rhys and most likely felt we would be over our grief by now and be moving on with our lives. This was so far from reality. By this stage I think I was just getting over the numb phase and moving into the other phases of grief. After the numbness came the raw pain of loss, then the, 'Why me? What did I ever do to deserve such pain?' Then came the bitterness and anger, which was hard to deal with. I didn't like who I became at all. I hated seeing a smiling pregnant woman. I felt incredible jealousy towards friends who were pregnant or had babies. I felt everybody who was ever going to have children should have to go through what we'd just been through so they didn't ever take pregnancy for granted. I cursed people who said they only wanted a girl or a boy. I wanted to scream, 'You should be happy that you have a baby at all.' Mind you, I was one of these people before the night of our fateful scan.

A really difficult thing for me was that people stopped talking about Rhys. They stopped saying his name. It felt like Adam and I were the only ones thinking about him, and we would talk about him all the time. I wanted to shout his name from the rooftops. If I ever brought his name up in conversation with somebody they would go silent or quickly change the subject. I found this so difficult to understand. He was our son. If he had have survived he would be in people's conversations, so why was this any different? If you lose a grandparent you don't stop talking about them.

Luckily for Adam and me, the social worker from the hospital called us about a week after we had Rhys. She felt we needed to talk to someone about our grief so she gave us the number for SANDS. I was at home in floods of tears one day and decided to call them. They put me onto a phone support person who talked me into attending one of their monthly meetings. This was our saviour. I don't think I would be where I am today if it weren't for those meetings. It was a place to go where you could talk about your situation, your thoughts and feelings and not be judged. The best part was, you came out of the meetings feeling normal and not the psycho bitch you thought you were that day at the shops. They reassured you that those horrible feelings you felt were all part of the grief process. I made a wonderful friend there whom I can ring and meet with and talk to about my little boy still and know she truly understands. I looked forward to the meetings and wished only that they were every week, not just once a month. Adam also got a lot out of those meetings as he could also express his feelings. People tend to forget about the father in his grief. Nobody ever really asked how he was holding up. If someone rang the house and he answered, they would always ask how I was coping rather than how he was.

SANDS also taught us something that is now so valuable, which was to create a memory box for Rhys. If I didn't have this I think I would feel distant from him as time went by. I will often sit down and look at his hand- and footprints, the letters Adam and I wrote to him and the little outfit he wore in hospital and have a good cry. I also smile when I relive the amazing, over-whelming emotions of love and pride that I felt when I cradled him after his birth. I really believe Rhys knew we were with him, giving all the love and comfort as only a mum and dad can.

We had a funeral for Rhys, which was beautiful. It was very personal and intimate; there were only our parents (who were back from holidays) and a couple of friends. The lady who conducted his funeral was a wonderful, caring person who made this day so special. She likened the loss of our baby to a butterfly: it lands on you for such a brief period of time but leaves a beautiful lasting imprint on your life. We now just love butterflies; they are a symbol of Rhys's short life. We have a butterfly tree in our bedroom and had them as a theme for our daughter's first birthday.

Losing our baby was so hard, but our smiles have returned. And our capacity to love our subsequent children – Eadie eighteen months and Bailey four months – is just as strong as it is for Rhys. I'm sure this is Rhys's gift to us: giving us our two beautiful living children.

We always wonder what he would look like and wish he was with us, bossing his sister and brother around. I say goodnight to him every night when I put Eadie and Bailey to bed. I give him a kiss and tell him I love him. It gives me comfort that he will always be in my heart. He will stay safe with me for the rest of my life and always be a part of our family.

It's so very sad that our little man never took a breath, never saw the sun and never smelt a flower; however, he does all these things every day through my eyes, from within my heart.

A butterfly kiss to you, our darling boy, from Mummy, Daddy, Eadie, Bailey and Leni Hope – another sister for Rhys, born 8.2.08 xxxx.

Dannielle Urquhart

Living with Broken Hearts

⅏

2.44 am to 3.30 pm
15 October 2004

It has taken me a long time to sit down and begin my story. I have always found something else to do. As much as I don't want to go back to that heartbreaking day, I do want to tell the world about my son, Jacob.

In October 2004, I was approaching my sixth month of pregnancy. Everything was going well: I was setting up the baby's nursery, was nearly qualified as a fitness instructor and my parents were beginning to come around to the idea of my being pregnant as I had just turned eighteen.

On Wednesday 13 October I attended my twenty-four-week check-up with the midwives at the family birthing centre. My partner Daniel had come along and we were both so happy – a happiness that I would later look back on and a moment I would cherish. I had a few aches and pains to report but it was put down to Braxton Hicks. Afterwards my partner and I went out to lunch to celebrate our baby.

That evening I was still in some uncomfortable pain, so back to the hospital I went. All correct tests and procedures were performed and I was sent home and told not to be concerned.

Thursday, 14 October, as my partner headed off to work, I decided I would miss my evening course. I was still having pains and the city was just too far to go. Daniel offered one last time to take me back to the hospital but I regretfully declined his offer and thought I'd be strong and put up with the pain.

By the time Daniel got home from work I was in trouble. I went from uncomfortable to agony. I knew there was a problem. We rushed to the emergency room and from there I was rushed in a wheelchair to the delivery suite. That uncomfortable pain I was in earlier was actually the beginning of labour. After that it was just a blur. I was in so much pain I don't remember even thinking. There are moments I remember, like when you wake up after a dream. Those moments, though, haunt me and to this day I can still feel my heart and soul breaking.

A doctor put her hand on my shoulder and gazed at me for a moment. I suppose she was trying to find a nice way to say that I was about to have my baby, and he was going to be very premature. We saw our darling for a short moment before he was rushed to the nursery. We were so happy. We had hoped for a boy and we got one. Daniel had a son he could name, and he chose Jacob, a name he'd always wanted for one of his sons. We were told to have a rest. We eventually fell asleep.

When I woke up the light had been switched off for our comfort. I whispered to Daniel to wake up, I wanted to go to Jacob. I asked a midwife if we could visit him. He was just about to go with NETS (Newborn Emergency Transport Service) to a larger hospital.

I fell so in love with him when I saw him. He was only a tiny 630 grams but a long 31 centimetres. His tiny chest was rising up and down as we spoke to him. Long blond eyelashes, with beautifully proportioned features. I held his fragile hands. I felt okay and I felt he would be okay. As I waited for Daniel to return to the hospital with clean clothes, midwives kept walking into my room. I didn't know what to think. Had something happened to my son? But every time they were just checking on me and asking me how I was feeling. I realise now what was happening, why they were checking on me, why they were trying to comfort me.

Daniel and I rushed to the other hospital to reunite our family. It seemed to take forever to get there. I wanted my son. I practically ran from the car to the elevator and to my son's bedside. When I was approaching the NICU (Neonatal Intensive Care Unit), a doctor turned to her colleague and said, 'There's the mother'. It almost sounded like a warning. It wasn't welcoming and it wasn't positive.

Jacob was surrounded by doctors. I screamed, 'What's happening to him?' Jacob seemed to have lost all his colour and was trembling. We were ushered away into a small room and asked to sit down. I wanted to stand right up and go back to Jacob. I wanted to protect him from all the needles and tubes. I already felt an unbreakable bond with my son.

The doctor tried to explain what was happening, but as far as I was concerned he was stealing precious minutes away from being with my son. I now knew he was not okay; now I was really scared for his life. I started praying in my mind, I began to ask for God's help.

It was eventually okay for us to return to Jacob's bedside and he was bright pink again. He had a tiny beanie on and a nappy that was far too big. A plastic sheet covered him to help keep him warm. He wasn't in a humidicrib as the doctors needed access at all times. Soon the feeling that he would be okay returned and the panic disappeared. Daniel and I spoke positively to one another. We agreed that his breathing needed to improve, but that he would be all right.

My sister-in-law had come along to see her nephew but as the day went on she needed to return home to her own son, so Daniel said a sad farewell to Jacob and drove his sister home. Watching Jacob, I couldn't help peering over to some other babies. A mother attending to her child in a humidicrib returned my gaze and it was as if we had an entire conversation with the one glance. I watched the doctors turn knobs and check tubes. I didn't understand what they were meant to be doing, so I asked a doctor and she showed me what Jacob's blood pressure should be. For the next half hour I watched that machine, staring at it and praying for the numbers to increase, but they didn't. They continued to decrease. Soon my son's blood pressure was low and I knew it would not be going back up.

The doctors looked at me sympathetically as I began crying uncontrollably. Jacob's tiny body was picked up with all the tubes still attached and placed into my arms. A screen was placed around us for privacy. I looked at the machine and watched Jacob's blood pressure drop under ten. I whispered to my son that I loved him so much and that his daddy loved him too. I whispered that I knew he tried so hard to be here with us, and I watched him slip away. In a second my life changed forever. A nurse waited for the right moment to switch his machine off. His heart rate flatlined on the screen and just like that my baby was gone. In that same moment my life, my soul, the person who I was had gone too.

I thought of Jacob's dad. He would be on his way back. How was I going to tell him his son was gone? I asked if I could take Jacob back to the small room we were in previously. Each step seemed like a mile and I could barely see through all the tears. The nurses stood behind their desk as if they had seen this so many times. In the room I could only hug my son's lifeless body and cry while I waited for Daniel.

It seemed like hours but soon I heard some distressed voices outside. Daniel burst in. His face looked so devastated. He begged me to tell him otherwise. He nursed our son and sobbed. I will never forget the sound. He cried so loudly, burying his face into Jacob.

He later told me that when he returned to the NICU the bed where Jacob was beforehand had been cleared, and for a moment he felt happy thinking Jacob had been moved to a less intensive area, and that his breathing had improved. When a nurse approached him and asked, 'Are you Jacob's father?' his heart sank and exploded all at once.

Time went so slowly after that. Although the hospital didn't seem to waste any time asking us what we wished to do with Jacob. Would we like a post-mortem? Would we like to donate our son for research and help science discover why these premature babies cannot survive? Would we like Jacob buried by the hospital with all the other babies that had died that month?

We decided to go ahead with a limited post-mortem and we refused the idea of donating him, despite doctors' efforts, and we decided to bury him privately so we could visit him at any time. Jacob was bathed and re-dressed, and his hand- and footprints stamped onto cards. I was handed a box specially decorated to keep what was to show for my baby's life – a few photos, some cards, hand- and footprints, and some tubes. That was all.

I wrapped Jacob for the last time that night. We let Jacob rest; he needed to go wherever babies are taken. We must have kissed him a thousand times. I can still remember the softness of his skin on my lips and fingertips. I closed the door behind us, leaving him alone in a bassinet. I went back one last time to kiss my angel. Daniel gave him a kiss and we walked out with our arms around one another. As we walked down the hall, I looked over my shoulder at a less intensive area. All those babies will be going home, I thought, and my little darling wasn't.

Going through the hospital towards our car was just another heartbreaking moment. People had no idea what had just happened. I wanted everybody to disappear. I wanted to fall to my knees and sink into the ground. How could I go on? I was leaving my baby with strangers. I was said goodbye to and just expected to continue.

I fell into bed and didn't bother getting out. I just curled up and cried. Daniel was put in a position where he now had to look after me. I couldn't eat, I couldn't sleep and it hurt to talk.

I had a reality to face. We needed to find Jacob a final resting place. Finding the perfect place for Jacob gave me some strength. Amongst other babies, surrounded by flowers and gum trees, and a pretty fountain with birds and butterflies dancing around, and some cheeky bunny rabbits to keep him company, I found that place.

From then on I feel it's the same for everybody. Your friends and family are there for you to say goodbye. They understand your quiet company and your fearful appearance but after a while they begin laughing again. You cannot join in the cheerful atmosphere for you are still heartbroken. All your thoughts are of your baby and the fact your baby has gone. Denial and shock still make the tears flow and the questions, Why did this happen? and How could this happen? repeat themselves over and over. Questions that will never have answers.

Months go by. No day you haven't counted. No day your baby has ever left your mind and no day you have felt honestly happy. Soon those same friends and family wonder why they haven't heard you laugh or seen that sparkle in your eye, for they feel you should have reached acceptance. So you learn how to hide your heartache from them. You smile but when you are alone you return to the heartbroken parent, for nothing has changed since you walked out of the hospital. This is just a new you now. The old you, you left with your baby and just as you need to accept this, so will they. So do what you have to, to get through this, as we are all trying to do the same thing. We are all just trying to cope.

Stephanie Rouillon

1984 – Stillbirth, a Prophecy from George Orwell

To Liam

It was a Wednesday evening in August. You were due any time now, and we were due for a routine antenatal visit the next day when I noticed that it had been some hours since I had felt you move. Sit down, take it easy, relax with a warm drink, I told myself. But still there were none of those familiar kicks and drummings. Why had you stopped moving? What was wrong? Try not to panic. Just keep the scheduled appointment tomorrow.

On Thursday, driving to the appointment, I noticed faint but regular contractions. The lack of movement was of major concern to the obstetrician. The fact that you had 'turned', unknown to me, and were now a breech presentation was also of major concern to me. This meant exclusion from the Birth Centre, our strong preference for delivery.

I was admitted that afternoon for monitoring, which indicated you were okay, but if I felt no movements overnight, delivery next morning would be considered. I'd have the dreaded caesarean but at least we'd have you soon. Must get our priorities right. I wandered, musing, looking at the babies at the postnatal end of the ward.

After numerous comments from the staff suggesting that he depart, your dad left around 11 pm. Getting out of bed to settle for the night brought on the contractions we'd been timing together for some hours. Before long I was up to the labour ward, contractions coming hard and fast, unlike the long, lingering affair of your sister's birth. My body had triumphed to deliver you. Was it because of the threat of the 'knife'? But now they couldn't find your dad! Where was he? No mobile phones for immediate contact.

One hour into Friday, then a gush. Things moving, waters breaking. No! It was blood, bright and flowing. The nurse's anxiety surfaced in her snappy response to my pathetic question 'Is it normal?' As if I didn't know. Filling space. The anxieties of the last day built up into a solid wall of fear, which numbed and encased me, helping me to focus on those regular contractions, meet them with relaxation, obliterate any thoughts. Then your dad arrived. Two separate people. I had no space for him. He may have opened a chink in my protective wall.

1.30 am   That lovely heartbeat sound.

1.45 am   No heartbeat located . . . painful shoving inside, no time to wait for a contraction to subside. You moved. Hooray!

2.00 am   A foot delivered, the other pulled down.

2.04 am   Liam James, you were born and whisked to the paediatrician for attention.

Silence, save for the sucking and pumping of the labour ward machinery. Two frozen people clung to each other. The wall was slowly cracking.

Through the silence I cried out, 'It's too late, he's dead.'

The paediatrician came to my side. 'I'm sorry,' was all he said.

Where to now? How could this be? To be robbed of the joy of childbirth, the reason for the sufferings of hard labour. Not just denied the joy we'd experienced last time, but death put in its place. How could this be real? How much more unreal this would be if you were firstborn. What made me think this then?

My beautiful son was tenderly wrapped and placed in my arms. Big, fat, beautiful boy. I held you, unwrapped you. Hands, body, boyhood, chubby thighs, toes. All perfect. Your forehead, just like my dad's. Your hair – were they tiny curls still stuck wet to that head? I held that little hand, caressed its soft fingers, my quiet stare of shock captured in a photo. Tears of incomprehension.

The day not dawned, the photo tells, as I sat on the bed cradling a beautiful baby, my head sunk, my face from the camera view. A big sister, three and a half, leaning over to kiss her 'sleeping' brother. Quiet, sad face, a tear captured in her eye. My parents had brought Fleur. They were quiet. How to reach us in their loss? How to protect their granddaughter?

My mother held you tenderly to her shoulder. My father paced the room, later remarking that your photos hardly did you justice. Two grandparents, two parents, two children – a family in this moment, knowing what was not to be.

My parents took Fleur home. An onlooker would have then seen parents together, the new baby wrapped and lying in the basket. But how would they explain the flat faces, the heaviness in the air? What should we do? What *could* we do? Somehow, we had to pull the pieces together. No-one suggested anything. Your dad took photos. But, no photos of you with the cameraman. A cloudy day was emerging.

Then it was time to go. We left our son with a final, lingering, backward look. How could we, how did we, leave you? That was just the next thing to do.

From my single room, well away from any newborn cries, I telephoned friends and cried with each one. I planned your birth notice: *Beautiful, but not alive. Sadly missed.*

In a daze, a dream, can this really have happened? We got through the day. Some visitors and flowers. That night the emptiness overflowed. Sobbing, we clung to each other. Thankfully your dad had not taken up my suggestion he go home for a more comfortable night's sleep.

Next day. Home. The empty bassinet hidden in the boot. Our beautiful boy somewhere, left behind. A new decision had to be made.

What if the hospital should bury you in the communal grave before I could make up my mind about the burial options? Was two weeks enough to make this decision? If I let them 'take care' of you, I could pretend that it was all a bad dream, get pregnant again, have another baby – somehow avoid my grief, my loneliness, my painful emptiness. But my empty arms were aching to hold you.

At home I stood at the door of the nursery that had been prepared in readiness for its small occupant. The little outfits, nappies, all soft and clean – the way they would stay for now. At the bassinet I closed my eyes and tenderly patted the blanket curved over my sleeping newborn. I felt you there. I knew you were not really there, no matter how much I wished you could have been. We knew you were real but would our friends acknowledge you? Would they come if we had a funeral for you?

Monday. We spoke with a recommended funeral director. No other choice to make. Our baby deserved a proper funeral to say our final goodbye, his own resting place in perpetuity. We deserved acknowledgement of our loss and support of friends. Funeral plans gave us a focus – buying a tiny bonnet and bootees to go with the beautiful smocked gown bought earlier in anticipation of showing you off.

Tuesday. We returned to the hospital to see our boy with his hair washed. 'Why do you want to see him again?' the pathologist had previously asked. I understood the horror that flooded my body from his question. My world caved in and any remnant of that protective wall shattered. Tiny form, wrapped in a sheet on a big bed. No washed curls. No curls. Forehead deformed by autopsy. What did they do to you, my darling? This is not what we'd been told to expect. I could not even touch you, I'm sorry. Your dad was able to caress your cheek. As we left I clung to him, paralysed. My beautiful baby was gone, disfigured, dead. No more tender fantasies. I had to block out this terrible image of what they had done to you.

Friday, the funeral. Your photo there – cold comfort. Please tell me he was beautiful. Before the service, we saw you snug in the little casket, bonnet concealing your 'hurt', in your hands the remaining links of the paper chain, one with *Fleur* written with love from big sister. In the countdown to your expected birth she had removed a link each day but your coming one week early left some still intact. The service was a tribute. We shared the hopes and dreams we had for you, the choice of your name, a verbal tribute from one friend, a musical tribute on the flute from another, the climax when we formed a 'ring of love' around your grave as you were lowered.

This was your 'life'. Where to for us now?

Making sense of it all

The ritual was over, the flowers wilting. How to pick up the threads of our lives? The agony ever-present, sometimes inconsolable. Rejecting Fleur for fleeting moments, wanting the baby I couldn't have rather than the child I did have; suffering the suspicious looks, which said *How is she coping?*; facing women everywhere with hordes of children; the note from the council informing me of the clinics where I could take my new baby. The question: *Why?'* Why had this happened to us?

Something outside the range of possible outcomes. Babies died today? But I knew that despite medical technology and improved antenatal care, it still happened. So why should this *not* happen to us? I also knew that when one door closed, others would open: a week's family holiday interstate; joining a local gym and getting fitter and slimmer than I'd been for some time; returning to work and being offered an interesting move, a one-off opportunity. Things outside the plan with a new baby.

Although our routines resumed, my thoughts and conversations were on little else but a single topic. If friends didn't bring it up, I did. Most would let me talk. Many would just listen but some would attempt to be consoling.

'Aren't you lucky that you didn't know the baby?'

'At least you've already got a child.'

'You're young, you can have another.'

'Perhaps it was for the best.'

On they went. Did I really have nothing to grieve for? Even a psychiatrist commented, 'You seem to have taken your baby's death very hard.' Was I supposed to tell my story without *any* tears? If he didn't understand that, he'd have no sensible advice to my question: 'When will I be ready for another baby?'

I knew that my grief was real, normal, okay and just plain necessary. Liam had been alive and very real in my body: nine months preparing and expecting to parent him. The focus of our love, dreams, hopes and plans had suddenly gone. A child deceased, against the natural order. Someone mentioned SANDS. All these feelings were confirmed by other parents I met who had also experienced the loss of a baby. This contact was invaluable. Understanding ears listened to long tirades without the need to add empty 'consoling' comments. People really do survive the experience. While some had none, we did have memories of our Liam.

As the months rolled on I accused my husband. 'You never mention Liam, have you forgotten him?' Did he think he was protecting me by not mentioning him? I had to understand that's just how it is for men. His grief was real but more private. We could share an understanding cuddle without words. Our memories of Liam came to represent a special bond, a connection that we alone share that is quite different from the shared experience of our living children.

At Christmas, and every Christmas since, there was a special decoration on the tree – a silver bird with a letter in its beak. For many years a gift for a child of Liam's would-be-age was placed under a charity tree.

Planning ahead

Part of the plan was, of course, another pregnancy to complete what we had embarked upon – to have another child. I resented the implications that this would 'fix it all up'. When would I be ready? It seemed so long to wait for another baby. It was already eighteen months since I'd conceived and miscarried a previous pregnancy, and here we were again back at square one!

Holding back the desperation. Yet no-one had a clear answer to my question about emotional readiness. I decided that I wanted to start trying after a couple of regular periods, concerned that it may again take many months.

A concerted effort, and as 1984 switched over to 1985 did I feel rumblings? No! You can't feel conception, can you? I must be mad, so desperate. The wait. Period due, the test positive. Thank goodness, maybe not so mad? The excited call to my obstetrician, the ultrasound at six weeks showing a heartbeat and Blair's first picture – a dot on a background. Wow!

Down following up . . . fear following joy. How to cope with the next eight months? The messages were double: 'pretend it didn't happen and have another baby' contrasted with 'get pregnant but remember your last baby died'. Being treated as high-risk, even though the chance of a repetition was minimally higher than before, had benefits and losses: more attention, but the new low-key care option, the Birth Centre experience I wanted, was out and intervention was more likely. Although I wanted a healthy baby at delivery I was aware that the quality of the delivery experience had a powerful impact on the relationship I would develop with my newborn child. This meant minimal intervention, minimal separation. We refused to agree to an automatic early induction of delivery unless some discernible problem arose, and also managed to obtain permission to spend time together as a family in the Birth Centre after the baby's birth.

There was no way to quite recapture the carefree experience of my first two pregnancies. The experience of any trauma reduces that. But I was able to focus on the positive experience of connecting with this new son whilst separating my grief for my first son, and focus on knowing that if the worst happened again we'd be more prepared this time whilst desperately hoping it wouldn't, as the score on chance indicated. I knew that relying on constant reassurance with many tests had its downside: reassurance lasted only as long as the results were being gathered and maintained the focus on 'stopping the baby dying' rather than accepting fate sensibly and getting on with enjoying our living baby before and beyond his delivery. And luckily we had an active boy on board who deserved a happy pregnancy too.

Yet my mind tangled with feelings of disloyalty towards Liam because I was 'replacing' him and resentment towards others who implied that our experience was over now that there was a new baby on the way, a new focus at last. How could other pregnant women understand these complexities? Consequently, the contact and support from friends in SANDS was again invaluable.

As the pregnancy became more obvious, the constant reminders: 'How many babies have you had?' 'Is this your first?' Hard to avoid the topic. Less so for fathers. Bill had, throughout the whole experience, received little acknowledgement of his loss and any comments to him had focused typically on inquiries about me. He was locked into the supportive-husband role.

Liam's first anniversary occurred towards the end of this pregnancy. My anticipation of this day was far worse than the day itself turned out to be. We burnt a scented candle all day, a ritual that will never die, and made a birthday cake at Fleur's insistence. Over the years his siblings blew out the candles and for his eighteenth we had a birthday party and raised three thousand dollars for SANDS.

A month after that first anniversary, Blair was born. A living son at last. This delivery was induced several days early, as I was having uterine niggles of impending labour and was, unsurprisingly, as anxious about the delivery as was the obstetrician. The discomfort and endurance of Blair's delivery contrasted with the effective efficiency of Liam's. But this boy was here, delivered to my chest, a moment needed to take it in. His father and sister cooing close, eager to touch, hold and bathe.

At Blair's first birthday, I experienced a glimmer of release, as though I could relax with him now. Was this his graduation from 'baby' to toddlerhood? Liam's anniversary had passed – two candles on his cake. Time and a living, growing son were distancing us from the experience and pain of our loss. There was now less need to talk about what had happened.

At three, Blair had asked, 'Will you get a boy baby in your

tummy, Mummy?' Was this *his* sense of loss, and desire to replace? But four months after having five candles on Liam's cake, Elena was born. This pregnancy took the cake. It was more relaxed and we got the Birth Centre experience. Blair was first to hold his baby sister. Now my most cherished photo frames four newborn faces – two girls encircling two boys.

A few years later a chat with a midwife scaled the medical wall erected when I'd pestered for answers – we can't guess *why*! A low-positioned placenta, partial placenta praevia, would have made a head presentation uncomfortable and explained the blood at delivery. Perhaps they could not admit this was missed. The rumblings of litigation were evolving over these years, but I knew it wouldn't bring our baby back.

To Liam I owe much. Knowing him has changed the focus of my life; his impact on my personal and professional development, immense. Yet as my living son Blair now requests, as many sons do, 'Mum, can I borrow your car today?' I know that little is different from other parents' experience. But when asked, 'How many children do you have?' I know that my experience is different from many.

So, George, when I read you a decade or so before, could I have guessed what 1984 would bring?

Penny Brabin

When Something is Wrong
with My Baby

❦

Every day I wake up and think that I am *so* lucky. I have four wonderful, healthy children. Kylie, nineteen; James, eighteen; Gemma, nine; and Nathan, eight years of age. It is November 2006, and our third child, Lorelle would have just celebrated her fifteenth birthday on 1 November. Which also means our fourth child, Adrian, would have been fourteen in October. I have had seven pregnancies, have four children, and one of them is adopted. Not a very good average.

Let's go back fifteen years, when I wasn't feeling very lucky at all . . .

My name is Leanne, I am married to Eddy, and we own a dairy farm. Our lives were great, with Kylie and James looking forward to the arrival of their new baby brother or sister. Lorelle was born on time, healthy, with no complications. So we brought her home from hospital, to live happily ever after . . . or so we hoped.

At four weeks of age, she caught meningitis, and was diagnosed at our local hospital. Here is where my life changed forever. The uncontrollable rollercoaster ride began at this point. Everything that was to happen from now on was now out of my hands. As a mother, I couldn't do anything to help my little girl. All I could give her was love and caring, but now this wasn't enough to make her well again. I hated that feeling, being totally out of control. I knew she needed professional help and care, penicillin and other things to keep her alive which I couldn't provide.

She became so ill so quickly; we thought we might lose her that day. The meningitis affected her so fast. At the start of that day, I had a perfectly normal baby, and by late evening the doctors had trouble stabilising her enough to transfer her to another hospital. When we finally got to the aeroplane, it couldn't take off from the airport because her observations started to go down again, so we waited for what seemed forever before we eventually took off.

She was flown to a major hospital, where she was put on drips, and monitors, and we were told she was gravely ill. The meningitis had affected ninety per cent of her brain, and so we waited another week, hoping for a change in her brain scans for some improvement. Not so. The miracle we hoped for wasn't happening.

We decided, after a couple of weeks, with lots of consultation with doctors, nurses and other professionals, to take her home. And so, on 22 December at seven weeks of age, Lorelle passed away at home with us. The timing was atrocious. My mum's birthday is the 21st, and I remember at the time praying for her not to die on that day. The little angel gave me my wish, and thankfully went the next day.

Christmas time came and went, such a terrible Christmas, I just wanted it to go away. Having to plan for her funeral at Christmas time was so hard; such a joyous time of year for everyone else around us. We had gifts for Lorelle for Christmas, not knowing if she would be here or not. God knows it was awful. Kylie and James still needed Santa, so with help from family and friends we got through it. Christmas Eve was Lorelle's funeral. I have lots of photos of her funeral, but I really can't remember much about it. If you were to ask me what hymns were sung, or what the priest said, I honestly can't remember. Most of it is a blur.

After her funeral we found SANDS. At the hospital were a few nurses that we got to know very well who had lost children themselves, and they contacted us about this wonderful support group. The meetings once a month were great for me. I really looked forward to them, and the need to talk to people with similar stories was of great support to me. I found it very difficult talking about Lorelle around friends and people with babies about her age. As soon as I began to talk about Lorelle, people became awkward, not knowing what to say to me about her. So, by being involved with SANDS, I was able to talk freely about her, with others wishing to talk about their babies and their losses. This was very therapeutic for me.

At this time, my husband and I decided we would still like to have another child. Nothing could replace Lorelle, but the instinct and the wanting to have another baby was still so strong. We also reasoned that Lorelle was a healthy baby, and would still be so, had she not caught the meningitis germ. So, we fell pregnant relatively soon after Lorelle's death, only for the pregnancy to go terribly wrong.

On 17 October the following year, Adrian was stillborn – fourteen weeks premature and weighing just 850 grams. I was admitted to the hospital the week before with a bleed. I was transferred to another hospital, where he was born soon after. I was diagnosed with placenta acreta, where the placenta pulls away from the uterus walls, causing bleeding. During his delivery I lost lots of blood, and doctors were concerned that they couldn't stop the bleeding. As soon as he was delivered I was taken for a curette, and was told if this didn't stop the bleed I'd have to have a hysterectomy.

Thankfully, the curette worked and the bleeding eventually stopped. I lost so much blood during his delivery, and was told that I nearly died. At the time I failed to grasp the seriousness of this. I failed to see how lucky I was just to be here. I wasn't feeling lucky at all.

What had I done? It was so unfair. Why me? Why us? Why my family again? Why did I have to lose another baby? We were good, hardworking people, never hurting anyone. My poor kids, having to go through all this yet again. How would they handle it? It's not fair.

After I came home from hospital I was tired and rundown. But we needed to organise another funeral. Second time around, and within eleven months of burying Lorelle, we knew exactly what we had to do. Kylie and James were more involved in Adrian's funeral. James picked out the coffin – navy blue for his baby brother.

We have so many photos of both Lorelle and Adrian, and we are so glad because they are all we have got. At the time photos are the last thing you feel like doing, but later on you cherish them forever.

So, back to SANDS again, I can't explain the feeling of déjà vu. Now I was in an elite group of people, feeling more alone, because not too many people out there have lost two children. But again the support from SANDS was wonderful, and yes, there are people out there who have lost two or more children. Now I was part of a group of people who you can share things with which no-one else can understand, unless you have lost a child.

The coming months and years were very difficult for us, especially anniversaries, birthdays, Christmas, or certain family events, or even songs on the radio that were around at that time. Christmas time in particular was bad. I must admit I really loathed the build-up to Christmas. Adrian's birthday in October, Lorelle's in November. She got sick on 1 December, died on the 22nd, her funeral on Christmas Eve, then Christmas Day. For quite a few years after, I could have just skipped October until the next new year.

After Adrian's funeral I was so rundown for many months. I lost a lot of blood during his birth and had to build myself up again. It was difficult with Kylie and James still needing me for everyday things, and not really wanting to do them. I was so lucky to have family, especially my mum close by to jump in whenever I needed her. Having to keep going for Kylie and James was the thing that got me motivated again. I think if I had lost my first two children, I doubt that I would have had any reason to get out of bed each day. They were part of the healing process. Having to function for them was so important.

So, after a time, we decided to try again for a baby. It was becoming increasingly difficult for us to conceive now, and we ended up going to specialist obstetricians for all sorts of tests. We had hystrograms, hystroscopys, blood tests, and more. So in the end we had to use fertility drugs to help conceive. And so, not long into the cycle, we fell pregnant, only for the pregnancy to peter out at about seven weeks' gestation. This happened twice, and our specialist told us that I didn't have enough lining on my uterus walls to carry the pregnancy to term.

This told us that enough was enough. My body obviously couldn't sustain a pregnancy, so that was it. No more trying for a child.

'Why don't you get a puppy?' someone asked me once. It's not quite the same though, is it? People who haven't experienced losing a child cannot comprehend the 'empty arms' feeling. Losing a baby is the worst thing in the world, I am sure of that. But life does go on, and it does get great again. It takes years, believe me, and you always go back there, every now and again. Sometimes the silliest thing sends you back, like the Jimmy Barnes/John Farnham hit song 'When Something is Wrong with My Baby'. That song just came out before the Christmas of 1991. When I spent countless hours beside Lorelle's hospital crib, the nurses would have the radio playing. And, I swear, they played that song over and over again. It still breaks my heart to hear it play today.

Life had been pretty bad for us to this point on the baby front. Eddy and I wondered about adoption. The feeling of still wanting kids was still so strong for us. We all still had so much love to give, and we discussed adoption with Kylie and James. They were so excited about it, so we looked into it, and after months of interviews, meetings, and social worker visits, decided to go for it.

Adoption is a huge process, and even if you never get to adopt a baby, after the initial process you will know yourself inside out. Well, the social workers will, that's for sure!

One day, after twelve months of being in the adoption pool, our social worker came out for a coffee. She had great news for us. There was a five month old girl for us to adopt. Her birth mum had chosen us, and really liked the idea of an older sister and brother for her. I was just beside myself. I was over the moon. We saw a few photos of her, and I fell in love with her from that moment. Kylie and James were ten and nine years old now, and we had ten days to decide.

Our lives had become relatively easy now with the kids. We could go places, and stay out later, not having the kids wanting to go home because they were tired. All that hard little kid stuff was gone – no nappies, toilet training, no running around to play groups or kinder. Life was pretty respectable and orderly now. The kids were at school, and we had some sort of enjoyment in our lives again.

So, the decision had to be made. Did we want to go back to all that stuff again? Sleepless nights of teething, bottle-feeding, nappies, and more. Yep, you bet! Yes, please.

So after a week Eddy and I went to meet her. She was in foster care; her foster mum greeted us at the front door. I remember that Gemma was wearing a little blue dress, and she was absolutely beautiful. As soon as we got out of the car, I grabbed her, and instantly she felt like mine. She was and still is absolutely fantastic.

When I bottle-fed Gemma, I could feel my breasts trying to let down. I was obviously very content. Gemma had my hormones running mad. I didn't really think much of it, just put it down to motherhood bliss. But what she had done was given me a huge fertility kick, and within no time at all I realised I was pregnant again. My body had a few years of rest from trying to fall pregnant and not thinking about it at all. Gemma was just the thing the doctor ordered. My doctor confirmed the good news. He was very positive about the pregnancy this time, so, after an ultrasound at about ten weeks, sent us home with positive thoughts and hopes. We were very cautious, and never told anyone about the pregnancy for two main reasons: we didn't want the children to be disappointed again if I did miscarry, and the adoption workers wouldn't be too impressed if they knew we were having another baby. But what was the point telling them if again it petered out at seven or nine weeks' gestation?

At twenty weeks we had an in-depth scan. We found out we were having a boy. I was beginning to show, and a few people said that they were starting to wonder if I was pregnant. Most were amazed, shocked. We had to tell the adoption workers, as they too were wondering. Most of the workers were very supportive, but a few were concerned about Gemma's well-being if a biological child was to come into our family. This

160

was very stressful for us, and the last thing we wanted was to have her taken from us.

Then, at twenty-three weeks into the pregnancy, having a routine check-up, my doctor said the membranes were bulging, and not to get up off the examination table. He called an ambulance, and I was taken straight to a larger hospital. Here I was again, out of control . . .

When I got there, they thought I might deliver that day. I was having slight contractions, and so they gave me drugs to suppress them. Well, they worked, and I was put into a general ward. I stayed there for four weeks, being given steroid shots for the baby's lung development. I was allowed out of bed to shower and toilet, then total bed rest. My thoughts were constantly for home, an hour and a half away from me. My parents had moved into our house to help Eddy with the three children. This was certainly a godsend for us, or I don't know how we would have coped.

I had done a pretty good job as an incubator so far, but one morning Nathan had different ideas. After morning rounds, and general observations were being taken, a junior trainee doctor noticed that the baby was well and truly on the way to being delivered. A code blue was called, and I was being prepped for an emergency caesarean. It all happened so fast. I was put under general anaesthetic, and Nathan arrived.

When I came around, I was shown a photo of him. He was in the Intensive Care Unit but *alive*. Now we had another fight to fight. A fight for life. He weighed 1100 grams, which is a good size for twenty-seven and a half weeks.

After Nathan was born Gemma's adoption worker contacted us. She needed to see us because she wasn't impressed about Nathan's arrival. Eddy and I went to justify ourselves to her. So we spoke to her, and after the meeting she was happy for the adoption to continue. She was worried about Nathan being our biological child and Gemma's place in our family. She could see that Gemma meant the world to us, and we don't even think of her as being adopted. She has fitted into our lives completely, and is definitely part of our family.

Nathan did really well in the coming weeks and had only one small infection to contend with. Then he was flown back to hospital for a further five weeks, and then home finally. Only to stop breathing on me after one day. After giving him CPR and calling the ambulance, he was re-admitted to hospital for a further ten days. I told the staff there that they could keep him till his eighteenth birthday!

He now came home with an apnoea monitor in his cot, which he didn't need, but for my peace of mind, I did. So, slowly but surely, we now had four children at home.

Eighteen months after Nathan's arrival, the final legal court proceeding went through to say that Gemma was now legally ours.

So, this part of our journey took fifteen years, from when Lorelle was born to November 2006. I can now look back with clarity and reason to myself. At the time, and for many years later, you question, 'Why me?' I don't know why Lorelle and Adrian died, or why I then had two miscarriages, but I do know that if these things hadn't happened, then I wouldn't have Gemma and Nathan.

Losing a child is the worst thing in the world, of that I am sure, but life goes on, and it is wonderful. It may not be wonderful for you today, but it will be wonderful tomorrow.

Leanne Rovers

Missing Angels

❦

My story starts in 1993 when my husband Walter and I were married in May. I had a ten year old son from a previous relationship and Wally and I wanted to start a family straightaway. I had been diagnosed with endometriosis and fibroids three years before and had to have ongoing operations and medication to help me control it. My gynaecologist put me on Clomid to help me ovulate. I did not fall pregnant. We stopped the medication in March 1994 and put ourselves on the IVF programme and were due to start in August. Much to our surprise, by May I was pregnant. We were speechless but extremely happy.

Our son was born two weeks early in January 1995. To our utter amazement, I found out I was pregnant again just five months later. After the initial shock, we were over the moon. Our next son was born nearly three weeks early in March 1996. When he was ten months old we decided to go for number four. I went through numerous operations and more fertility drugs but after three and a half years, nothing. Every month was like a knife stabbing my heart. I felt like I had done something wrong.

Then in June 2000 I found out I was pregnant again. I cried for days. I could not have been happier. The only downfall was that I was so sick. I used to have a bucket in the car with me as the nausea was so bad. I also got migraines that lasted for days. They were awful. I could not function normally. At work I would be running to the toilet all the time. (Not a good thing when you work in a kitchen.) I was put on a few medications but nothing helped.

At twelve weeks I was booked to have my ultrasound. My mum came with me. We had asked her if she would like to come into the operating room with us for this baby as it was going to be our last one. (I had to have a caesarean, hence the operating room.) During the scan, the doctor looked a bit concerned. When I asked him if everything was all right he answered, 'I'm not sure.' The baby was big for its dates and it had a thickening around its neck. He indicated that it was a cause for concern and added to the fact my age (I was thirty-eight years old) and I needed to go and have a chorionic villus sampling (CVS) done. So four days later I went to have it done. This doctor agreed that there was a problem but we would need to wait for the results. After an agonising ten days, our obstetrician rang us with the results. Our beautiful, much-loved and wanted daughter was gravely ill and would not survive much longer. All the specialists agreed that they did not know how she had lasted so long as nearly all babies with her number of problems do not usually pass twelve weeks. She had Trisomy 13 as well as heart and brain problems. We were told the best thing for her and me would be to terminate her. Our obstetrician gave us the weekend to think about it and we had to ring him on the Monday to let him know of our decision. Some decision. We felt we had no choice. My mum

---

Chorionic villus sampling (CVS) is a test that checks the pregnancy for genetic abnormalities. The pregnancy can be tested by taking a small sample of the developing placenta. The sample is collected using a slender needle which is inserted through your abdomen and into the placental tissue. The tissue (chorionic villi) is then examined in a laboratory.

CVS is a specific test for particular abnormalities, such as Down syndrome or cystic fibrosis. It is commonly performed between ten and twelve weeks of pregnancy.

looked after my boys for the weekend and we spent the time thinking about what we should do. We did as our doctor suggested. So, at fifteen weeks pregnant, I went to the hospital. I felt so guilty to be there. Our daughter did not ask for this but here we were. My only saving grace was knowing she would not be in pain or hurting. After a few weeks our obstetrician said that what our daughter had was a genetic problem, so Wally and I were both tested. It showed that Wally was a carrier. He was gutted to think that he had caused this problem. Apparently, his genetic problem only affects girls but is carried by boys. We had our boys tested straightaway. Thankfully neither of them are affected by it.

When I went home from hospital I could not function for weeks. Wally was inconsolable. We did not know how to cope. My sons did not know how to deal with it. They were only four and five years old. When it was nearing her due date, my younger boys asked, could we celebrate her birthday. It was a good idea. They also wanted to give her a name. We had names picked for her so we decided to have a little name-giving ceremony on her birthday, 5 March 2001. My two young boys decided we should plant an orange tree so that Madelyn could look after it and she would be with us always. So we did plant an orange tree. My children lovingly tended to the tree almost every day. It was lovely to watch them. My youngest son has high-functioning autism so he was very interested in looking after Madelyn's tree.

I am not sure where I heard about SANDS but in February of 2001 I attended my first meeting. It felt great that someone actually understood what I was talking about. I felt like it was home. I could cry or scream or yell or blubber and no-one thought I was weird or crazy. I went to monthly meetings and even took Wally a few times. He said it did help him to talk about it, but he understood it was my time to remember my girl and he wanted to deal with things his way. SANDS really helped me to cope with getting on with my life. Each month I reserved one night for SANDS to talk about my loss and to learn you can deal with life after a loss.

Much to our surprise, one month after Madelyn's birth date I found out I was pregnant again. What a shock. We were all ecstatic but I was extremely cautious. I went to my obstetrician but all was well. This little miracle was due three weeks after Christmas. A highlight for me was there was no morning or all-day sickness. I was rapt. I could continue to work and do everything with the boys. I felt great. At eleven weeks all was well. I was due to have a CVS at twelve weeks (on the Wednesday).

On the Sunday night I went to work as usual. About two hours after I came home I had a searing pain in my lower left side. It was so bad I had to sit down. It lasted only a minute but took me completely by surprise. I took a paracetamol and went to bed. The next morning I went to get up but had horrible pains. I rang work to let them know I would not be in. I also rang my obstetrician but he was away so I had to speak to his locum. He said if the pains got too bad or I started to bleed to ring him straightaway. As the day progressed the pains got worse. By late evening I had started to bleed. The locum booked me in for a scan on the Tuesday morning. By the time I got there the bleeding had stopped and so had the pains. I was a little relieved.

As the radiographer started the scan, Wally and I had our fingers crossed that it would be okay. It was not to be. Our precious baby had died. There was no movement and no heart-beat. They tried twice with two different people but to no avail. Our dreams were shattered. And for me at age thirty-nine,

I knew this could possibly be our last baby. So instead of going for our CVS the next day, we went to hospital for a dilation and curettage (D and C). I was devastated. I could not believe it could happen a second time. We told the locum we wanted to know the sex of our baby, so a week later when we saw our own obstetrician we were told it was a little girl. Another daughter taken from us.

My children did not know what to think and we did not know how to console them when we could not come to terms with it ourselves. I felt I just had to get on with everything. This time we sat the children down and explained, in a brief way, what had happened. When it came time for her due date, we named her Grace and planted another tree. Now our two girls were in heaven together. The hardest part was trying to answer the kids' questions about where our girls were and why they didn't live. How can you explain that to them when you don't understand it yourself?

I could not cope with things. I could not go shopping because if I saw a mum who was pregnant or who had a baby I would just cry. It did not matter where I was, I would just burst into tears. The two youngest boys would ask about their sisters and I had trouble answering them. I just did not know what to say. For us, the journey to have more children was nearly over. I went on the fertility drugs for another twelve months to no avail. At the age of forty-one my obstetrician said it was not looking good. If we wanted to we could try IVF: under the circumstances we could try embryo selection. They would test all embryos and only put back the ones that were not affected by the genetic problem we had. Wally and I thought about it. We even went to the first counselling session for couples undergoing IVF. Afterwards we realised it was too much pressure to put on ourselves to go through it all, and to have no result at the end would have devastated us. Money was never the issue, but I could not have coped going through all that and either not falling pregnant or losing another one.

I did what you were supposed to do: get on with it. I still attended my SANDS meetings. I would not have coped if not for these women. They helped me through a really tough time in my life and I will be forever grateful.

Each anniversary that came up we remembered our girls. A lot of people thought we were crazy as according to them, 'They weren't born so why are you upset?' Nothing makes me madder than ignorance. Only my real friends know how I feel and they are the ones that are still in my life now.

When I was pregnant with each daughter I had two friends who were pregnant with me.(One with each pregnancy.) When I lost Madelyn, I could not see my friend as I was not coping. She was a single mum and I felt envious that she still had her baby and I didn't. When her son was born, I went to see her a week after she came home. She did not press me to see the baby or to hold him but once I heard him cry I had to go and pick him up. It was a strange feeling knowing that I should have had my baby with me. My friend allowed me to do as I wished. So I bathed him and fed him a bottle and put him to bed. It felt so good to have a little baby in my arms. I didn't want to let him go but I did. After a few hours I went home and sobbed, but I felt okay. I am glad I did go to see her but I think if she had had a girl I am not sure I could have gone.

After I lost Grace it was too hard to visit other friends who were expecting their second child. I would speak to the husband to see if all was okay but I stopped visiting them. My husband still took our boys over to visit but I couldn't cope. After she had her baby it was her husband's fortieth birthday and they invited us. I went with Wally. If I found I couldn't cope he said we could leave. In a room full of people, the only one I saw was my friend. We hugged and cried and went into the bedroom to see her six week old son. My job for the night was to look after him. He was beautiful. I fed him and changed him and cuddled him. Again, I am not sure I could have done it if the baby had been a girl, but I don't know. After that night I was around all the time to help and look after the boys.

Even after all these years I can still have bad days. If it is close to an anniversary of my girls' birth dates or their due dates, I get very emotional. Sometimes I don't even know why. Last year when our then eleven year old son was getting ready for the first day of Grade Six, he started crying. When I asked him what was wrong, he informed me, 'Did you realise that today would have been Madelyn's first day in Grade Prep.' Of course there was soon more than one person crying.

The same thing happened this year only I was aware of it. This year Grace would have started school when her big brother started high school. I am sure we are going to go through many more 'firsts' and plenty of other things that go with everyday life. I only hope Wally and I and the boys are able to carry on with our lives. I find I am more emotional now over the tiniest things but I am working on it. And with the help of the great people from SANDS and my friends I am sure I will learn to cope one day.

Kerrie Sanders

'That Day'

This is my story. My name is Susan, thirty-one years old, primary school Physical Education teacher. Happily married to Magnus, thirty-five, works from home, computer programmer. At my twelve-week scan we discover we are expecting identical twins. Wow! We experienced feelings of joy and excitement; smiles beamed across our faces. Magnus had always wanted twins. He had told many of our friends even before I was pregnant.

I refer to this article as 'That Day', a song I often listen to by Natalie Imbruglia. 'That day' was Thursday, 19 June 2003. In the morning I was enjoying my twenty-third week of pregnancy. It had all gone to plan so far. No morning sickness or any discomforts. I was actually enjoying my body taking on a new shape. I was never expecting 'that day' to end with me being told, after coming out of a general anaesthetic, that we had lost both boys: Erik Leif who lived for five minutes, and Bjorn Alistair who was stillborn.

Let me fill in a few more details of 'that day'. Apparently I'd had a show in the morning. I thought nothing of it. I wasn't feeling unwell so went about my day. I went for a swim and then off to work. I was teaching Tuesday to Friday and was due to finish up in a week. After work we had plans to go to our niece's eighth birthday, (a seventy-five minute drive). I got home from work and just wanted to sit down and relax. I knew Magnus would drive and we had dinner cooked for us. Seemed like a fairly relaxed evening.

In the car on the way I started experiencing some pains. They came and went. When they came Magnus offered to turn back or go to a hospital. As they went I'd repeat, 'I'll be okay, I'll just take it easy when I get to the party.'

The pains got a little more intense and a little more regular. I rang my sister, Kerrie, who had had a baby boy four weeks earlier. She suggested I ring my doctor. So I rang the hospital I was booked into and they suggested I get checked out. I remember the girl on the phone saying, 'Maybe you're in labour.' I thought, I don't think so. I'm only twenty-three weeks.

We were stuck in traffic on the highway, in pouring rain with no idea where the closest hospital was. The girl from the hospital was to ring me back and advise us where to go.

On arrival at the hospital, we were directed straight to emergency. It wasn't until I saw a bit of concern on the faces of the people assisting us that I first realised maybe this was more serious than I'd been allowing myself to believe. Maybe I *was* in labour. I got a little teary.

Next minute I'm lying on a hospital bed being looked after by two midwives. They gave me a tablet to try and stop contractions. This was unsuccessful. They monitored the babies: two strong heartbeats. This was a positive. However, contractions continued. I was shown how to use the gas as I hadn't been to my antenatal classes yet.

Next minute my waters broke. The babies needed to be delivered urgently. As the boys were still high up in the uterus I needed to have a caesarean. I was given a general anaesthetic. My midwives had been a great support, explaining everything that was happening and holding my hand through each contraction. I appreciated being told the reality that the babies were being delivered early and that it would be touch and go. As I was wheeled into theatre I was repeating the 'Hail Mary' and 'Our Father 'and praying I'd read about my miracle babies in the paper the next day.

As I came out of the anaesthetic I was informed by the doctor of my little baby boys' passing. I was also experiencing painful contractions again. This didn't seem fair after all I'd been through. I was probably numb and in shock at this stage. I was asked if I'd like to see the boys. They just looked beautiful. We named them fairly quickly, agreeing on names with no fuss. We both liked Erik and Bjorn, and Leif and Alistair are our fathers' names. Magnus's parents and my other sister Jane and her husband were in the recovery room with me. It was comforting to see some familiar faces.

The next few days in hospital seemed to fly by. I had Erik and Bjorn in the room with me. In the mornings I'd wake early, watch TV and await my visitors for the day. The phone kept ringing and flowers kept arriving. The hardest was seeing my family for the first time. Not much needed to be said, just some hugging and some tears. For a family that doesn't normally express a lot of emotion it was comforting to feel okay to cry and hug. The nights were normally when I'd spend time with Erik and Bjorn: touch them, talk to them and shed a few tears.

The funeral was a day of mixed emotion. At times I felt numb. People were organising things around me. It had been a week since the birth of the boys so I wasn't too mobile. It was a day of overwhelming emotion. At one stage I stood by the couch with my lunch in one hand. I just stood there and began to cry – not able to eat or sit down, just cry. Dad spotted me and gave me that comforting hug I needed. I was then able to refocus – to sit down and eat.

I remember the funeral car arriving. For some reason I fought off crying. This was it – the day to touch Erik and Bjorn for the last time and say goodbye. Magnus and I travelled with the boys to the burial service. Whilst still in the driveway I remember looking out the window and seeing my sister Jane in Dad's arms being comforted. I often have flashbacks of that scene.

The funeral service was as pleasant as we could expect it to be. Apart from the final song I'd chosen not working in the CD player, it all went along the way we wished it to.

Magnus and I are now going along okay (three months on). Magnus told me that ringing family from the hospital was the toughest – that and coming home alone that first night to a house that was starting to get ready with baby gear. However, he has always put on a brave face for me. We talk a lot about what happened 'that day'. Magnus often fills in the details, some of which were a little blurred for me. I'm now experiencing a lot more happy days than sad. I think about the boys every day and daydream about what could have been. Sometimes the unexpected comes around and triggers a good cry. However, our daily lives are regaining a lot more normality. Erik's and Bjorn's existence will be with us forever, even as we move on beyond 'that day'.

Postscript: We are now five years on and are blessed with two more beautiful boys; Niklaus Magnus born on May 31, 2004 and Tommy Max born on February 10, 2007.

Susan Michelsson

The Life Journey of Braydan, Our Little Man

❧

What a rollercoaster we had been on! We had tried to conceive a baby for seven months when finally the signs were there: I was unable to drink coffee, was vomiting and had missed my period. Time to do a home test and wait to see those two lines. Then there they were and I had to wait to tell my husband that we were pregnant. We have a daughter who is four at this time. Do we tell her?

Once I tell my husband we decide to keep it to ourselves for a while, until we reach that magic twelve-week mark when things don't go wrong. How wrong were we! We decide to go to the doctor's to confirm the pregnancy and to arrange the medical support required. On this day our daughter complains of having an itchy back and tells the doctor over and over. In the end I ask if the doctor can look at her back. To my surprise she is diagnosed with chickenpox. I am concerned but am told not to worry as I had had it as a child and that will protect the baby.

My nausea increases instead of subsiding. Our poor daughter listens at the bathroom door as I vomit and at times wet myself from this. She even brings in towels for me to clean up with. How bad do I feel that she is being shown such a bad side to a joyous occasion. I am unable to keep water down, and become dehydrated to the point of convulsing. At this time I am only seven weeks pregnant and I am admitted to hospital for intravenous rehydration. After this we tell Sarah about the baby brother or sister she will have because we had to explain why Mummy was still vomiting. As she finds it hard to keep a secret we also tell others. Unfortunately this is not to be the last visit I have to the hospital. My third and final trip lasts for nine days, with a tube down my nose to my gut so that food can be given to me as I still can't take in food or fluids without vomiting, and there are no veins for intravenous drips due to dehydration. Charlie is extremely busy working all day, coming into the hospital to see me, caring for Sarah, who is being difficult due to her age, and caring for the house whilst I try to keep up the fight to save the baby and myself. The visits are terrible; we argue about Sarah and the behaviour she displays at the hospital and at home.

The obstetrician had performed an ultrasound prior to this admission to ensure I still had a baby. I was totally amazed to see the heartbeat as this was only nine weeks into the pregnancy. I lost more than twenty kilograms in weight. I grow concerned as the weeks go by because I am only able to eat certain high-fat foods and those that are high in protein. At fourteen weeks I felt Sarah kicking but at seventeen weeks I feel nothing, and despite reassurances that the baby is growing well I am not convinced. I am told that twenty years ago my baby would have been terminated to stop the nausea which continues and I get so low at times that I think this would be the answer, although never really wanting to let the baby go. I am sure it is due to exhaustion, but Charlie and I don't seem to be getting along very well and I feel as though he wishes the baby and I were out of his life, as well as Sarah, so he can just relax for a while.

At twenty weeks I have the routine ultrasound and to our amazement we see the baby suck its thumb. This image stays with me and I know I have to continue to fight and so does the baby. The nausea eases but never goes away. I had been injecting myself with anti-nausea medicine three times a day. At about thirty weeks the injections are down to once a day, with me keeping small quantities of food down and gaining a small amount of weight each visit. At thirty-two weeks I feel a pull at the side of my stomach when visiting the specialist, and advising him of this, am told that it is muscle-related due to stretching as the baby is growing so well and perhaps will be a big baby. The pain returns a fortnight later and once again I am told not to be concerned, so I ignore it and continue to do all that needs to be done. However, at thirty-five weeks I have another pain which intensifies three days later. The baby has not moved for twenty-four hours. I went to have a bath at this time but nearly pass out, so wake Charlie who then organises everything so that we can go to the hospital.

At the hospital we are told I am definitely in labour. A new midwife attends to us, who is unable to find the heartbeat. A more senior midwife comes in and the same process occurs. She says, 'The peanut is hiding,' and they will try other things when the doctor arrives.

Upon his arrival he says he is unable to find it either and the room is deadly quiet. The look on all their faces says enough without a word being spoken – in my heart of hearts I know that something is dreadfully wrong. He says he will put a scalp lead on. He then says there is a reading but it is very slow and the baby needs to come out.

Through our tears I scream, 'Get the baby out!'

Charlie is not sure what is happening. The midwife is not convinced and tells the doctor it is my heartbeat. After moving the scalp lead, he agrees and does an ultrasound. The baby's heart is still. We are told I will have to deliver naturally and the waters are broken. We beg for a caesarean section to be done, but are told this would be worse in the long term as I will always have the scar to remind me. We both break down in tears and ask, 'Why? What should we have done?'

Once the baby is moving during the birthing process I pass out, and Charlie feels he is going to lose me too. Later we found out why: the placenta was almost fifty per cent severed and therefore a clot the size of a watermelon had developed and somehow my body had compensated for it with no changes in my blood pressure or pulse. This was the reason the baby boy I delivered had died despite no blood being present in the waters or any obvious signs being shown on the ultrasound.

Once we have shed many tears together, Charlie states he had better make some calls. Although I don't want him to leave me, we agree this has to be done and he does what he has to. We name our son Braydan and have a Catholic priest bless him. We are fortunate enough to be in a hospital that cares for the family and baby in such situations. The midwives take photos, encourage us to do the same, along with our family, as nearly all our immediate family and close friends visit us. One midwife helps my cousin make plaster casts of Braydan's hands and feet, from which my cousin makes a plaque. They cut a lock of hair and make as many memories as possible for us, including putting him in the bed with me at night. This is really hard, as I listen to the other babies cry for attention and mine stays still. I pray for just one whimper, for him to just open his eyes so that I can see their colour or change a pooey nappy. This prayer is not to be answered.

As time draws near for him to go with the undertakers we find it difficult to say goodbye. This is made a little easier by them as they take him away in a cradle. I am taken to a room away from the new mums and babies but can still hear them cry and cry myself, especially when a midwife comes in to give me exercises to do to retone as I am not breastfeeding the baby of our dreams. The day I leave makes it all so real as I am empty-armed.

Planning the funeral is the next thing. Again I end up in hospital with a possible clot in the lung. Told I cannot leave the hospital until all tests are done, this adds to the pain as we need to plan the service. Why don't they understand? As this was a rushed thing, I have no supplies with me and I am told I am only allowed one pad for the blood. Have they not had a baby before and realised the amount of blood you lose and how embarassing it is to have blood everywhere? Finally, discharged and told it was a stress-related incident, we organise the funeral.

It is a nice service; we have a naming ceremony first. We have visited him several times in the lead-up to the day and dressed him. Last photos are taken as he is in the coffin. Prior to the funeral a viewing takes place and lots of family and friends attend to our surprise. Sarah is involved in lots of this, and now tells of her time with her brother and of the funeral and is not scared about death. We release balloons at the cemetery and this is very difficult for me. I don't want to let go but eventually Charlie talks me into doing it.

We visit Braydan regularly to begin with and then slow down but never forget him, especially on Anzac Day – a day for all to remember, but we remember a special little boy who was born still on this day.

We now have a new boy who has come to play, and whilst he has not replaced the little boy lost he does bring us joy which at times I thought we would never feel again.

Therase Hewitt

Gregory's Gift

❧

Australia Day holiday 1992 was not an ordinary day. It was the day Gregory Shane was born. He turned sixteen on his birthday (anniversary) this year. It's nice to say 'birthday' because he will never have a normal birthday with his brothers and sister.

The Australia Day weekend was moving day for us. We moved into our new house. I had been having some pain for a while but put it down to Braxton Hicks pains and stress from moving, I was thirty-three weeks pregnant with Gregory and having had a normal pregnancy with my first son, I didn't think anything was wrong.

The first day in our new home was Australia Day and that first night at around 2.30 am the pains wouldn't stop. I went into labour. But this was so different from my first pregnancy. At 7.10 am my husband rang the hospital to say we were coming in.

While my husband was moving our cars, I went to the toilet and my waters broke and I started to bleed a lot. It seemed like a long time but I couldn't get up off the toilet. When Alf came in he said to get on the bed. I wasn't going anywhere: the baby was coming. I felt the head soon after getting on the bed and told Alf to ring the ambulance. Then Alf helped the baby out. It was 7.30 am when our little baby boy Gregory was born. Alf rang the ambulance operator again and they told him what to do with Gregory. Alf held him, he checked his airways and with gentle puffs blew air in his mouth. Then the ambulance crew were there and they took over.

Gregory was warm and had good colour. I didn't even think

he was going to die, as babies have a good chance of surviving at thirty-three weeks. The ambulance officers cut the cord and took Gregory to the nearest hospital fast. We lived five minutes from a non-maternity public hospital and the ambulance took Gregory there and came back to get me. We stayed at the hospital all morning and a Newborn Emergency Transport Service (NETS) ambulance came and worked on Gregory. His lungs were underdeveloped and he was too weak.

Gregory fought for life for two and a half hours. His little heart was straining to beat and the machines were taking over. His brain started to lack oxygen and after twenty minutes the doctor said he would have severe brain damage. It was better to stop the machines and to give him a cuddle. Gregory was not going to make it.

The doctors didn't know what was the cause of his heart and lungs not functioning properly. They thought it was Down syndrome, but wanted him to have an autopsy done to find out the cause.

The autopsy came back to say that Gregory had Potter's syndrome, that he didn't have any kidneys, and the heart and lungs also were affected. The genetics counsellor told us this happens to one in two thousand babies and we had a five per cent chance of it happening again with the next pregnancy.

Some of the pain I had as Gregory grew bigger inside me was because he was unable to make any fluid. No kidneys meant no urine and so therefore his body squashed against my insides with no protection by fluid. I didn't know there was anything wrong, I was so busy moving house and looking after my son Darren.

I remember having a week's holiday two weeks before moving and having a couple of pains then. It was all coming back to me. Why didn't I know the signs that something was wrong? I can't answer that but I am so grateful to have had thirty-three weeks with Gregory inside me.

We had questions for the doctors and we wanted to know why the problem wasn't picked up at the twenty-week ultrasound. We had a video of this so we took this back to the ultrasound specialist and he said that the adrenal glands were in the same position as the kidneys and would have been mistaken for the kidneys because Gregory had a bladder and there was fluid around him at that stage. Had they got me back for another ultrasound a few weeks later it might have been picked up because less fluid would have been present, but this was not done because everything looked fine at the time.

Gregory was 4 pounds at birth, a good size, and lived for two and a half hours, and I held him for one hour before he was transferred by NETS ambulance to a larger maternity hospital. It was a confusing time with so many decisions to make. I was asked if I would like to go with Gregory and I was confused. I didn't know what to say. My heart was tearing. I wanted to be with my baby; however, I thought I was being rational and said I would stay because I was booked into a local maternity hospital and it would be easier for my family to come in. I regret that decision now. I should have gone with Gregory, as at least I could have had more time with him. I didn't hold or see him again. I should never have been asked to make that decision; I should have automatically gone with my baby.

The local maternity hospital was really helpful. They gave me a lovely blue outfit for him and I have it as a lovely keepsake. They also helped me with funeral arrangements. My mum and dad came in to see me and we showed them the hospital pictures taken while Gregory was still with us by the staff in the emergency department of the non-maternity hospital as we didn't have a camera with us. I am so pleased the staff did this for us because our hearts were being ripped out and we didn't even think of this at the time.

Gregory Shane was a beautiful boy with dark hair and deep-blue eyes. We think he would have been very tall because he had long legs and big feet.

I was given the book *Your Baby Has Died* and I couldn't put it down; I just wanted to read it. The comfort this gave me was so helpful and after one week I contacted SANDS. The support was invaluable, and with the help and support I received in that first year I was able to deal with the difficult feelings I had. I went to my first meeting two weeks after Gregory died. The emptiness I felt inside was unbearable and at each meeting I would just listen. At first it was difficult as the pain was so raw, and right down in the pit of my stomach I felt so empty, and then slowly I would start to talk. I couldn't wait to get to the next meeting: it was a chance to share my feelings and to know I was normal and there were others feeling like me.

I remember going to the shops in the first few weeks after coming home and a shopkeeper asked me where my baby was. Did I leave my baby at home? I was devastated I had to explain my baby had died.

From then on when anyone asked me, 'How are you?' I would tell them my baby had died and I would come home and I would go into my bedroom and cry. I didn't want to be seen crying all the time, so after a while I found that the best time to have a good cry was in the shower; this was my time. There were times when I would be watching a show and the tears would just flow. Darren would say, 'Mum what's wrong?' and I would tell him, 'I miss Gregory' and he would give me a big cuddle. He just knew; he is a sensitive and caring boy.

Creating memories was important, and going to group meetings and making friends with other parents helped. The first Christmas was a difficult time. I remember going out and looking for a special bear ornament to hang on our Christmas tree and I wrote *Gregory Shane* on the back. Then not long after we had his first anniversary. We went to the cemetery and put flowers on his grave and afterwards had a picnic in the park nearby with our three year old son Darren. We also bought a soft teddy bear and that evening we sang 'Happy Birthday' and ate birthday cake together with Darren and our special teddy bear. It was emotionally hard to do but very worthwhile in creating memories and the healing process for me. Each year we go to the cemetery and take a picture of our kids. They are growing up and this year they asked more questions about what happened. It is so natural and healthy and we always do something special on Gregory's anniversary.

The doctor said I should wait six months after Gregory's birth before trying again. After eight months I fell pregnant and miscarried at eight weeks. I was devastated that this could happen, having had a history that included two other miscarriages at about the same time, and endometriosis. It shouldn't happen; why did it have to be me? I already had my fair share of loss. When I went into hospital for the curette I thought they had made a mistake; the baby could not have died again. I prayed that it was a mistake. This was hard to deal with at the time. I went to my local SANDS support meeting and I cried and told my story. With the support and comfort I received I gradually got back into living. It was Gregory's first anniversary. We were told to wait two months this time and then we could try again.

I found out I was pregnant again eighteen months after Gregory died and I was very scared. What if the baby dies again? How would I cope? At least I knew what to do and could be prepared just in case. Each month I would go to the SANDS meeting and share my thoughts and feelings, and I used these meetings as milestones to get through the pregnancy, especially when I had to have a thorough ultrasound test to check for Potter's syndrome and all was okay. I was reassured that the baby was going well. I still was very anxious until thirty-eight weeks, when Brendan was born to a relieved mother who cried and cried when he was delivered. I got to enjoy having a baby again.

A year later I was pregnant again and having had three boys I was hoping for a girl. I had to go through the same test for Potter's syndrome and all was well. I was scared of going into labour at home but was reassured by the safe arrival of Brendan at hospital. But things were different with this pregnancy. I had been labouring from Christmas Day for two weeks. I went for check-ups and the doctors kept sending me home.

Then one night at 1.00 am I had this urge to go to the toilet. As I got up my waters broke, and while sitting on the toilet I could feel the head. My husband Alf was scared, thinking of our previous experience. I got on the bed and Jessica, my little girl, was born fifteen minutes from the time I woke up. Alf didn't have time to call the ambulance. The cord was around her neck twice and he was just wonderful. He flipped the cord over her head twice then called the ambulance and told them what had happened. I was very lucky to have such a wonderful, switched-on husband who didn't panic and was able to remove the cord from around Jessica's neck. When the ambulance officer arrived they cut the cord and took us to the local maternity hospital. I had lost a lot of blood because the delivery was so quick and the placenta was difficult to deliver, and felt very weak and a bit out of it the first day after Jessica's birth.

I am very lucky to have had a good experience with Jessica's birth at home. I didn't have time to think about things. I know

now that Jessica was a blessing to us and having her at home gave us closure.

I have had four babies and three miscarriages; three wonderful kids and one beautiful baby, my angel in heaven. Gregory gave me so much. I cherish his memory. The insight he gave me into my feelings and the experiences I have had have enriched my life. SANDS gave me a lifeline that helped me to help others, and over fifteen years I have been involved in helping other families: this was truly Gregory's gift.

Sabina Nyssen

Our Little Star

❦

How did I get to this point in my life? Was I just having a bad dream? I was lying in a hospital bed in labour and about to give birth, with a feeling of total disbelief and powerlessness. I did not understand how my life had got to this point, and what I had done to deserve this.

Going back to the day I found out I was pregnant, it was a joyous day. Paul and I had been trying for a couple of months and I really did not think it would happen for us so soon. I raced home from work just knowing that I felt different and knowing that the pregnancy test would be positive. I cried with joy and showed the test to Paul, my fiance. We both laughed and cried at the same time. I felt as though I had been initiated into some special woman's club. I was thirty-nine at the time and never thought it would happen for me. Circumstances in the past had not been right, but finally my time arrived to become a mum. I felt special that this tiny soul had chosen me to be its mum.

We began to tell family and friends. As the weeks went on, the morning sickness started. I did not sleep very well and I woke at 6.00 am most mornings. Some would say that my body was preparing me for the lack of sleep I would experience after the baby was born. It was like clockwork: at 11.00 am every day the nausea and dizzy spells started and continued for the rest of the day. I would sit and talk to my belly, pondering the questions, such as what the baby would look like, what colour the hair would be. This was the most important job that I would ever have in my life.

I took care of my health, taking vitamins, eating the right foods, exercising when I could. I was nine weeks pregnant on my fortieth birthday, and I allowed myself one glass of French champagne to celebrate. My sister and I were wondering what to call my little 'embryo', and we decided on 'Bubbles', as I sipped the exotic bubbles that I held in my hand.

I was amazed at how protective I became over Bubbles. I would walk through my day with my hand instinctively on my belly. What an amazing feeling of unconditional love. The connection that occurs so early in the mother/child relationship is very strong and grows quickly. Such a complete love.

In one of my reflective times, I had an insight, almost like a lesson for the day. *Enjoy every moment of this joyous time.* This is a lesson that has come to me before, especially after the death of close family members, but now it became more important and immediate for me.

I had a full-time job at this time. As fate would have it, I was working with another lady who told me that she was six weeks pregnant when I was eight weeks pregnant. Wow, it was great to have someone to compare notes with and talk to about being a first-time mum! Over the next few weeks Paul and I discovered that we knew of three other women that were pregnant and all due within weeks of our baby. It was an exciting time and I felt as though it was fate.

I had a disturbing dream when I was about nine weeks pregnant. I woke in an absolute sweat and I knew on an intuitive level that there was something wrong with our little Bubbles.

Our first prenatal visit to the hospital was fairly routine. We sat in the waiting room with all of the other growing bellies. I could not wait to have a belly full of baby. I would look at the size of some of the other bellies and wonder how big mine would grow. The time came for our twelve-week ultrasound and we were so excited to finally see little Bubbles in my tummy. As the machine scanned my little bump, we could see the form of a body taking shape on the screen. I had tears rolling down my cheeks at the most beautiful sight I had ever seen. The little arms and legs were waving at us, 'Hi, Mum and Dad, here I am!' Various pictures were taken and measurements done. The radiographer started to talk about the nuchal folds on the back of the baby's neck. He was concerned with the thickness and took measurements of that also. He suggested that we may need to see an obstetrician about the results and there was a high possibility that there was a chromosome abnormality. We left the hospital feeling quite deflated and numb. This was to be the start of many hospital visits. Fear and anxiety started to replace the joy.

The obstetrician called me the next day, and I started to panic. We went back to the hospital within a couple of days. During the appointment the obstetrician discussed the different outcomes with us. My heart began to fill with fear. She discussed the different chromosome abnormalities and the associated disabilities and consequences. I wanted to scream. Why was this happening? We decided to have the amniocentesis done to give us some conclusive answers. The results of this test would change our lives forever. If this child has a disability, how would we cope? When this child is twenty I will be sixty. How do parents do this? Paul and I were asking ourselves some very hard questions and not coming up with many answers. My morning sickness was still with me and the stress of attending work every day, plus not knowing our future, was exhausting and debilitating.

I had the amniocentesis done and then the waiting began, three days for the initial results. They call them the FISH results and test three of the twenty-one chromosomes for trisomy 13,

18 and 21. The rest of the results would come through within two weeks. I don't know how I got through this. I know that I cried a lot, sat in solitude and was very reflective. I have never felt so out of control in all my life. My life was not in my hands anymore. My fate was being decided for me and it was such an excruciating feeling.

The wait in the hospital on this particular day was particularly long. When we finally saw the obstetrician, I was so nervous that I was looking over her shoulder at the results. I saw the word 'female' and was overjoyed. It was a little girl. The obstetrician looked over the results and finally said the words trisomy 21, which is Down syndrome. My joy turned to anger and pain. I swore and cursed, Paul put his head down and I could see his eyes well with tears. I don't remember much else about that appointment but I said to Paul that I had a strong urge to name her there and then. We decided on Megan. I think I knew that my time with her was short and I wanted to bond with her as much as possible while I had the chance. As the news sunk in, my emotions went from shock to anger to sadness. I felt sadness for our little girl who may suffer from illnesses and learning challenges throughout her life, and I felt sad for us. At no time did I love Megan any less. If anything it made me love her more and I became more protective.

We did some research on Down syndrome and approached the appropriate organisation for help. We also saw a genetics counsellor for further information. The more information that we had the better equipped we felt to handle the new life that lay before us.

Now that we had some answers, Paul and I were asking the hard questions again. My well-being was fading quickly with the morning sickness and stress. I was unsure how much more I could cope with. After much discussion and thought, we decided to terminate. At least that is what I thought Paul wanted. We did not want Megan to suffer. Oh, what a disgusting and shameful feeling that decision left me with. We were driving to the hospital to organise the termination when Paul pulled over to the side of the road.

He said to me with tears in his eyes, 'I want birthdays, not memoriams. I cannot do this.'

I was relieved that he had said this as I was in no frame of mind, nor did I have the strength to be making these decisions. We drove home and called the hospital. We would be going ahead with the pregnancy. This was a huge lesson for Paul and me about being totally honest with one another in our relationship.

I still could not get the dream that I had had out of my head. I still felt that all was not well and there was more to this journey. I could not look at baby clothes or furniture. Our families were eager to start the collection but I asked them to wait and they respected that.

As I reached nineteen weeks, the morning sickness started to ease and I began to feel a bit better. I was finally enjoying my pregnancy. Paul and I went away for a weekend to a friend's holiday house by the sea. The weather was warm and inviting. We walked along the beach and ate nice food, and generally relaxed after the emotional and tumultuous time that had swept through our lives. We went to a surf beach and I laid in the sun soaking up the sea breeze and warm ocean air. I dipped my toes in the cool water, and the little child within me was beckoning for a swim. I ventured into the water and the waves consumed me, covering my growing belly. I chatted with Megan and felt the joy of our connection together. We rolled in the waves and I swam freely and without a care in the world. It was certainly the best I had felt in months. My life with Megan had certainly begun.

The twenty-week ultrasound was about to tell us another story again. I had experienced three months of this uncertainty, sickness and stress and it had taken its toll on me physically and emotionally. I often felt guilt for the thoughts that I had. In my dark times, I just wanted this to end. I don't know how many times I apologised to her, telling her that I loved her deeply but I was struggling. The ultrasound pictures were not as they were supposed to be. Megan's little body was swollen with fluid. This is not a good sign. Her heart rate had dropped slightly but was still strong.

The obstetrician's news was devastating. Megan had severe hydrops, a swelling and fluid retention throughout her body. We were told that Megan could die at any time. If the pregnancy had been more advanced they may have been able to do something for her, but we were at twenty weeks and she was too tiny. I do not ever recall crying so hard. I told Paul I could not do this any longer. I was spent. We decided that I would book into the hospital to be induced. It was the hardest decision that I have ever had to make. We had to wait nine days before they could fit me in.

A couple of days later everything was taken out of our hands. I was standing in the kitchen at home, and all of a sudden I nearly fainted and vomited at the same time. It was a very over-powering sensation, one that I had not felt before in the pregnancy. God had taken Megan back. There was no movement, no life, just a swollen belly. The despair and sadness was overwhelming. I cried, I felt frustrated and angry. I felt afraid at what was to come. How does someone move on from this sort of tragedy? My heart ached for my little girl, who did not have a chance at life. I would never walk her in a pram down the street and feel so proud. 'Hey, look at my beautiful girl, my special little girl.' I did not really give a thought to the fact that she had Down syndrome. She was perfect to me. She was life, she was the sugar and spice that existed in all little girls, the pigtails and frilly dresses.

My week was spent at home trying to keep busy but I felt restless and sick. Saturday was coming too fast, as I would have to let go of Megan's body from mine. I reflected on the decisions that we had made and wondered how this would affect me in the future. Decisions were made out of love and I had to keep reminding myself of this. What gives me the right to terminate a life that God has sent to me? It was a painful and shameful feeling. I was so afraid of the physical side of giving birth. Paul and I mourned together. He was a little bit distant, keeping his feelings to himself. During the pregnancy he would touch my belly, but as things changed he touched my belly less and less, maybe to distance himself from the pain. I know he felt enormous pain as well. Men just grieve differently to women.

We arrived at the hospital early on Saturday morning, and were shown to the birthing suite. I was told that I would have the room to myself for as long as needed. My midwife was very supportive and helped set me up in bed. I told her that I felt that Megan had died and she used the foetal monitor to check. There was silence, no blood rushing around, no thumpety-thump of life in my little baby girl. My worst fears were confirmed. I felt a rush of sadness and loss that I have never felt before. I had experienced the loss of my mum and dad, and my beautiful brother Jeffrey, but this was a different pain. I was soon to learn that the depth of pain in losing a child is like a bottomless pit that never seems to fill up in your lifetime.

I knew that I was in for a long and uncomfortable weekend. I was induced and the labour went for about twenty hours. The pain was excruciating, and the medication that they used to induce labour gave me a fever, shaking, nausea and sweats. The painkillers were in constant supply, and I was told that I could have anything I wanted as there was no prize at the end for me. I felt like a walking drug cabinet. I was not allowed to eat or drink until after the birth as I may need surgery to remove the placenta.

My water broke early on Sunday morning after a very restless and painful night. Oh, here we go, I thought to myself with some relief. Paul and my midwife assisted me to the toilet, and Megan slipped out. Megan Joy was born at 9.36 am on the 30 April 2006. I felt strange and the emptiness in my tummy was immediately apparent. The afterbirth was yet to come out and I was told to push. I pushed with all my might, as I did not fancy the idea of having surgery to remove it. But I had no strength left. I had nothing left to give.

Megan and I lay on the bed together still attached by the umbilical cord for about an hour. Finally the cord was cut. Megan was released from my body; we had run our course together for this life. The placenta refused to come away from inside me, so I went into surgery. Paul and my midwife were there by my side supporting me the whole time. The room was soon filled with people in gowns, and a trolley was brought in to transport me to theatre. I was wired up with drips and tubes. I was moved onto the trolley and wheeled along the sterile corridors of the hospital, weaving in and out. I remember going into the lift and then up a couple of floors. What the heck was I doing here and how do I wake up from this dream? I felt so spaced out. A man started to ask me questions about allergies and previous operations. I was then wheeled into the operating theatre. Looking around the room, there was the usual big light in the middle of the ceiling, lots of strange-looking metal implements and medical staff fussing over machines and tubes.

They could have done anything to me at that point and I would not have cared. I was depleted. I wanted sleep. The anaesthetic liquid was soon pumping through my veins and I was off to sleep. It was a heavy black sleep. I am sure that I wanted to stay there forever and not wake up. The bliss of nothingness and the absence of pain.

While I was in surgery the midwives had wrapped Megan's body in a bunny rug especially made for tiny babies like Megan. She was covered head to toe and was so little, just 190 grams and 19 centimeters long. They had placed her in a cot. Paul had some time with Megan while I was in surgery. When I had woken up sufficiently he placed her tiny body in my arms. I felt quite numb. Her little body was limp. I remember smelling her and my nostrils filled with a sweetness like that of a newborn baby. The softness of her blanket pressed against my cheek. I wanted to squeeze her so tight and never let go. All the medications and drugs that were swimming through my bloodstream were messing with my emotions, and my hormones were going crazy. There was no clarity in my thoughts. The midwives took photos of Paul and me holding Megan, and they made up a beautiful memory book containing poems and her cot card and our photo. I will treasure this all my life.

I said to Paul that every little girl needs a teddy bear, so Paul went to the gift shop in the hospital and bought Megan a cute pink teddy. We placed the teddy beside Megan in her cot and the scene somehow looked complete.

Megan stayed in the room with us all day, and that night we said our final goodbyes. I knew that we had to say goodbye eventually and I was so physically and emotionally messed up that I did not put up a fight to let her go. If I had my time over I would have held on to her for longer. I did not look at Megan when she was born. I did not want to remember her that way.

I wish I had held her tiny hand in mine, and felt her bare skin on mine.

Leaving the hospital the next morning was very difficult. Empty arms. The tears came in buckets and as we drove away from the hospital I just cried all the more. The intense grief had started. I felt cursed. I held Megan's teddy bear so tight, and I could not stop crying. I felt incomplete, battered and bruised all over. No prize and all that effort and energy, and nothing to take home but a broken heart and a broken and battered body. Now I understand what a broken heart truly means.

Paul and I had not made any preparations in terms of baby furniture or even buying her clothing. One thing happened after another, and we were focused on just getting through each day and each event. This somehow made it a bit easier to go home as the bigger reminders were not there. Megan's ultrasound pictures were hanging up in the kitchen and I had some pregnancy books and some small gifts from friends. That was okay to handle; I just put them in a cupboard. Flowers started to arrive from friends. Paul's sister came over with flowers and balloons with smiley faces on them that her young boys had chosen to cheer us up. People did not know what to say to us, and we just said, 'That's okay, we don't know what to say either.' No words can soothe such a broken heart.

The next day I was walking around the house with cabbage leaves on my breasts as they had started to swell with lactation. I was given a tablet in hospital but the swelling still occurred. I told Paul that I smelt like an old washerwoman. I have often felt that my sense of humor had got me through some difficult times; maybe it just masks the pain. It was certainly helping somehow.

Meditation has been extremely helpful to me. I was meditating one day, not long after coming home from hospital. I believe that we have a spirit and that it lives on after we die. I felt that Megan was an angel in heaven now. I asked her, *How do I move on from this? I don't know what to do now.* I heard a little voice say to me, *I will be a shining star and guide you forward, Mum.* Wow, that really took my breath away! It was so reassuring. I know now that Megan is with me always, my Little Star.

We chose to have Megan cremated. Paul picked up her ashes from the funeral director and brought her home. He said that he never thought he would be bringing home his daughter in an urn and a paper bag. Megan sat in our kitchen for months; she was part of the family now and it helped us to see her there every day. She has now been placed in my mum's crystal cabinet, and we bought a lovely rose bush in her memory. The rose is called Angel Face, which is very appropriate.

Moving on from this experience has been very difficult. I was mentally preparing myself to have a child and live a new life. Life has thrown me some curveballs but this takes the cake.

A couple of weeks after giving birth I went back to work. All the staff were very supportive and kind. Nothing seemed to change too much, but I had changed. I will never be the same person again, and I don't want to be. I am now a mum. At the start I had more bad days than good, and I wondered if that would ever turn around. It seemed to go on for months and months. I got out of bed every day and tried to find a purpose for the day, set my goals and work on projects around the house. I was determined to move forward but I also had to give myself the space to grieve. There were times when I wanted to scream. I ended up leaving my job three months after Megan was born. I did not have the emotional energy to deal with the job anymore.

If Megan were still with us she would have been due on 8 September and I got very emotional around this time. Instead of having a sad day on this day, I decided there was going to be a birth of some kind, a celebration to take away some of the hurt. Paul had asked me to marry him on my fortieth birthday, but at the time I was just pregnant and I had a gut feeling it was not the right time. He had given me a beautiful engagement ring and it needed to be resized so I took it to the jeweller's. The lady told me that it would be ready on 8 September. For me that was a sign. Something good would come out of this tragedy.

We started to hear about the other babies being born around September. There were two boys and a girl. I was happy for them but it was difficult. I felt jealous and bitter, and I told myself that this was a normal emotion. I could not hold a baby without bursting into tears so there were not many visits to new mums around that time. I found that there were some triggers for my tears, such as an advertisement on the television about babies or seeing a child with Down syndrome.

Christmas was a difficult time. I thought about how to include Megan in our Christmas celebrations each year and I thought I might buy a gift that I would have bought for Megan and give it to a worthy charity. But every time I walked into the shops where the children's toys were, I burst into tears. Too hard for the first Christmas so I will try again next year. Instead I bought a lovely pink star to be included on the Christmas tree every year. This will be Megan's star. We went to a friend's place on Christmas Day and there were the usual people there. There was a little girl running around. She was about two years old, and we started to play together. On a nearby chair there was a big yellow star made out of cardboard. She walked over to the chair, picked up the star and handed it to me. I had tears streaming down my cheeks. Megan was with me. My Little Star was spending Christmas with us after all.

It is now a year since I gave birth to Megan. The sadness and the tears are coming quite consistently again on a daily basis. We have just had her first birthday. We attended a memorial service the day before her birthday which seemed like a nice way to remember her. I cried a bucketload of tears again and the sadness remained for a couple of days. We lit a candle and I said a special prayer for her. I have more good days than bad now but the sadness still remains.

Does Megan hear my thoughts and prayers? Is she happy in heaven? She is with her nannas, and Poppa, and Uncle Jeff. She would be surrounded by so much love. Where does my story go from here? I don't know. I will continue to be strong and work through each day, each feeling, each moment that I miss her. She has taught Paul and me not to sweat the small stuff. Life is too short.

It has taken a year but I have finally seen pictures of Megan's tiny body. I contacted the hospital as I was told that they normally keep photos in patient files under these circumstances. She has tiny arms, hands and feet, just sleeping peacefully. I can just make out her facial features but she looks very sick and as though she had a difficult time. That breaks my heart. She is a beautiful sight to me. She is my flesh and blood and such a huge part of me. I feel like something has shifted inside me emotionally after actually seeing her. I feel like I can move forward a bit more now, as if I now know that I have done everything I can to help Megan and myself. There just seems to be a feeling of a little more peace inside me. I just want my Little Star to be at peace too.

Christine Warren & Paul Dooley

Kate's Legacy

❧

My pregnancy was perfect, with only a few days of morning sickness, and I was able to continue working until the end of my fifth month. I only finished then because I was prepared to stay home to await the arrival of this child whom we wanted so much. I had read everything I could lay my hands on dealing with pregnancy, childbirth and breastfeeding. I was really eager to breastfeed and felt ready to conquer any trouble which may be placed before us.

I entered hospital very excitedly, thinking that by the end of the day our child would be born, to receive all the love we had stored up. It was only two hours later that our world shattered. There was great hustle and bustle and instinct told me that our baby had died.

Following the very exhausting seventeen-hour labour and difficult forceps delivery, our precious daughter Kate Louise was placed in my arms. I had agreed to a suggestion by one of the nursing staff to see and hold our baby. This was a very important step toward accepting our loss. The memory of holding and seeing our baby and pointing out family resemblances will remain with us always.

Brian and I received so much love and support from our doctors and the nursing staff. We are deeply indebted to those people who all became so involved with us. They showed that they are humans with feelings and not machines as so many people seem to think.

One thing that you don't even think about following the loss of your baby is that your milk still comes in. I spent a very uncomfortable day forty-eight hours later, and found hot showers very relieving. My doctor also provided tablets to help me dry up the milk.

Kate had been baptised at birth, but we decided to wait and have her funeral the following week after I had been discharged from hospital. The decision was completely up to us. (The funeral can be held immediately and the mother can be let out of hospital for that day.) I found it very important to have been part of laying our daughter to rest, but it is a very personal decision.

We felt as though we were the only couple in the world to lose a child but it is amazing how many people will say, 'I know how you are feeling, we lost a baby too.' While in hospital I was able to speak to someone who had suffered a stillbirth some time ago. By speaking to that person and asking questions, I was able to accept my situation a little more easily.

Don't be afraid to show your emotions. Find comfort in your partner and talk about your feelings. It is very possible that either of you will have guilt feelings. Discuss your feelings with your doctor and have him explain the circumstances to you. He will also be able to discuss the possibility of further pregnancies and the chances of stillbirth reoccurring.

We found that many of our friends were frightened to phone or visit because they were unsure of how we would react, especially if they had children themselves. To those people who have a friend who has lost a baby, remain their friend for it is now that you are needed most. Be prepared to sit and listen, or to ask questions about the baby. That child has been part of life, even though it has been lost prior to delivery.

Overcoming grief takes a long time. The baby has been planned and carried for so long – the memory cannot be erased overnight. Given time the pain diminishes, but the scar of having lost a child remains always. There have been floods of tears since we lost Kate and I guess there will be many more in times to come. People have told us not to think back but it is very hard not to. I have found comfort in frequent visits to our baby's grave but only time will heal our hurt.

We are hoping to have another baby soon, but no-one will be able to replace our firstborn child.

Footnote: This story was written late in 1981, prior to us finding out we were expecting another baby. What joy, what excitement, what trepidation! In October 1982 we became the very proud, yet anxious parents to Mathew – a boy, what joy as HE could never be seen as a replacement for Kate. Emma was born in 1985, almost a replica of her older sister. The family expanded with Laura's birth in 1990 and culminated with Samuel's arrival in 1992. Our family complete, but still the unfilled void left by Kate's death.

Our subsequent children have all grown with the knowledge of Kate. They all say there are five kids in our family.

I will always wonder what could have been . . . teething, talking, walking, kindergarten, school, deb balls, uni, boyfriends, marriage, children . . . but I will only ever experience these things through the lives of my living children.

Bring on the sleepless nights or dirty nappies – I know they are much easier to deal with than the grief and despair not only felt by parents, but one's entire network of family and friends.

Janette Reynolds

Learning to Breathe Without You

❧

A short story for all the members of my family, whom I love dearly, especially those that are still to come.

How did this happen to us?
Feeling so hopeless. Helpless. Powerless.
Just less. Less than alive.
Much less than alive.
Much less.

The nightmare begins

Like any couple, newly married, expecting their first child, we fronted at the doctor's office soaking in anticipation and pure joy. It was a Tuesday evening and we had been counting down, almost holding our breath, looking forward to our twenty-week ultrasound.

We'd made it to halfway. Beyond the expectations of most, we'd fallen pregnant, relatively easily, survived the first trimester, and made it (safely) to four and a half months.

I handed the already-cued video cassette tape to the doctor and climbed up onto the bed. Your dad, Robert, positioned himself in the chair next to me and we readied ourselves to watch you as the doctor made his checks and measurements.

We were both so excited. So eager to see how much you'd grown, how much you'd developed since the twelve-week ultrasound we already had on the video and had watched so many times. Robert was bursting to know if you were a boy or a girl.

I wasn't. As per our agreement, this was not going to be the day we found out (although your dad was not-so-secretly hoping he would be able to see for himself).

Over the next three-quarters of an hour or so our joy, and all our hopes, would decidedly, and oh so painfully, turn to worry, stress and deep hurt. *How could this have happened to us?*

We saw your head, your brain, your cute little nose and 'perfectly formed' lips. The doctor showed us your heart, pumping away with its fully-developed chambers. We watched with heightened anticipation as the doctor found your two legs, two arms, left hand . . .

'Where's the right hand?' Robert asked.

The doctor had been searching for about fifteen minutes (at least it felt like at least fifteen minutes) and I could see that your right hand was not looking quite normal. We could only make out a thumb and three digits. Only four fingers. And the three digits didn't seem to spread apart as they should.

Okay, I thought, so we'll have a left-handed child. But I could sense that Robert was getting very worried. Agitated. Unnerved. I thought I would be able to calm him down, make it all okay for him. But that was before the penny really dropped and we realised how bad things were.

When life was good and breathing was easy

My life has been full of ups and downs, and some of the downs have been really well below sea level. There's a bit of a joke amongst my family that if there's a hole in a piece of straight ground, and someone has to fall into it, the someone will be me.

I was recovering from a rather nasty car accident when your dad and I met in August 1999.

Robert somehow understood my pain. Not just the physical

side of it, but also the psychological and emotional torture the debilitation was causing me. He became my rock, my backbone. As long as he believed I would recover and be able to walk and dance and swim and be 'normal' again, I could get up in the morning (well, most mornings anyway) and bear the pain for another day.

In January 2001 I finally began working full time again and seemed to be as recovered as anyone thought was likely to be possible. I was driving again, swimming again, able to ride my bike again. And your dad and I were living together and planning to move into our first home, which we had purchased the previous month. Life was basically great.

We moved into our home in May 2001. On 31 July that year your dad managed to build up the courage to tell me that he'd like me to be his wife. We were married in December at the same place that both sets of parents were married – and it was truly a magical day shared with our family and closest friends.

The next step was children. Actually I should probably go back a step or two to make sure you fully understand how eager we were to be parents.

Your dad had just turned thirty-one, and I was twenty-six, when we started going out. We were both living out of our parents' homes, independent, single (obviously) and ready to 'settle down'. I had been wanting to be a mum for quite some time (some would say I was clucky before I could walk and talk).

When your dad did (finally) manage to breathe out the words on that cold day, sitting on a rock at the beach at Cape Shank, and we started to plan our wedding, his preparedness for parenthood suddenly became very apparent to both of us. We had walked about three kilometers through the bush to the (somewhat) secluded beach, and after we'd sat there (in the wind) for a while and soaked up the romantic atmosphere, we decided to head back up to the car. We hadn't yet been engaged for a full half-hour, had not yet even told anyone about it or set a date for the wedding, and your dad turned to me to ask, 'So, when do you think we can have a baby?'

Everything (and I mean our whole lives) from that point on was wished for and planned around the fact that we wanted to have our first child, if at all possible, before the end of the following year. Not that we told anyone that.

So in early 2002 we found ourselves married, sublimely content, and trying to have a baby.

Effortless breath

With my history of endometriosis, and the length of time I had been on the contraceptive pill, no-one could tell us how long, or difficult, it might be for us to fall pregnant. They told us not to hold our breath, and to be patient. Two years was not likely to be improbable.

I was worried about the endometriosis coming back, and we both wanted to be parents so much, I spared no expense in our endeavour. We bought books, thermometers, ovulation-determination kits. Anything that I thought would help us make sure we were giving it our best chance. I also started a journal. Your journal.

In January we had a false alarm that got us all excited. After that we put away the books and thermometers and tried not to try so hard. It wasn't easy. We were both so eager to be Mum and Dad. Both wanting to grow our family so desperately.

I don't know exactly how I knew, but I knew. Before I really could have known, I knew. We were trying to be patient, cautious, trying not to jump the gun after January's experience.

Mother's Day was the following Sunday and we decided we

would wait until Monday before we did the home test. We weren't sure we would be able to keep the news to ourselves in front of all the family, but we were determined not to say anything until the twelve-week mark.

That was the theory anyway. But I couldn't wait, so even though I woke up on Friday before six o'clock needing to go to the toilet, I held on. And held on. And held on.

Until eight o'clock, when I jumped in the car and drove forty minutes to a pharmacy (there and back) crossing my legs the whole way. I ran into the house and straight to the toilet and before long we had two pink lines on the stick. What joy! We were pregnant! Now how were we going to contain ourselves on Sunday?

The first trimester was pretty tough. While I wasn't having as bad a time as some people I know, it wasn't all that pleasant either. I was tired, nauseous, forgetful, growing. And it was really hard to contain myself and keep from telling absolutely everyone. Especially with one of my best friends giving birth to her first little boy when I was about eight weeks.

Also, the doctors had warned us that the chances of you surviving the first twelve weeks were not as great as most because of my history with endometriosis. When we made it to the first ultrasound and heard your heartbeat for the first time, we were both absolutely over the moon. And I breathed a huge sigh of relief. I also starting telling absolutely everyone.

Suddenly my life, which had been basically great, became oh so fantastic, and I don't remember a time when breathing was so effortless.

How do you make a choice when each of the only two paths open to you presents an equally unimaginable option?

Loving you till it hurts

The most horrible thing about this nightmare, besides not being able to wake up, and having lost you, is that I was totally unable to take myself out of it for even one minute. Each moment of the following two weeks was oh so real and suffocating, and I could not make myself stop feeling it so intently.

On our first day in the hospital I commented to Robert how terribly unfair it was that on our wedding day I had to constantly remind myself to stop, and breathe, and take it all in so that I wouldn't miss any of the detail I wanted so much to remember forever. Yet during this time, no matter how hard I tried, I couldn't make myself miss any of it.

From the moment the doctor started to explain to us what further implications your deformed hand may have, we started to fall apart. I can't describe it any other way. As individuals and as a couple, with such wonderful expectations, we literally began to come loose. Like a jumper caught on a nail, we started to unravel. And there seemed no end to the devastation we felt.

The air became heavy and as we were given added information, each breath became more and more difficult.

Without your dad sticking by my side, and I mean literally, basically twenty-four hours sticking by my side for those two weeks, I would not have been able to continue breathing. We would find ourselves unable to part from each other's company and hours would pass without our realising it. We sat together, washed together, tried hard to continue breathing in and out together. It was literally impossible for us to not be touching each other. It was like letting go would mean we couldn't each continue to draw breath.

Our parents were amazing and, despite the disappointment and pain they must also have been feeling, managed to fully support us through the most horrible time of our lives. They brought us food, washed our clothes and our dishes, held us, listened to us, talked to us. Listened to us. Without their unfaltering support – no matter what decision we finally made – this ordeal would have been monstrously worse.

Although I can't erase a single moment of that first week from my mind, I find it very difficult to translate it to the page. It was the longest week of my life and also the shortest week of my life. It was the week I most want to remove from my life. It was the week I stopped being able to breathe.

While your dad was able to somewhat distance himself from you as soon as we saw your right hand, I was not. Not physically. Not emotionally. I had grown to love you so, so much, eagerly reading a week-by-week account of how you were growing and developing, what you were doing. And then I started to feel you moving.

I felt like I was being forced to make a totally impossible decision. There was no way that I could, in good conscience, force Robert, or myself, or you, or any of your future siblings, or our extended family, to live with the altered dynamic that continuing with the pregnancy would have created. It wasn't fair on anyone, least of all you, to put our family through the certain stress, uncertainty and relationship difficulties that your cleft hand presented to us.

On the other hand, how was I going to live without you?

How was I supposed to continue to breathe with you no longer in my life?

It was a completely untenable situation.

And I had no idea how I was going to get through it.

How was I going to be able to do what I had no choice but to do?

Monday 2/9/02

To my dearest darling, sweet & innocent, tiny little baby,

I am oh so sorry that this has happened to us and that we are going to lose you before we even get to meet you.

I am so so sorry that there's nothing I can do to fix it – to make it better – to take it all away and protect you (and us) from this horrible thing. My greatest wish is that we wake up tomorrow and find that the last week didn't really happen, or that it was a big mistake and everything is ok and we can go on as before and wait until January to meet you. But the reality is that this most terrible situation is not going to just go away and tomorrow will be the most terrible day of my entire life.

I want you to know that I love you dearly and with every ounce of my being. And though I haven't yet met you I feel as though I've come to know you over the past four or five months. I have definitely become very attached to you. I promise to never forget you, and if I can, I will endeavour to let your future brothers and/or sisters know you.

You brought a joy and strength into my life that I want to thank you for. Through you I have learnt so much about myself, life, love . . . and I carry it all into the future. It's my way of making sure that your short time with us was not in vain, that it had a purpose. It's my way of making sure that you are always with us – always in my heart – from now until forever.

I love you, baby, and I thank you. Please forgive me for not being able to do, or be, more so that things could maybe have been different. You are a valued and necessary part of our family and I will always love you – please don't forget your mum loves you with all of her heart! Goodbye my sweet little darling baby.

Mumma will miss you . . .

Breathe in, breathe out

Giving birth to you was the most incredible, painful, amazing, difficult, fantastic, horrifying thing I have ever had to do. I asked them for as many drugs as they could give me – I had to numb the physical pain in order to help me breathe through the emotional and psychological pain. A pain that was excruciating beyond belief.

They started the 'procedure' at about eight o'clock on the Tuesday morning. You were born at 5.33 the following morning. It was a long and unfathomable night. Your dad was, once again, simply amazing. He was there for me and made sure I was able to keep breathing through it all.

I think the waiting was maybe one of the hardest parts of the day. They would give me the labour-inducing drugs, then I'd have to lie still for an hour, then I had two hours to kill before they gave me the next lot. Somehow, though, just like the preceding week, the time passed slowly and quickly, both at once.

We were told it should all be over by mid to late afternoon and we may even be heading home that evening. At 7.30 pm the doctor was worried that he may have to try something else because nothing seemed to be happening. And your dad got very worried. By eleven o'clock the doctor was satisfied that we'd see you before morning.

The hospital staff were tremendously helpful and the support we received was just fantastic. At nine o'clock there was a change of shift and the midwife who delivered you arrived. She was an absolute angel. And I'm glad you waited until she was there because it was all the easier for me due entirely to her presence.

We had spoken to a counsellor the previous Friday, and the hospital had organised for one of their social workers to visit us while we were waiting for labour to kick in. There were so many issues to consider, so much to discuss.

Did we want to see you? Hold you? Name you?

Since the ultrasound, your dad and I had made a complete swap as to wanting to know your sex. He immediately no longer wanted to know. I immediately did. I think it was part of Robert's way of distancing himself, making it less emotional. I felt I needed to know you as fully as I could. To have some closure. To be able to say goodbye.

When the time came, the midwife told your dad he should probably leave if he didn't want to risk seeing you. He was out of the room for about an hour and half (I think).

The epidural hadn't fully worked so I could feel the contractions, which meant that I could help by pushing. You were born bum first – breech – and at the last minute seemed not too sure that you really wanted to leave my body. They wrapped you up and put you in a cot. I had said I wanted to finish with the birth totally before they gave you to me to hold. I wanted to be able to fully focus on you, and not be concerned with the placenta or anything else that would have been going on.

As is very common with premature deliveries, the placenta was good and stuck. At about 6.30 it still hadn't moved and our wonderful midwife would finish her shift soon. I decided to spend some time with you while she was still around and then have her take you out so that Robert could come back. I needed him with me.

You were so small, and yet so fully a baby. You had a face, and a body and arms and legs and feet and hands. Hands. The minute I saw you I said, 'She's got Robert's nose.' I checked your ears too. Your dad had spent the past few months teasing me about you having my ears. It was hard to tell – they were a bit squashed to your head after the delivery – but I think you had Robert's ears (thank goodness) with my earlobes.

Your eyes were still fused closed so I don't know what colour they were, but they were big. Although I think that may have been because you were born at only twenty-one weeks. I traced your tiny lips and touched your tiny, cute tongue. You were so beautiful and perfect. So real. So mine.

I had expected that seeing you, holding you, knowing you was going to be terribly difficult and painful. I expected that I would fall apart and totally lose it over you. I felt that I was not going to be able to control my sadness and pain, but that I really was going to need that 'big bad ugly' cry in order to be able to continue breathing. Surprisingly, none of that happened.

From about four o'clock on that Wednesday morning I was strangely very calm, almost not totally present (maybe it was partly the drugs, partly the tiredness). And when you were born I felt very matter-of-fact and okay. Then the midwife put you in my arms for the first time and I was so happy to finally meet you.

It felt strange to be so calm and contented, but somehow, also so right. I think it was a bit strange for everyone else too. Robert and my mum were really concerned and worried for me. I think they believed leading up to your birth that I shouldn't spend any time with you because it would be too hard for me. But I seemed to spend Wednesday reassuring them and keeping *them* calm. I felt strangely very much in control.

I spent some more time with you later in the day. I held you and undressed you (they put you in this hideous white dress that I would never have chosen for you) and looked you over. I rocked you and talked to you and tried to memorise every part of you.

And then I told them they could take you away.

Hour by hour, day by day

When terrible things happen, when people are grieving, all the 'experts' say to just take it day by day. For a long time I was only able to make it hour by hour, moment by moment.

Thursday morning, when we left the hospital, and we had to leave you there – go home without you – I began to fall apart again. I not only had trouble breathing, I felt I couldn't take another step as we walked along the path, away from the hospital door, closer to the car, closer to home. Further away from you. *How had this happened to us?*

I have spent so much of the past few weeks feeling so lost. We came home from the hospital and I had no idea what to do. No idea what I wanted to do. No idea what I needed to do. Just no idea.

Breathe – in, out, in, out.

That's about all I could manage, and even then I had to try really hard.

In the hospital that morning Robert and I had talked about our different ways of coping, of dealing with what was happening. We talked about how good it was for me to spend time with you and how it was going to make things so much easier for me in the long run. We talked about how hard it was going to be for me not to give away any of the details to your dad, who had started to ask me some questions but was still unsure about what, if anything, he wanted to know.

He had asked me to tell him, without giving him any specifics, if I thought you looked like one or the other of us. He asked me, without giving him any specifics, if it was obvious that you had any of his features. He asked me if it was going to be too hard for me not to use pronouns (like he and she) when we were talking about you.

213

I could see that the effort of trying to work out whether it would be better for him to know or not was eating him up more than the pain of knowing would have. But I was not going to tell him anything unless he specifically asked. He had to make the decision as to whether he needed, or wanted, to know or not. Then, finally, he asked. And just as well; it made things so much easier for both of us.

Your dad can sometimes be a typical male and he is a 'doer'. He likes to 'do' – it makes him feel he is in control and helping in some way. When we left the hospital they gave us a lot of paperwork and forms, just the sort of thing Robert loves to take charge of. If he hadn't allowed himself to know that you were a girl, I would have had to fill it all in and lodge it by myself, something I was not really in an emotional position to do.

We bought a special pink box and put all the photos, the video, your journal and the memory book the midwives at the hospital prepared for us inside. It has all your details and photos and prints of your tiny hands and perfect feet. I know that one day I will be able to put it away in the cupboard, but not just yet. For now it sits on the chair near my bed, where I have easy access for when I need to see you and speak to you again.

Robert went back to work on the Friday after you were born. I waited until Monday, and found it extremely difficult. The first week I didn't make it every day, falling apart again at times, not being able to be around people yet not being able to be on my own either.

I missed you terribly and longed to have you with us. It was a sickening, painful longing that ripped me apart inside and made it almost impossible to draw breath.

Two weeks after you were born your dad took me away. We spent four days at a little bed and breakfast cottage and it was perfect. I needed to just get away and be away from the house, away from people, away from any have-to activities. I wanted to spend some time just being. Without doing.

Our first morning there I woke up with the start of what would develop into the flu. It was perfect. I had no reason not to just sit inside, by the log fire, with my cross-stitch and a warm drink. Just being. Without doing.

We came home last Sunday and I felt so much better. It had been so good to be away, to leave you at home. And it felt oh so good to come home, back to were you are. I was now ready to start breathing again, slowly. On my own.

Looking to the future – continuing to breathe

When we had the original twenty-week ultrasound the doctor said he thought there may also be something wrong with your left hand, but he wasn't sure. When I held you, I checked it very carefully, more than once. The two middle digits were fused together, and as we had seen, your right hand was cleft and missing a number of the bones.

Next week we are going to meet with the genetics specialists again. They will have the final results from all the tests, including your autopsy, and hopefully will be able to give us some more information. I say hopefully, but it's a mixed feeling of hope.

On one hand we want to hear that there was (definitely) nothing else wrong and that it was a one-off event with as little likelihood of re-occurring as there was of it occurring in the first place. That would make us feel more at ease for when we are ready to try to give you some brothers or sisters.

On the other hand we want to know that there was (definitely) more to the problem and they have pin pointed exactly what it was, what caused it, and what to look for next time.

That would help us to feel even more certain that what has happened is the right thing and give us hope that we can work with the experts to ensure it doesn't happen again. Or at least that we can catch it earlier so that if we have to make a decision it may not be as painful and traumatic.

The likelihood is that they won't be able to give us any more information than we already have, leaving us as much in the dark about what, why, how . . .

For now I'm just taking things as they come. I do what I feel like doing, when I feel like doing it. And I continue to breathe. In and out. I'm leaving my doors open and not making any decisions, about anything, until I can feel more alive again. Until I can be more sure that the next breath is not going to require a conscious effort. And right at this moment nothing else, and no-one else (except of course for Robert), matters.

In and out.

In . . . and out.

In . . . and . . . out.

In . . . and . . . out.

In . . . and . . . out.

Epilogue: After a number of rough years and miscarriages, we now have a beautiful fifteen month old girl who carries her older sister's name as a middle name. We are also pregnant again with another precious baby hopefully joining us is four months.

E. Sal

My Butterfly's Story

❦

Last March, after struggling with fertility issues, we found out we were expecting. My first two pregnancies to another partner ended in early miscarriages but we were lucky to fall pregnant with our first daughter (who was six) very easily. So we had a focus of getting past that twelve-week mark and boy, was it rocky. At six and eleven weeks I had bleeds and went off to the emergency department thinking it was all over. But both times we saw our baby. I had lots of nausea but not much followed through. I was getting bigger and proud to wear my maternity tops which I had made.

I remember spending a lot of time fishing out in our boat and thinking that this kid will be one knocked-around bubba but needless to say very seaworthy!

From around twelve weeks I was having lower back pain and just put it down to me and my usual ailments. My partner was working afternoon shift at the time and on Friday, 10 June I was having lower back pains again and he got me a heat pack and went off to work. That evening my daughter took a picture of me and my belly and I did a few things on the computer. At around eight o'clock I went to the toilet and felt a pop and then my waters rushed from me. I knew straightaway that it must have been nearly all of the waters.

I screamed for our daughter to get the phone and I rang my sister to come and take me to the hospital. I also rang my husband and told him I would ring him when I got to the hospital but to stay at work. I rang the birthing suite as I wasn't sure where to go; they say you can go there after twenty weeks and I was sixteen weeks six days. They told me to come there.

The whole time I was finding pads and towels, our daughter was telling me to calm down, it would be okay. Oh, to be that innocent again! I didn't want to walk into the birthing suite because I knew it would mean losing my baby for good.

I still held out hope so I told my husband to wait until we knew what was happening. Well, I went to the toilet and was bleeding, so I rang my husband and he came straightaway. By the time he got there the obstetrician came in with a portable ultrasound machine and put it on my tummy.

I couldn't look. This doctor then told us that baby was alive but there was only a tiny amount of fluid surrounding him/her. Then he explained all of the things that could happen and that the most likely was that I would go into labour. I asked if the baby was going to be alive and he said no, but what he should have said is that most babies of that gestation will pass away before they make it out of the birth canal. I was aware our baby had no chance of life outside my womb.

That night we had a fantastic midwife that went through what our baby would look like and other things. We tried to sleep but I couldn't. I actually pretended I was so that hubby would sleep. In the morning after having a long contraction, I woke him up so that he could move our car and go home and shower. While he was gone I went to the toilet and upon wiping I felt something. I called the midwife and she had a look and told me it was my baby's foot. My heart broke.

The doctor came in and rang my husband to come back in. He did and I just cried and cried. In the end I said to him that I was just going to have to push because I did not feel the urge. I did, and with every push my heart broke more and more.

We didn't see our baby straightaway but I was told by the midwife that she was alive. She cut her little cord and wrapped and gave her to me. She was the most perfectly amazing little human I have ever seen. She looked like her daddy and I marvelled at her tiny finger- and toenails. Her nostrils were still closed, as were her eyes.

We actually thought she was a boy, as girls at that gestation can have enlarged genitals. The midwife took her and wrapped her and placed her in a sleeping bag for us. I had to have a curette to get the placenta out.

We decided that they would take our baby and have genetic testing done. So we were given her sleeping bag and when I got back from the curette a midwife had done her foot- and hand-prints for us.

Next day I left the hospital without my baby to find our car had been stolen with the box we were given to bury her in, her sleeping bag and prints. So we had to wait for my sister to come to drive us home. During all of this we decided to name her after my husband's mate who had died just before we met.

The days after were a blur, apart from having to work out the exact requirements for the box our daughter needed to be in for cremation. In the end a funeral home lined a box that we bought. In the early hours of Tuesday morning our car was returned, with the box in the boot of our car.

Later that day we went to pick Catharine up from the birthing suite which was so hard with pregnant women all sitting around waiting to be seen. I wasn't going to look at her but I did and she had changed for the worst. My husband placed his daughter in the box and sealed the lid. We brought her home and when our daughter finished school we took Catharine out to the crematorium and left her. Driving away was so hard. We now have her ashes in an urn with a carousel on it in our glass cabinet along with special keepsakes and gifts.

Five weeks after her birth we found out she was a girl after naming her Kyle Joshua. It was like grieving for another child. We then decided to name her after my great-grandmother and my grandmother on my dad's side.

I like to think of Catharine Ellen as my butterfly and nine months later I still cry but I can smile when I think about the life that she was. I think my healing has been helped by the fact that I am a talker and like to talk about her anytime I can. My support group really helps me and I have become involved in putting together clothes for various gestations for hospitals, even tiny outfits that should have been there for my butterfly. If there is one thing that eats away at me now, is that no-one took photos of Catharine. We also had a plaque made for her at our local cemetery with some of her ashes buried underneath. We have the verse 'A butterfly counts not months, but moments, and yet has time enough' on her plaque and she has some very special friends at the cemetery with her.

I fell pregnant again after one cycle but we found out at nine weeks that the baby had never developed. It was a blighted ovum. It hurt because it brought back losing Catharine again. After having all sorts of tests we are now trying again and know that it is going to be a long, stressful road. My new doctor thinks it may have been strep B that caused my waters to break and will monitor it. As well, I am taking aspirin daily for a clotting disorder. We are also getting married after almost eight years of being together.

Catharine came into our lives for a reason. We don't know why she had to leave so soon but if I can help other people in our shoes, it will help me heal.

Erica Manser

Many in Heaven

Gary and I married in January 1995 and always wanted to have four or five children. Much to our joy and satisfaction our first two children were born without complications – a daughter, Kaitlyn Jade in August 1999, and then in April 2001 a son, Jarrod Carl.

When Jarrod was five months old I found I was pregnant again. At first I was upset. We hadn't planned to be pregnant yet as I was recovering from a very low iron count and consequent postnatal depression. However, this new little life growing inside me quickly attached itself to my heart and soon I was looking forward to having three children under three years.

At ten weeks I went for a dating scan. Later that day my doctor told me that 'no heartbeat was detected'. I cried with shock. My babies don't just die, I thought. I went home and waited to miscarry naturally, opting not to have a curette. During those days of waiting, Gary and I had to come to terms with the loss. One of the things we did that helped a lot was having a little memorial service just for the two of us. We had a clear picture of our baby from a second ultrasound. We lit a candle, talked to the baby, cried, prayed and read from the Bible, then we blew out the candle and had a glass of port. It was extremely therapeutic for both of us and I told the baby that it could now leave my body.

I was nearly twelve weeks pregnant when the miscarriage happened. I experienced full labour contractions and lost a lot of blood. After six hours of losing blood at home, I went to hospital and they kept me in overnight. I lay in the hospital bed in the middle of the night trying to process the loss of our baby. Expecting a baby changes your perspective on everything in your life as you think about the future with your new child, but then having a miscarriage changes it all again. I discovered that's a lot of change to cope with in just a few short weeks.

Christmas was a sad time, but by the time the new year came around I was feeling much more positive and hopeful and determined that 2002 would be better. I spent the year getting fit and healthy again preparing for another pregnancy. In November I fell pregnant and had terrible morning sickness from four weeks on, but was told that this was a good sign. When I was five weeks and five days I started bleeding. At the sight of the blood I began crying with shock and disbelief. When I lost a couple of clots I knew for sure I had lost this baby too. The next day I had an ultrasound and the sonographer told me there was nothing left.

I was shocked that I could have two miscarriages in a row, especially when I had spent so much time preparing for this pregnancy. My response was to rebel against all the healthy things I'd been doing. I stopped taking vitamins and going to the gym and I ate whatever I wanted. Gary and I decided to try again straight away. My period came again and the grief returned. It just reminded me of what I didn't have.

The next month I fell pregnant, but instead of being anxious to confirm with a pregnancy test we decided to try and forget all about it in an attempt to detach. We were so scared of being hurt again that we thought it better to pretend the whole thing was not even happening, so we didn't talk about possibly being pregnant or the baby. I did finally go to the doctor and have the pregnancy confirmed at six and a half weeks, but we carried on as if it wasn't happening. At eight weeks the pregnancy symptoms disappeared and I began bleeding. A scan in the emergency department revealed a six-week sac but not much else. We left the hospital, held each other and cried. It was all too much. Our attempts to not bond with this baby and avoid pain did not work. If anything, it made our grief worse because we felt awful that we didn't acknowledge our baby's life while we still could.

Two days later the miscarriage bleeding got heavy. I spent about four hours in pain and losing a lot of blood and clots before things started to settle down. With the previous two it had ended there, but with this miscarriage I bled for sixteen days, still losing clots till the end. I returned to the hospital every few days for a scan and had terrible pain. In the end I was glad I never needed a curette, but the physical trauma dragging on just added to the emotional trauma of losing our third baby in a row.

The next few months were a battle of tiredness, grief and depression. I wrote this in my diary:

'It has now been almost seven weeks since that miscarriage. Gary and I have been knocked flat by the grief this time. It has been far more intense, as if we are grieving for all three babies at once. I have sought help this time, from support groups and counsellors and reading materials, and all have helped in the grief process. What has not helped are some comments from family and friends – "Maybe you're too tired, or not eating right, or maybe God doesn't want you to have any more children." There is also the expectation that we'd be over it in a couple of weeks and that we would carry on as usual, giving our utmost to everyone else. Our busy lifestyles just don't leave us much time for grieving properly. I feel the grief deep in my bones, and know that it will be a long road. We have been changed forever. If Gary and I do ever have any more babies, it will never stop me from missing my three babies that have died.'

I wondered whether we would ever have any more children. My life was full of day-to-day activity but my life was also empty without my baby.

At this time we also made contact with a recurrent miscarriage clinic and had a consultation that included blood tests. In June of 2003 we got results back revealing that I had a balanced translocation – a chromosome abnormality. It basically meant that for us any pregnancy had a fifty per cent chance of failing. I also had a high level of an antibody that restricted blood flow to the placenta. The doctors also told us that the chromosome abnormality may result in us carrying a child to term that was deformed in some way. I remember leaving the hospital that day in a daze. In some ways it was a relief to discover a cause for our miscarriages as I knew that many recurrent miscarriage sufferers never found a reason. On the other hand it was devastating to learn that the problem rested with me and there was nothing we could do about it. We were left amazed at how our reproductive history had turned out so far – two beautiful, healthy children, and then three miscarriages in a row.

We cancelled everything for the next four days in order to process and absorb this new information. What did it mean for now trying for another child? No-one could make the decision except us, and there were plenty of factors that made it the most difficult decision we had ever made. Trusting God with our future and being prepared to accept responsibility for the result of our decision, we decided to try again.

In October of 2003 I fell pregnant again. The early days of pregnancy were not the joy they used to be. But I had an ultrasound at around seven weeks and it revealed a tiny wriggly baby with a beating heart. Our confidence increased ever so slightly. Much to our joy and relief the pregnancy continued, full of tiredness and morning sickness, and I joyfully gave birth to another delightful daughter in the early hours of 30 July 2004 – Rebecca Mae. All the trying was worth it for that moment, and all the moments she has given us since.

It was wonderful and triumphant to now have three children, but our quiver was not yet full and we knew we were prepared to risk more to have more. I got pregnant again when Rebecca was five months old and again an ultrasound revealed a beating heart at seven weeks. My excitement grew until just past ten weeks, when I began to bleed. My heart plummeted into the depths and we again experienced a sad and physically difficult miscarriage. We shared this loss with our children and we ceremonially buried the pregnancy sac in our back garden. The children asked many questions, which we answered openly and honestly at their level, and we cried together as a family.

We were due to move from city to country at the beginning of 2006, so waited a little while before endeavouring to become pregnant again, as we didn't want to make such a big move and possibly have another baby too close in time. In October we tried again. As I got ready to do the pregnancy test on the morning my period was due, I realised that there had been a pattern with my tests – every time I had miscarried, the pregnancy test had only been faintly positive, but positive nevertheless. With Kaitlyn, Jarrod and Rebecca's pregnancies, the test had come up with a strong positive line quickly and definitely. I did this pregnancy test and the line was faint. I was convinced that this meant I would lose this one. I just prayed that it would be sooner rather than later. Ten days later I miscarried. Anticipating this miscarriage made it different from the others and I was relieved that it had not continued too many weeks. That was my fifth miscarriage.

We began thinking about just how many pregnancies and miscarriages I could endure both physically and emotionally before we decided to stop having children. I felt I had one more attempt in me and still desperately wanted a fourth child. On 2 January 2006 I found I was pregnant, for the ninth time, and this time the pregnancy test came up strong and positive.

Gary and I were thrilled to finally be having our fourth child. We had endured so much to get to this point and we were thankful beyond words to be 'finishing our family on a good note'. I felt so strongly that this was our last, and I was so happy and excited at the prospect of our family of four children. The weeks of pregnancy ticked by so slowly. I just wanted my baby in my arms. I was tired and heavy and had nausea and headaches for the first half of the pregnancy. But the ultrasound at twenty weeks showed that our baby was doing well and we were relieved beyond belief.

We crept up past thirty weeks and the countdown began. The children were excited and put a calendar up on the wall and began crossing off the days left until baby's due date, 6 September. We decided to hire a private midwife who would take over my antenatal checks and be with me during labour. I still intended to give birth at the hospital, but she would provide the familiar touch that was lacking after moving to a place where we didn't yet know our health providers well.

I finally got to thirty-nine weeks and had an appointment with my doctor, whom I had not seen for a few months due to her long-service leave. All checks were fine except when I lay on my back and she checked for baby's heartbeat. Gary and I could tell that the heartbeat was slower than usual. My doctor asked me to lie on my side and immediately the baby's heart rate picked up. That was normal, she said. Babies don't like you lying on your back so late in pregnancy.

That evening Gary and I got talking about our pregnancy history. Ever since all our miscarriages we knew about how things go wrong, and although we didn't speak about them much, we both had fears. Fears that something would go wrong with this baby. Perhaps he would be abnormal in some way, or something might go wrong during labour. We talked about all of this, deciding that it was better to get our fears out in the open and admit honestly the realities of things taking a turn for the worse. I said, 'We have to face the reality that there is a possibility that we won't bring this baby home from hospital.' We prayed and left it all in our loving God's hands.

During the night I awoke and found myself on my back. Remembering the slow heartbeat from the doctor's office, I panicked and quickly flipped over onto my side. Patting my belly, very full of baby, I went back to sleep.

The next morning I had some errands to run and noticed that I did not feel my baby move from the time I woke up that morning. By lunchtime there was still no movement and I mentioned this to Gary. Baby had had some slower times in the last few days and it was typical of babies preparing for labour so I didn't worry too much. By mid-afternoon, after we had picked up the children from school and been to an appointment, I was more worried and was poking my belly in an effort to get baby to respond.

We went to the hospital and I told the midwives I had not felt my baby move that day. They put the heartbeat monitor on my belly and there was silence. They told me not to worry as sometimes babies curl up and it's hard to find the heartbeat, but after half an hour of trying to no avail they called on my doctor. My midwife, who also worked at the hospital, was there working her shift and they both appeared, wondering what was going on. My doctor made one quick attempt to find the heartbeat and then scribbled a referral for an ultrasound. Gary was white and worried. I was patient and not panicked at all. I tended not to worry until there was something concrete to worry about. I guess I really knew something was wrong, but I was going with the flow of things for now. The stress began to sink its claws into my mind when I started towards the ultrasound department and both my doctor and midwife accompanied me, a hand on my arm for comfort. That's when I knew things were bad. They knew what I had not yet had confirmed.

The sonographer began the ultrasound and I could see my baby's head and heart. The heart was not beating. I lay there in silence, refusing to speak first. I wanted them to tell me, so I waited. My doctor spoke, and after all my deliberate waiting I recall nothing of what she said.

I spoke to her in response. 'Are you telling me my baby's died?'

Straightaway she answered me. 'Yes, I'm telling you your baby's died.'

The floodgates broke open and I began to sob uncontrollably.

The disbelief and shock was all-consuming. Gary and I held each other and wept. I was saying over and over, 'How can this be, how can this be?' It was unfathomable that our baby could die six days before my due date. Through my crying I began asking questions. What had happened? Why? Haven't we had enough babies die? What happens now? The thought descended upon me that I would have to labour and give birth to a dead baby. How in the world was I going to endure that? My doctor gave me some preliminary answers to my questions but ultimately none of us knew why my baby had died so late in pregnancy.

We told the children the news in a room prepared at the hospital. Kaitlyn (seven) cried immediately, Jarrod (five) looked sad but two year old Rebecca continued to play, having no idea what we were saying. We went home, our lives completely turned upside down, the weeping not ceasing. For the next twenty-four hours, our emotions in turmoil, we began to call our family and friends, sharing with them our very sad news.

In consultation with my wonderful and understanding doctor, we decided that the best course of action would be to induce me, not too soon, but not wait too long either. It was late Thursday afternoon when we learned of our baby's death. My doctor made the necessary arrangements for me to be induced on Saturday morning and my midwife would be there during my labour and delivery. It is insufficient for me to say that I was terrified of going through labour only to deliver a dead child. The thought was deeply distressing. With Gary's help I spent that Friday coming to the decision to fully embrace the difficult experience and give it my all as it was going to be the last thing I could do for my baby.

'We are still our baby's parents,' Gary said to me, 'and our baby deserves the best we can give.'

I cried, prayed and enlisted the support of as many friends and family members who were all sharing our grief and praying for us. And by the time I went to bed on Friday night by God's grace I was calm . . . and ready.

I woke around 3.00 am to contractions. Relief washed over me as I knew my body was naturally ready for this event even as terror hovered in the background. By the time I got to the hospital at 9.15 am on Saturday morning I was two centimetres dilated, so my doctor broke the waters. The labour progressed. I tried to remain calm and strong, drawing upon the support of the many I knew who were praying for me and listening to inspirational music as each long contraction came. At 11.50 am, just as I was beginning to feel that I could not endure any longer, a voice deep within assured me that things were just as they needed to be. At 12.02 pm our baby girl, Hayley Grace, came into the world, stillborn.

She was beautiful, with a perfect mouth and crop of black hair, and she weighed a healthy 7 pounds 10½ ounces. It was soon apparent that our lovely healthy girl had died from a cord accident. The umbilical cord was looped around her neck and the midsection of the cord had kinked and become trapped between Hayley's head and my pelvis. My midwife found the cord next to her head as she was being delivered. We deduced that as she had descended further in preparation for labour, the life supply from her cord had been cut off. It was a rare and tragic accident.

The hospital staff were marvellous to us, and Gary and I were blessed with twenty-eight hours to spend with Hayley. We took over a hundred photos, captured video, and with our lovely midwife's help took foot- and handprints and a lock of hair. We held her, loved her, studied her little face, cried and told her she was cheeky for making us think we were having a boy. We slept for some of the night, but not wanting to miss a moment with her, we paced the floor with her in our arms, just as we would had she been alive. We talked through the night with each other about our grief and pain and marvelled at God's care of us in such a tragic time. Many of our family and friends supported us and came to the hospital to meet Hayley, which meant so much. However, it was so very hard to watch our children hold her in utter sadness, except for Rebecca, whose excitement about her baby sister finally being born was evident. Her innocence broke all our hearts.

There is no doubt that leaving the hospital the next day was one of the most difficult things to do. Gary was determined to be involved with Hayley's every move – from our room to the hospital mortuary, and from there to the funeral home. One of the midwives sat with me as I cried when Gary and the hospital porter left with her. Babies are never meant to be taken away from their mothers.

I was thrown unwillingly into a surreal land. Instead of breastfeeding, changing nappies and enjoying getting to know my newborn and showing her off, I was planning and preparing for her funeral. We tried to make Hayley's funeral true to everything we felt and believed. We were overwhelmed with love and support, as many people in a town that we had only just moved to, as well as many family and friends from long distances, went out of their way to come to her funeral. People shared our sorrow deeply and compassionately, and those who had also lost babies in the past wept for their own. I was strengthened and given hope as endless cards, flowers and gifts flooded into our home, some from complete strangers. Visitors hugged us and told us they didn't know what to say, but cried with us anyway. The phone didn't stop ringing with people sending their love. We never anticipated this response from people. After enduring each of our five miscarriages, we experienced a range of insensitivities by well-meaning people who really didn't know what we were going through and didn't really try to find out. Perhaps we expected the same again, but although there were some hurtful things said by some, they were few. And we were grateful. It was evident that Hayley's life and the shock of her death rippled out far and wide. This we never expected. Losing a child is much less taboo than it was in the not-so-distant past. We are thankful that laws and attitudes have changed so much and we know this is helping us heal and move through our grief.

It has now been three very short and very long months since Hayley died. For me, losing a child has been like having my arm cut off. We are trying to move through our grief as best we can. Sometimes it turns out positively as we direct our energies into a variety of things – crying, talking about her, journalling, building a garden in her memory, caring for ourselves and our children, and trying to inject as many positives into our family life as possible. On other days it has been all too much and I wonder if my sanity will stay intact.

Our lives will never be the same and we will always long for her and wish this never happened. But we do know that we would rather that she came and died, than not have come at all. Our grief is only in its early stages and my many thoughts and feelings to this date are too numerous to write about. I do know that our story is not finished. We have been given much joy through our three children here with us, and we have endured much grief and tragedy as we lost five babies from a chromosomal abnormality and then a precious longed-for daughter at full term from a cord accident. Our story will continue as we decide whether to embark on another pregnancy knowing it can end in such unspeakable heartache. Another thing I know for sure is that children are a precious gift from God and the joy they bring is worth all the risk. Life throws at us many things and makes us who we are. I don't want to have any regrets. Today I say, 'Bring it on!'

Postscript: Gary and Natalie went on to have a sixth miscarriage in mid-2007. Then much to their joy and relief, thankfully welcomed a healthy baby boy, Cody James, born safely on 10th June 2008.

Natalie Stephens

Always Her Dad

❧

When our first two children were born healthy and without any complications, my wife Natalie and I thought that our desire for a family of four children would come quite easily. However, Nat has been pregnant seven more times since and only one of those children still lives in our house. Those losses have left a deep imprint on who I am.

The three miscarriages that followed our first two children, Kaitlyn and Jarrod, hit us with a compounded grief that took us many months to recover from. The future shape of our family had a much hazier horizon but we took the risk head-on and decided to try again, prepared to embrace whatever would follow. Ten months later we joyously received Rebecca Mae into our family.

The optimism following Rebecca's birth was short-lived – two further miscarriages made us face the question of how much more loss we could endure. In early 2006, when Nat's ninth pregnancy passed our miscarriage danger period, we were relieved, overjoyed and looking forward to the day we would hold our final baby and finish our family.

One week before our fourth baby was due to be born I joined Nat for a standard check-up with her doctor. Little did I know that this day I would hear our baby's heartbeat for the last time. All the next day our baby was quiet, still. When we visited the maternity ward to check our baby, the heartbeat monitor found no sound. No heartbeat. No woosh of the cord. Silence had never been such an enemy. Forty minutes later an ultrasound confirmed our baby had died. Nat found out before

I did because I had been caring for our children. When I arrived the ultrasound was finished, the monitor was black and I held my wife tight, as she cried and questioned why. As I held her, I saw that two paths lay ahead of me. The first was a path that would avoid dealing with the death. This path would eventually eat me away inside. The second was one that would see me face death and seek to care for my family despite the pain it would bring. I turned to the sonographer and said, 'Can I have a look please. I want to see for myself.'

On the monitor I saw our baby, still, lifeless and floating. It is difficult to remember the feelings of that moment. Initially the shock of the discovery made it more fact than emotion, yet the tears were coming fast. Amid the growing heartbreak I prepared myself for the task of telling our children that their brother or sister they had so longed for died just a few short days before it was due to be born. Their previous experience of our miscarriages had made them even more joyous that this baby had lived and now made this tragic turn all the more sorrowful for us to share with them.

I stepped out of the sonography room, internally in turmoil but externally calm so as not to distress the children. As we approached them, Rebecca was upset, as her sultanas had spilt across the floor. I collected the sultanas and gently told the children that we needed to go back upstairs. We seated the children in a private room.

I looked at them and said, 'I have something hard to tell you. You know we were having some tests to make sure the baby is okay. We found out that the baby has died.'

Kaitlyn cried, Jarrod sat bewildered, Rebecca, yet to understand death, played as if nothing had happened. We spent a few minutes crying with our children and answering their questions and then we came home, empty inside, turned upside down in life and with our children still needing us to supply the routine things of dinner, bath and bed.

That night the phone calls to gather support, our own conversations and much crying left us completely wrung out. We found ourselves tempted to sidestep the trauma of birthing a dead child and seek a caesarean delivery as soon as possible.

As we went to bed that Thursday night I made a milk drink for us both in the hope it would help us sleep. As I stood waiting for the milk to warm I remember imagining that moment in time when, curled safe within its mother's womb, my child's heart stopped beating. It is a thought that still tears my heart apart. The silence and invisibility of our child's death stood defiantly and laughed at my deep parental desire to protect. I wanted to reach in and stop whatever it had been that had caused this baby to die so late and unexpectedly in the pregnancy when all seemed to be going so well. My legs gave way beneath me and I sat on the floor and cried. Late into the night we finallly crawled into bed and barely slept at all.

Somewhere between Thursday afternoon and Friday night I had come to the conclusion that though the baby had died it was still our child and its story was not yet finished. I wanted to love this child just as much as we would love any of our others and parent it with the same care and concern that we would give to our others. I knew that I would regret anything less, and our short time with this child meant embracing everything that was to come – birth, our time with the baby while in hospital and its funeral. We shared this goal and knew it would help with our grief, but Nat was still daunted. However, by the end of Friday night she had herself ready for the birth that would come either naturally or by induction on Saturday morning. Her willingness to enter this darkness deepened my love and respect. Together we were ready.

Nat woke with contractions around 3.00 am Saturday morning. She found it a relief that the labour had started naturally while I found myself vacant of the excited anticipation that came with the onset of labour for our previous deliveries. When we woke in the morning the contractions continued and we arrived at the hospital about 9.15 am.

It was a smooth and simple birth. There were just us and our midwife. Our doctor appeared occasionally and another midwife kept in the background as our baby was delivered. Emotionally we survived relatively intact, strengthened by the prayers of friends and our commitment to love our baby by delivering as well as we could. For me the most difficult moment came as our baby's head began to crown. I had been in this place before with my wonderful wife as our cherished children were born, awaiting their arrival, seeing their faces for the first time as their heads emerged, taking them from the midwife after they were born, hearing that distinctive cry as they began to breathe on their own, and feeling their little uncoordinated bodies kick as they discovered freedom after the confines of the uterus. This birth would be so completely different and I had to work hard to remain focused on being involved instead of retiring to a corner and weeping from the depths of my heart. Within a few moments, at 12.02 pm, our beautiful baby girl, Hayley Grace, came silently into the world.

Soon after her birth we discovered she had tragically died from a cord accident, an unbearable thought given our miscarriage history. While we stayed in hospital with Hayley, we tried to do all we could to take hold of the moment and create memories of her in our family. We made prints of her hands and feet, and took many photos and video footage as we cleaned Hayley and talked. We cried a lot. We had moments of laughter too. Our family arrived and when we were ready we brought our children in to meet their little sister. Rebecca still did not understand death and was as excited and eager to hold Hayley just as if she were alive. More than once she said she thought the baby was very tired. Kaitlyn and Jarrod were subdued, crying occasionally and holding Hayley too. Eventually we were ready for others in our family to meet Hayley. I walked to the waiting room, Rebecca coming with me, and ushered them in. As we walked back to our room Rebecca danced with joy at the arrival of her new little sister and all our hearts were broken by her uninhibited innocence.

For me, expecting a child brings with it much anticipation and shapes all thinking about the future. I can still recall that joyous first month of a newborn's life (that period before the really serious sleep deprivation sets in!) as a family settles into life together while this new little person swamps your heart, and how we shared the joy with family, friend and stranger alike. This time I sat in a hospital room introducing my child to our children and family, hearing tears of sadness instead of cries from our baby, undoing all my thoughts of the future and thinking about my daughter's funeral. It was a contrast as strong as black and white.

Yet even in the midst of all this, our time in hospital with Hayley was priceless. In all, we had twenty-eight hours with her in our room. We continued to talk, cry, pray, laugh and make more memories. I cherish those times now. I soaked up as much of her as I could and did everything possible to compact all my longings to be her father into what little time we had. I held her and stroked her and kissed her. I paced the floor like I had so many times with our others when they were restless and needed comfort. We let friends visit and hold her so we had memories to share with those around us. We fussed over her and dressed her and cleaned her and changed her nappy. All these things helped us to express both our love and our grief over her death.

Late on Saturday night we needed to change her clothes. Hayley lay on our bed in just a nappy for some time. I studied her little body and held her baby hand. I looked through all the years ahead in my life when that little hand should be in mine and wouldn't be – trips to the park, beginning to walk, crossing a road, the first day of school, a dance we might share, guiding her down an aisle to get married. When Hayley died so much had been lost and I did all I could to capture some of it while I still had her with me.

On Sunday afternoon, twenty-eight hours after Hayley was born, we left the hospital. Nat had given birth and was no longer pregnant but there was no baby in our arms and our extra car seat remained empty. The walk from our hospital room to our car was difficult, some of the heaviest steps I have ever taken. We went home, I played with the children, we talked and cried more with each other and with Nat's parents who were staying with us and eventually we went to bed.

Early on Monday we began planning for Hayley's funeral and on Friday Hayley was buried. I had been involved in every step of her journey. I carried her from our room to the hospital mortuary, transferred her to the funeral director's, carried her into the church for her funeral, spoke at her funeral about the impact her short life had had on me, placed her coffin over her grave and held the ropes as her little coffin was lowered into the ground – ropes I never wanted to let go of. Everything seems wrong when a parent has to bury their child, yet Hayley's funeral also provided a wonderful moment as our children created a beautiful memory.

After Hayley was buried and we talked to gathered family

and friends, Kaitlyn, Jarrod and Rebecca crouched with a friend around Hayley's grave. They peered down into the grave, talked and sang 'Happy Birthday'. It was extraordinary.

On the Monday following Hayley's funeral Nat's parents returned home and we began the task of working out how to live this new life full of heartache, a heartache made all the more acute by the deafening silence that is life without an anticipated newborn living in our house.

Just as we had with Hayley's birth through to her burial, we decided to dive deeply into the process of grief, convinced that the more we resisted the harder and longer it would be. It has been a torturous process but with each hard word that we write, each tear that wells and falls, and each hard memory that we share, we rebuild slowly. There are times when it seems like the darkness will just never go away. The constant presence of unshakable sadness is inexplicably tiring and temporarily threatens our sanity. I have had all kinds of moments: times when all I could do was sit by her grave and cry, times when I just held her photos and longed to hold her instead, times when I could barely resist the desire to dig up her body and hold her just one more time even though she was dead. We stand at Hayley's grave and can't believe that we have buried our child. Sometimes I wonder if it is all true. Was Nat pregnant and did Hayley really die? Sometimes I wonder if it will all be over and we'll finally get to have her back and watch her grow up. I ache when I see Nat cry for the baby she never got to bring home, for her desire to nurture that never got fulfilled. I feel helpless because there is no answer and I am still learning what it means to just be with her in the middle of her sadness. We have 'meltdown' days (our house rule is to ensure we both don't do this at the same time!), times where we feel terribly distant and more times when we feel particularly close. We do not have the mental and physical energy to run life at its normal pace. Our children have said things that are blunt and unintentionally stab at our aching hearts, and yet they have offered their own fair share of comfort with their cuddles, their simple perspectives and their playing, which sometimes includes Hayley in their make-believe games.

As I look at our lives, even now, just three and a half months since Hayley died and was born, and as we work hard at grief, I can see the process of healing taking place, though we are far (maybe years) from being healed. I have moments of hope as I see some emotional and mental energy slowly returning, as my enthusiasm for other activities gradually awakens, and as I find myself less overwhelmed by life's normal events. I see moments of hope when, as I remember holding Hayley's hand in the hospital, my mind is not only flooded by the ache of not having her but also has thanksgiving that I got to hold her hand at all. For me Hayley's story has been one of both joy and sadness. Her story has been short but it has not been small. It has affirmed all I believe, it has strengthened my love for my family, it has lessened my preoccupation with the 'stuff' of this life and caused me to think about caring for people and to long for heaven more than I did before. Having Hayley die has not robbed me of fatherhood but has given me a different kind of fatherhood to embrace. For me as a man, as a husband and as a father, that is what lies at the heart of my story with Hayley. I will always love my little girl and part of me will always wish she lived here with us, but for as long as I remain alive on this earth I will still be her father. I would not change this for anything else. When Hayley died I encountered more sadness than I ever could have imagined. Yet as long as I live, in my memory of Hayley, in my day-to-day tasks and in my facing of grief, I will seek to be her father with all the love, respect, attention and involvement that I devote to the children who still live under my care. Her short life brought love into mine, has taught me much and so has changed me in ways for which I am grateful. I thank God for bringing Hayley into our family and I would rather she had come and died than never have come at all.

Thank you, Hayley, for being a precious and wonderful daughter. Thank you for being you.

Gary Stephens

Remember Sarah

The worst day of my life was a cool Saturday in early September 2003. Late in the afternoon my husband and I were outside pruning some trees. I was tired but still had lots of energy, even though I was three days overdue in a trouble-free pregnancy. When we were finished the sun was setting and we sat down outside the kitchen door to have a rest and admire the view from our patio. I could feel the baby kicking hard and being very active, and it made me very happy.

The pregnancy had been quite enjoyable, and being my first pregnancy it was all new and unknown to me. The pregnancy began to feel real at the twelve week ultrasound, where I could see a tiny little baby on the screen and see the arms and legs move. When I could start feeling the baby kick I really fell in love. The baby seemed to have favourite positions, and used to push its bottom really hard against the left side of the tummy. At my twenty week ultrasound it was discovered that I had *Placenta Praevia*, but at the thirty-two week ultrasound I was told this problem was no longer of concern.

After all the hard work with the pruning, we were about to start preparing dinner. While I was tidying up in the kitchen, my waters broke. I rang the hospital to let them know and they advised I wait until the contractions were regular and less than ten minutes apart before heading in.

We finished dinner and I had a shower while counting the minutes in between contractions. As it was my first pregnancy, I didn't know what to expect and wasn't worried at all.

After dinner the contractions were getting closer and closer, so we decided to go to hospital. The drive took forty-five minutes and half way there the contractions became very intense and frequent. When we arrived at the hospital I was in very strong labour.

The first thing the midwives did was to check for the baby's heartbeat using a CTG scanner, but they were not able to detect it. They brought in another machine to try and find the heartbeat and they brought more midwives in to see if they could somehow find it. After a while they decided to call the obstetrician and ask him to come in. As this was happening at 9.30pm on a Saturday night, it took another forty-five minutes for the doctor to get to the hospital. When he finally arrived, he put a probe on the baby's skull but didn't get a heartbeat either. He said, 'Let's get this baby out as soon as we can,' and took out the forceps. As it was very urgent, they didn't have time to wait for the local anaesthetic to take effect, so it became a very painful birth. Luckily it was very quick. It took me three pushes and the baby was born.

Immediately after the birth the baby was taken away to the revival unit. At this point I was so exhausted and so relieved the pain was over, I closed my eyes and relaxed. Time seemed to be standing still. I could hear people talk around me but nothing grabbed my attention. Not until I heard the obstetrician say, 'It's no use, you can stop now.' He came over to me and said 'I'm sorry but she didn't make it.'

That moment is forever etched in my mind. Up to this point I had been too busy focusing on the pain to register what was happening around me. I was later told that the midwives were trying to revive our baby for over five minutes, but to me it seemed like less. When I was stitched up and the obstetrician had left, the midwives were hovering around making sure my husband and I were all right. One midwife asked what we were planning to call her and my husband answered 'Sarah'.

We were still in shock but we managed to call our family in Sweden to let them know what had happened.

The next morning the obstetrician came back and told us what had most likely happened. We were told we had a rare condition called *Velamentous Insertia of the Cord* whereby the umbilical cord does not have its protective cover between the membrane and the placenta. The blood veins were properly attached to the placenta and worked perfectly throughout the pregnancy, but they were exposed and very vulnerable. On top of this condition, we also had *Vasa Praevia*, a condition in which the cord is blocking the cervix. All of this was most likely caused by the placenta moving upwards in the uterus during the second half of the pregnancy, and the cord being attached low on the placenta. When the placenta moved, the cord did not follow, but instead the blood veins inside the cord extended themselves on the outside of the membrane to reach the placenta. When the waters broke, the pressure of the fluids, or the pressure of the baby descending into the birth canal, broke off one or several of the blood veins. Sarah probably died from the loss of blood within half an hour after the waters broke.

Sarah was brought back to us after being weighed and measured, and my husband and I broke down and cried for a long time. It was just so heartbreaking to see such a beautiful girl and know that we would never see her open her eyes or hear her take a breath.

We called a couple of close friends in the morning, and two of my best friends came to see us in the hospital in the afternoon. When they arrived I was so immensely proud of my child and wanted them to see how beautiful and perfect she was. I asked them if they wanted to hold Sarah and when they did they each cried. I really wanted other people to see her and touch her so they also had a memory of her.

We were able to have Sarah with us almost the whole time during our hospital stay. She was taken away for a day to be embalmed, and every minute she was away from us was painful. I just kept thinking about how little time we had with her and every minute apart was a waste of precious time.

The midwives at the hospital were very caring and supportive, and helped us through this difficult time with great professionalism. Without them we wouldn't have done even half of the things we did with Sarah. They helped us bath her, and dress her, and they took lots of photos of her to take home. They also compiled a little book with her birth details, some poems and a hand- and footprint. We were also given a flower arrangement and a card as we left hospital, and a few weeks later the midwife who was present during the birth came to visit us. We talked about Sarah and the birth, and looked at all the photos of Sarah. It provided some closure for us and I guess for the midwife as well.

When we left the hospital we brought Sarah home with us and kept her with us until the funeral. When friends came to visit us my husband told them at the door that Sarah was in a cot next to me, so no one was shocked or surprised that there was a dead baby in our house. Some people chose not to look at her at all and others were keen to see her. We respected their decision and they respected our decision to keep her at home with us.

A few days before her funeral Sarah's casket was brought to our home. It was a tiny white casket with a beautiful satin and lace lining that just fitted our precious little girl. We found some photos of her Mum and Dad, a little teddy she had been given by her grandparents, a little rattle we had bought for her and we wrote lots of cards with poems and notes to her from ourselves and our family, and put it all inside the casket.

Eight days after she was born we had a small and very beautiful service for her with only some close family and four of our best friends attending. My best friend organised a beautiful wreath for the casket with yellow hyacinths and yellow freesias. It lit up the church, added a soft fragrance, and gave us something beautiful to look at throughout the service. We had brought the casket to the church but we didn't place Sarah in it until five minutes before the service was about to start. This was the hardest moment of my life – seeing the lid being placed on the casket and knowing that I would never see her again. I had never believed that you could feel heartache, but at that very moment my heart was physically hurting.

It was really hard after Sarah was born to think about the strong kicks she used to give me and how active she was all the way to the end. Even the last hour she was alive, I could feel her strong kicks and this is probably one of the most painful memories I have. It is hard to think about how alive she was and an hour later dying from something that could easily have been detected with a thorough ultrasound, and prevented by doing an early caesarean section. For a long time I blamed myself for not going to hospital when my waters broke. Sarah would probably still not have survived, which in a strange way makes it easier to cope with.

We had a lot of support from family and friends for the first four to six weeks after Sarah's birth and it helped us get through the first month quite easily. When they disappeared into their normal lives I felt a bit lost and very lonely. There was no one to talk to about all the intense feelings and the strange thoughts I had. I still had a big need to talk about Sarah and what had happened, but all of a sudden there was no one around who wanted to listen. Most close friends had heard my story many times and I guess there is only so much energy you can put into someone else's grief.

To fill this emptiness and to get an outlet for all the grief we started attending SANDS meetings. Through the SANDS meetings and forums on the internet, I got to know three other women that had had very similar experiences to me. We started writing to each other and telling each other about our stories, thoughts and feelings. This was the best therapy for me and it really helped me to know that I was not alone and that someone else was feeling the same as I did.

I remember very clearly the first few weeks after Sarah was born, I was reading about losing a child and about the grieving process. I initially thought that I would grieve intensely for a few months, and then it would subside and become sad memories. How naïve of me. I read about other women who had lost their children talking about grieving for a whole year, and some even grieving for several years. I remember thinking I don't think I can handle the pain for so long, I don't want to do this. For a long time I felt very lonely and angry, and I remember being unfair and unrealistic in my thoughts about people and in my expectation of them.

Everything I did for the first time after Sarah's birth was a major hurdle for me to get over; the first time I went back to work, the first time I went to the canteen, the first Christmas and birthdays. I kept anticipating how horrible it would be and I would feel sick to my stomach in the days leading up to the event. Meeting colleagues and acquaintances for the first time after Sarah's birth was painful. Most people didn't know what to say, and subsequently didn't say anything at all and pretended that nothing had happened. This was the most difficult thing for me, I wanted nothing more than to hear people talk about my child, and to ask me questions about her. To have her completely ignored made me feel that she didn't mean anything to anyone except those directly touched by her; parents, grand-parents and close friends. I quickly learnt that if I told people that I wanted to talk about Sarah, they were quite happy to listen. Other than close family and friends, no one ever asked how big she was when she was born or what she looked like. One thing that struck me during this time was how concerned everyone was for my wellbeing, but almost no one asked about how my husband felt.

The grieving process is exhausting and very difficult. For months I felt numb and almost like I was still getting to grips with the whole experience. In the first three to four months after I lost Sarah I searched everywhere for literature about losing a child, reasons for stillbirths and how to cope with grief. I found a few good books but most importantly I found a paper that describes what's called 'umbilical cord accidents' and it talked in detail about different kinds of umbilical cord compli-cations causing stillbirths. It helped me a lot in understanding why Sarah died and at least brought me some peace. But it also made me very angry thinking that she could have been saved had the obstetricians and the ultrasound specialists taken some time to investigate the *Placenta Praevia* and the way the cord was attached to the placenta.

Even after all this has happened I still feel I had a very happy pregnancy, and even the labour was exciting. In a way I am glad that I didn't know what happened to Sarah until after she was born. At least I have had one happy and carefree pregnancy, and a normal 'worry free' labour. I will never have that again.

We were desperate to get pregnant again, and five months after Sarah was born I discovered that my period was late, so I went to the doctor to do a pregnancy test. It turned out to be positive, but instead of getting really happy about it I just wanted to go back to bed and cry (which I actually did). I was so scared and kept thinking about all the horrible things that could happen to the baby. At first my husband couldn't understand why I wasn't happy being pregnant, but we talked about it and he understood a little better how I felt. I told him that he needed to be happy for both of us until the end of the pregnancy.

At the time when I fell pregnant I was very angry with my obstetrician, so I decided to find a new one. At the first meeting my new obstetrician asked a lot of questions about Sarah's birth and he answered all of our questions. I wasn't one-hundred per-cent happy with his answers but I wasn't expecting him to be able to answer everything to my satisfaction. He was able to confirm a few things, brushed away other things and raised a few more things for me to think and obsess about. But he was very caring and understanding of our situation and he did every-thing he could to make sure we had a happy outcome this time.

Throughout the pregnancy I worried about big and small things and was never relaxed. My husband was sometimes even more worried than I was, possibly because he felt he had no control over the pregnancy, and could do nothing to make it a happy outcome. Every ultrasound would make him happy and relieved for a few days whereas I hated them. I worried for days before each ultrasound and by the time I was in the waiting room, it was so bad that I felt sick to my stomach. After each ultrasound I was very relieved that everything was well but rather than make me happy I felt depressed for a few days.

At the twenty-week ultrasound we made a special request for the ultrasound specialist to investigate the way the umbil-ical cord was attached to the placenta. All the doctors kept telling us how unlikely it was that the same thing would happen again. Even so, we were adamant that the check be done. At least we could be sure that the cord wasn't going to cause the death of another baby. We were relieved to see for ourselves and hear from the ultrasound specialist that the cord was in a perfect condition and attached the way it should be.

One year and two months after Sarah was born our son Liam was born two weeks before his due date. He was in breech position and was delivered by elective caesarean section. When he was pulled out of the womb feet first he managed to inhale some amniotic fluid. A short while after he developed breathing difficulties and was put in an incubator with extra oxygen, and he stayed there for six days. After eight months of worry it was frustrating not to be able to hold and cuddle our precious little boy, and again I was recovering in hospital without a baby to look after. For the first few days we could hardly touch him as even the lightest touch would cause him distress. Three days after he was born we were able to hold him in our arms for the first time, and after ten days we finally brought him home.

Liam's arrival made us so happy; finally it felt like we were a family. Two years and two months after Liam was born, we had another son who we named Mattias. This third pregnancy was easier than the second, but it was still a worry every day.

We think about Sarah every day, what she would look like and what her personality would be. We celebrate her birthday every year and our parents send birthday cards to her, and always give her Christmas presents. It is very important to us that she is remembered by others. It makes her more real. There is nothing that makes me happier than when family and friends bring her up in everyday conversation. She is important in other people's lives and not just ours.

I love her so much and miss her more and more every day.

Annika Enell

Our Shattered Dream

❧

Where do you start to tell the life of someone who never lived? A life so dear and precious that your whole world will never be the same again.

So I will begin at a time way before my babies were even thought about, as you need to understand how they came into being and how losing one was ever so tragic.

In 1986, at the tender age of twenty-three, I was diagnosed with an inflammatory bowel disease (IBD) called ulcerative colitis (UC). Coincidentally, my elder sister (by two years) suffered from Crohn's disease, which is another IBD. UC is a very physically debilitating disease of the large intestine and is usually well managed with drugs and diet. I won't go into the terrible nitty-gritty of what I had to actually experience, but the time came when the drugs were no longer able to keep me going. So in 1989 I had surgery to remove my diseased large intestine, and had an ileostomy fashioned. This means I do not have normal bowel function; my insides have been bypassed and this means my poo is collected into a bag on my abdomen, which I empty when necessary. This surgery in effect cured me of UC. I soon went back to work, and being married only since 1985, Carlo (my dear husband) and I thought about the prospect of adding to our family.

I did all the relevant pre-pregnancy checks deemed correct at the time, for instance rubella immunisation status. My GP stated that he could see no reason why a pregnancy could not be achieved. He later came to eat those words. We tried for about eight months with no success and were then referred to an IVF specialist.

In April 1992 I had an extensive laparoscopic investigation, which confirmed my worst fears that I was indeed infertile with blocked tubes and my only chance of a baby was with IVF treatment. I cried solidly for a day. IVF was expensive, had a long waiting list and very poor success rates. I would never have a baby. I resigned myself to a childless existence and I was determined to get on with life, whatever that meant to us now.

The following week I was back to see the specialist for a review, and he said that I had the best kind of infertility, as all the other reproductive bits were working. There was no reason why IVF would not work for us.

There was no waiting list, it was not that expensive (well, it cost hundreds per cycle, not the $10,000 I had envisaged) and success rates were quoted at about twenty-five per cent. So we began the long depressing merry-go-round that is IVF, the very next month in fact. I read everything I could lay my hands on about the subject. I told only my parents and a few close friends. I secretly dreamed that we would be the magical couple who got pregnant on the first cycle, but how wrong I was.

The hormone drugs made me so ill that I could hardly drive in to the clinic to get the next dose; I could not sleep, could not eat and came up in large welts at the injection sites. But I had to persevere. They said that the result would make it all worthwhile, although I couldn't see any further than the following day's needle. So after many internal ultrasounds (Yuk!), blood tests and more hormones (Yuk. Yuk!!), I was knocked out to retrieve about a dozen precious eggs. Sounds a lot, but after fertilisation we had five embryos. I shouldn't complain – some people don't even get an egg retrieval – but after all that suffering I wasn't prepared to go through too many cycles to get a result. Implantation was three days later. It was fingers crossed, or to be more exact, legs crossed!

Three embryos were frozen, hopefully to be used at a much later date. From the time of embryo transfer to the time of the 'pregnancy' blood test is the worst two weeks you could ever wait. I always wished I could find out the next day, and so have saved myself all the unnecessary hope and grief I experienced. Of course, the first cycle didn't work. And neither did the next one using the frozen embryos. Another stimulated cycle ensued, during which a single, childless girlfriend drove me for the injections a couple of times. She could not fathom why I would put myself through all this pain. I told her I had to, as at least this way I would have tried all avenues open to me.

It was about this time that I was having serious trouble with my rear end. To cut a long story short, I needed to have an abdomino-perineal excision to relieve an oozing tail. I had been putting this off for a while to concentrate on our fertility experiment, but seeing as we were not having any success I thought it was best done now. Our frozen babies could wait. So I had another lot of surgery that my wonderful surgeon could not 'guarantee' would work, but at least it was over with and healing. About six months later it was healed, only five years after the first crater was dug!

By this time it was mid-1994, and my original gynaecologist wondered what was happening in the baby-making department. I told him we had really given up all hope but would use the few embryos left before deciding on our next journey.

So it was back to IVF and that wonderful merry-go-round that is so hard to get off.

On our first cycle back I had a positive blood test. Joy of joys. We danced, we hugged, we cried, we laughed, we called everyone we knew. It was a miracle and we were going to be parents. How naive I was! The next nine months were a nightmare, but I can't tell you here about that dramatic time. All I can say is our precious Dean was born with relatively no problems in July 1995.

When Dean was two years old, we began on IVF again. The thought of those horrible drugs was enough to put anyone off, but I was determined that he was not going to be an only child. There were still two frozen embryos in storage, and I hoped that they would do the trick. But this time round things took even longer, even though the yucky drugs had been replaced with more user-friendly ones. I was able to inject myself, or get Carlo to do it, and I was not incapacitated at all. This is good when you have a toddler in tow. My medical history took a turn for the worse too. I had a blood clot diagnosed in one leg, due to the IVF drugs. So I was on warfarin for six months, meaning I could not even contemplate pregnancy. In early 1998 I had a strangled bowel. This meant another eight months out of the IVF circus. I was becoming very disillusioned and forlorn at the prospect of never having another baby, as I was now thirty-seven years old. Dean was soon to start kinder and what would I do with my lonesome self?

In February 2000 I finally received the news that I had waited so long to hear: 'Your pregnancy test is positive.'

Dean was very excited at becoming a big brother, not that he really knew what that meant. Dad was also excited at the prospect of having another little munchkin to play with. My pregnancy progressed with relative normality. The only major hiccup was the emergence of another deep-vein thrombosis. This time I was sent to a maternity specialist. I attended the appointments with happiness instead of nervousness. I slowly prepared the new arrival's things, kept in storage for so long. We also moved house to accommodate our growing family, getting a wonderful backyard for our kids to play in, cubby-house, jungle gym and all. What more could I have asked for?

At both the thirty-two- and thirty-four-week visits to the obstetrician, he commented on the large baby I was having. I didn't pay much attention as I was definitely eating better this pregnancy.

By the thirty-sixth week, I had just about had enough. I felt like a giant elephant and could not get any comfort from sitting or lying down. I hung on knowing that it would soon be over and my little bundle of blue/pink joy would make it all worthwhile.

My appointment on 11 October was no different to the others, except I mentioned to the doctor that I wasn't feeling as much movement as previously. He ordered an ultrasound to be on the safe side, arranged my final appointment for the following week and left me with his nurses, who thankfully arranged the ultrasound for right then. I waddled across the road, and proceeded to the radiology department where I had been so often for my IVF scans for the last eight years.

As soon as I was in having the scan and the doctor was talking to me, I suddenly became aware that all was not going well when she said, 'Have you been well this pregnancy?'

What did that mean? I did not do pregnancy well at all. No, I have not been feeling too good.

'I'm sorry to have to tell you that your baby is very sick and not likely to survive.'

Surely you have made a mistake. I think I need to get a second opinion. Get a paediatrician; I'm certain that my baby can be saved. This is not happening to me. You have got it all wrong. Do the scan again, *please*.

So I was put in the little room where the patients go that have had bad news. 'Ring your husband.'

'I can't, can you please do it?'

It seems like an eternity before Carlo arrives, but it is only about twenty minutes. I hope he doesn't blame me. Maybe the doctors can make it all better; they do really amazing stuff for babies now.

So together we go back to see the doctor who can't give me any good news. She still has no hope for us; she has contacted our doctor, who is writing a referral to another doctor at the hospital. We need to go over the road and get it. I cannot bring myself to face the doctor who has let me down so badly. Carlo is quickly back with the letter. An appointment awaits us tomorrow. I can't understand why I have to go to another hospital from the one where precious Dean was born. My baby can't be born in a different hospital with a different doctor.

We drive home in silence. We collect Dean from kinder. I can't face anyone; Carlo tells the kinder teacher what is about to happen to us. He tells me she cried and sends her love. I have only known her for about two months.

Dean knows something is wrong, but I cannot speak. I cannot breathe. I am in a daze, stunned, dying slowly from a broken heart. I cook tea but can't eat. I go to bed but cannot sleep. I get up and look in the nursery that my baby will not see. I look at the clothes that my baby will not wear. I cry into the blankets knitted by Nanna, who will not hold my baby. Maybe tomorrow this new doctor will tell me everything is going to be all right.

Thursday 12 October is my girlfriend's birthday. She has no children but treats Dean like a nephew. I can't bring myself to ring her; I don't want to ruin her day. Mine is already ruined.

Carlo calls some elderly friends, who will look after Dean all day. He tells them that things do not look good, and that I am too upset to speak to anyone.

We arrive at the hospital and there are lots of pregnant mums, but only one is crying. The doctor in charge of perinatal medicine is very sorry for us. We are now in his hands. He asks if we want to do genetic testing. This will help us find the cause of our baby's terrible deformity: hydrocephalus. We can also have amniocentesis; our baby can't be harmed by this invasive procedure now. I feel totally out of control. Luckily Carlo is on the ball. He asks what, why and when questions.

I am so in shock I wish someone would offer me a stiff drink. The doctor has said I can go home after the amnio and wait for labour to start. *What!* I scream inside. I can't possibly have a vaginal delivery, not after all my medical history.

Carlo tells him that this is a mistake, I need to have a caesarean, to ring my usual doctor as he knows my history. But this doctor is adamant; there is no need for unnecessary surgery. Carlo is even more adamant; speak to our doctor, my wife cannot give birth naturally. After a short while the specialist returns to tell us that a caesarean will happen, but doesn't admit he was wrong.

Soon the amniocentesis is done. As I wait to go home I start to cramp. I now don't want to go home. I can't possibly go home to face a nursery with no baby. An hour later I'm still cramping and am asked if I want to stay. Luckily I have an overnight bag in the car, just in case. There seems to be some difficulty in finding a bed. Carlo tells the clerk that we have private cover. What is the delay? But I will have to go to the public hospital.

By teatime a bed still hasn't been found and I get wheeled to a delivery suite. At least I now know what a labour ward looks like.

The next morning a bed materialises. It turns out that this is a special bed, located on a ward where other mothers have lost their babies or their sick babies are in another hospital. It is a large double bed in a larger than normal single room, right outside the nurses' station. I am sure this is so they can keep an eye on me.

I have a phone and decide I need to ring people and let them know the latest. My friend, who had her birthday yesterday, drops everything and is at my side within half an hour. My dear friend Anne says she will ring all who need to be told. I give her my address book to write out names and numbers.

The doctor arrives. I tell him that Anne is not leaving. We hear the news that there is not a definite finding from the amniocentsis. He asks if I want to hear for a heartbeat. No, I think that will be too painful. He says I can go home for the weekend. I decline. How can I face my 'new' empty house? I want to hide here until I recover. Carlo arrives; Dean has been farmed out again. I can't bear the thought of seeing him; he reminds me of everything I won't have when my baby is born.

Later my mum arrives; some of her friends have brought her in to see me. She is staying with them and is reliant on their transport. They do not know what to say so they say nothing with any meaning. My mum hugs me, but is not sure that she has a role here. One says it is very much like a hotel here. Well, if it is so nice you stay here. The 'friends' leave us alone. I tell her everything I know to date. She is from an era when things like this were not talked about. Dead babies were not held, named, loved or grieved for. How can another mother not feel the pain I am feeling. Or can she too be in shock and not be able to ask for help?

The doctor returns when Carlo arrives. He is having trouble getting a surgeon to assist (with the possibility of bowel trouble in mind!). Any operation will not take place before next week. Am I sure that I don't want to go home? I am being selfish I know, but I can't face home yet. The nurses on duty are very, very nice. They are empathetic and explain everything until they are sure we know what will happen. They tell us that we are allowed to do anything we want with our baby, even take it home if we want. There seems so much information to digest, but we try to make the best choices possible.

The nurses ask if we want anyone contacted, any religious person or social worker. I wish to speak to pastoral care. All my experience has not prepared me for this, but I know that pastoral care can arrange and/or organise certain things. We meet a lovely person who talks us through even more things we can do for our baby. She talks about what-ifs, because for us there are now two choices: what we want if our baby is born alive, and what to do if our baby is stillborn.

In the afternoon the doctor is back to tell us that surgery is planned for Monday afternoon. He asks if I want to hear the baby's heartbeat. No, I don't want to know if my baby is dead or alive, but in my heart I do know that there is no life inside of me anymore. But I do wish this baby could be out of here right now. I've had enough.

The evening brings more friends. A lot of people don't want to see me. It might upset me, they say. More like it will upset them and gosh, how would they cope with that? Now is not the time for self-pity, is it? Am I not allowed to feel just a little bitter and resentful? I put out orders for no flowers; there is no way I want to stay in this room looking like a florist shop.

By Monday, 16 October I am not sure if I want this day to pass. We complete all the necessary medical forms and are asked some questions no parents want to hear. 'Do you want your baby resuscitated?' 'Do you want your baby put on life support?' and 'Do you want your baby to be christened as soon as possible after birth if delivered alive?'

As the afternoon arrives I begin to be filled with trepidation and anxiety. Would I like my baby alive for even a short time, or would it be better to never hear it cry? 'What names are you choosing for your baby?'

My mum has arrived by this time, and she is upset to know that she will not get to know grandchild number eight. We have not really talked; we have spoken about a lot of things but she hasn't asked how I am feeling or if there is anything she can do for me.

I am wheeled off to theatre and she slowly lets go of my hand. Maybe she's glad it is not me that is dying. We are met by a huge team of people, and of course the specialist, who now checks for a heartbeat. There is not a baby heartbeat to be found. I have killed my own baby and nothing or nobody can make me believe otherwise. There is no time to think of the whys and what-ifs as half of the medical staff quickly disappear (I mean, how many do you need to deliver a dead baby?) and a spinal block is quickly inserted. The tears roll down my face and then I begin to hiccup from all the crying. I try to calm down as I know that there could be trouble if I hiccup in the midst of a surgical incision. It seems like an eternity, but it is really only a few minutes before I hear, 'It's a girl.'

My daughter, Sarah Elizabeth, is whisked off to the side so that her large head can be drained of fluid, and made a bit more presentable. She is swaddled and given to me to hold. I can only wonder if my little girl would have been beautiful in another life. She has lovely brown hair but unfortunately her eyes are not really open and I guess they could have been brown, just like mine. She has been dead for maybe two or three days, and I have a moment when I think that, yes, a mother always knows. Her dad has a cuddle next. Is he wondering what a daddy's girl she could have been? This experience is not like when my precious Dean was born. We were the centre of attention, all the staff was congratulating us and we were thanking the medical staff. Now I am alone in my thoughts and there is nothing to console me. Sarah will never breathe, she won't cry out for me and she won't be coming home with us. The morphine is quickly pumped up and after being stitched back together I get wheeled back to the room of gloom.

My mum, Anne and the pastoral care person are waiting. There is now no rush for a naming ceremony, which will happen tomorrow. We are left alone and we cuddle our daughter. I am too drugged-up to be in any emotional or physical pain. Sarah can stay in my room overnight but I have been told that deterioration will be quicker in a warm room. So with a final kiss and cuddle she is taken from me, to 'sleep' in a much colder place until I can have more time with her tomorrow. After more morphine and sleeping pills I soon succumb to a fitful sleep.

The next day Anne brings an unexpected present for Sarah. She always seems to know what to do in a crisis and this is no exception. My daughter gets a lovely little pink teddy bear, a beautiful hand-knitted matinee jacket with matching bonnet and a small gold guardian angel. I could not have asked for a better friend.

Sarah's naming ceremony is attended by only a handful of people: Carlo and me, Anne, Sarah's nanna and two of her friends. I am still in zombie land and don't even shed a tear. But the pastoral care person shares Sarah with the room as if she does matter to all. We take photos and film the event, probably more for Dean than for anyone else.

I stay in hospital until the following Sunday, the 22nd. I am reluctant to go home. Anne has offered to clean out the nursery, but I know that is a job I will get around to when I am ready, if at all. I have prolonged my stay to also recover physically, as I know that I am in no mental state to cope with running a household. I don't get a lot of visitors, to be honest. Less than a dozen would be pretty accurate. Most of them do not want to hold or look at Sarah, and I wouldn't force them. A surprise guest is our specialist, who doesn't have a lot to say and certainly doesn't apologise for anything that occurred. Obviously he thinks a lawsuit is imminent and the less said the better. A 'sorry' may have healed my broken heart a lot quicker.

We have a lot of time with Sarah, and take what we think are plenty of photos but in fact later will prove to be less than thirty. Dean visits and we take a 'family' snap but it appears staged and he looks like he is trying to get away from his sister. We have a photo of the three Elizabeths: Sarah, me and her nanna. We have her hand- and footprints and a lock of hair. We don't get to give her a bath as her skin was peeling, and I have a horrible thought that I may hurt her. We have a beautiful pink/purple shawl given to us by the hospital and we have lots of other mementos from her stay in hospital, but there are not enough. I have kept lots of things that would not mean much to anyone but me, but they are the only tangible things that tell me Sarah was here.

No-one can ever tell you about the awful, terrible physical pain you will feel when your baby dies. My arms ached for Sarah. I started to cuddle one of Dean's teddies, then when my mum asked if there was anything I would like, I suggested she buy me a cuddly teddy bear. It made me feel less empty.

Sarah's funeral was held on Friday, 27 October. Carlo had courageously made many of the arrangements whilst I was still in hospital. We had a wonderful celebrant, who had great empathy for us as she had lost an adult son. We chose all the songs for our daughter's short ceremony. A friend wrote a poem, which she very graciously gave to Sarah, and tried to read it through a well of tears at the service. Angel dust was sprinkled by many, many friends who turned up that day. At the end we released balloons to signify the letting-go of our high-flying angel. Sarah had a lovely day and I know that we did all the 'right' things. My only real regret is that I did not take a photo of her coffin, although I have kept all the small tokens that were there at her funeral. We requested no flowers but that the money be donated to SANDS instead.

This is when my friendship with SANDS began. I proudly read the next SANDS newsletter with news of all the wonderful donations made in Sarah's name. I hoped that her small contribution could help ease the pain in someone else's tragedy. I also thought how wonderful it would be if SANDS had no reason to exist, wishful thinking I know, but what a dream to behold.

In writing this story I have had to think back to those dark days when life just seemed too hard to bear and I ached for someone I could never replace. Certainly time has healed some of those terrible pains, but not a day goes by when I don't think of my daughter, Sarah.

Susan Iovenitti

Losing You

❧

The day had finally arrived when my husband and I would be able to see our baby on a 3-D ultrasound. I was about twenty weeks pregnant. I took my two young boys to the ultrasound centre and met my husband there. I had so far had a normal pregnancy. The doctor told us that he would begin using a 2-D ultrasound and move onto the 3-D one later.

We never did see our baby using the 3-D ultrasound.

Watching the screen, things were fine at first. Then the doctor told us that there could be something wrong with his hands and feet. It was unreal. How could something be wrong with my baby?

The doctor told us that he was sleeping and we needed him to move so that he could have a better look at him. We were asked to have a walk around and come back in a little while for another scan. We walked out of the centre and down the street to a cafe to have some food. I was sitting at the table eating my lunch and couldn't stop quiet tears from falling. It was as if I were living in a bad dream.

The second ultrasound confirmed the doctor's initial concerns and he gave me an immediate amniocentesis. My husband drove home with the two boys. I drove the other car with tears streaming down my face the whole way home.

We were booked in at hospital for another ultrasound in a week's time. That was a very difficult week for me. I felt very low. Strangely, by the end of the week we had some faint hope that things would be okay. Maybe whatever our baby had could be fixed.

After about three hours waiting for our turn we finally had our ultrasound. Unfortunately it was confirmed that our baby had adducted thumbs and club feet.

We were referred immediately to a genetic specialist that same day. While waiting for our appointment, I couldn't stop the tears as I sat at the hospital cafe with my husband. After seeing the genetic specialist and talking to my obstetrician, it was recommended that we terminate the pregnancy in a week's time. The geneticist said the baby had arthrogryposis. Arthrogryposis is a term describing the presence of multiple joint contractures at birth. A contracture is a limitation in the range of motion of a joint. In the 'classic' case of arthrogryposis, hands, wrists, elbows, shoulders, hips, feet and knees are affected. In the more severe cases, nearly every body joint may be involved including the jaw and spine.

My face felt numb. I felt a real depth of sadness. Smiles were far, far away. The rest of the world was distant. Tears would come in waves, unexpected and suddenly. There was an overwhelming feeling of sadness and grief. There were sleepless nights and constant thoughts. My hands and fingers were always tense. I would forget what day it was.

That week was one of the longest weeks in my life. I had many periods of crying. I told my young sons that the baby was sick. I wouldn't go anywhere public as I was obviously pregnant and I didn't want people saying, 'When are you due?' I couldn't look at myself in the mirror as I would see my pregnant bump. I wore large maternity black tops and a blue jacket every day. The blue jacket hid the bump very well. I couldn't talk much with anyone except my wonderful husband. I didn't answer many phone calls. I borrowed lots of books from the library about people with similar experiences. I read fiction books all day to enable myself to forget the pain for at least some time. I watched movies to escape the pain. I didn't feel hungry so I didn't feel like making breakfast, lunch or dinner for the family. Luckily my husband took over in this area. I stopped taking pregnancy vitamin tablets. I threw away all my pregnancy magazines and hid away my pregnancy books. My home was my cave.

The inevitable day finally came. We went to the maternity ward at a private hospital to have our baby. I was induced. My husband was with me all the time. We spent the night in the delivery ward. My husband slept in a recliner chair. Finally, in the early hours of the morning I started getting contractions. I was given morphine to help but I still felt extreme pain.

In the early hours of the morning our baby was stillborn.

As soon as he was born it was like the end of something. My husband and I cried together for a long time. The midwives left us to be alone together.

Presently I was able to meet our baby. He was wrapped up and looked very peaceful. He was a beautiful little baby who reminded me of his two brothers; like a full-term baby only smaller. Wonderful people from Bayside Church had provided a little suit and blanket for our baby to wear. We were given a little booklet with his birth details and tiny hand- and foot-prints. He was 29 centimetres long.

We had a little funeral for our baby at a cemetery in the outer suburbs, with a little section for babies, overlooking cow pastures and gum trees.

All the professional people involved with our situation are to be highly praised. Our obstetrician and the midwives were very caring and empathetic. One midwife who delivered our baby was so comforting and shared her own loss from many years ago. Somehow it was helpful to hear her experience and made me feel that she understood what we were going through.

She gave us a plant that is now growing in our garden. It's called Yesterday, Today and Tomorrow.

About six months later we learnt that our baby probably had amyoplasia that has no known cause. Amyoplasia is a generalised lack in the newborn of muscular development and growth, with contracture and deformity at most joints. It is the most common form of arthrogryposis. It is characterised by replacement of skeletal muscle by dense fibrous tissue and fat.

We now have a gorgeous new baby boy whom our two older boys adore.

In our house there lies a beautiful wooden memory chest, full of our memories of our little baby boy whom we lost too soon.

Ann

Byron our Star who was Stillborn but Still Born

We were over the moon when we got the result that we were expecting our first baby in November 2005. Our very much planned and wanted baby was now a reality. Oh, how much our little one was going to change our lives! Little did we know that it would be a different type of change in life.

I went into hospital on my birthday in September as I was tired of the pains I had had for a week and I felt my belly was getting big really quickly. I was told by my obstetrician I was 'having a big baby'. The pains were ligaments stretching. I protested but was corrected and sent off home again with sleeping tablets and painkillers.

That weekend I went interstate for a party. That Saturday morning I had a tiny, tiny amount of blood. We had just learnt of this possibly occurring so decided we would keep an eye on things and go to the function. Once there, I started getting back pains and remember saying jokingly, 'I hope I'm not in labour!' It turns out I was having pre-labour pains that stopped by themselves.

On Monday, 26 September at thirty-two and a half weeks' gestation, we took ourselves back to hospital due to severe pains. The baby was monitored and we were told the baby was fine, though a little sluggish. However, they were worried about the pain I was getting as it was an irritable uterus (wanting to go into labour), so I was admitted for observation.

Later that afternoon a midwife came to me and she wanted

the baby to be monitored again as she was not happy about the morning's trace. Lying there I remember listening to the faint little heartbeat. That little heartbeat was not a healthy one and all of a sudden we were rushed into an emergency as the baby was in distress and I needed an emergency caesarean.

I was transported to another hospital. I remember looking out the ambulance window and looking out at the clouds. We had just had a huge storm and the sun was setting. The clouds were so dark but above them they turned pinky red, and along the top of them was this incredible golden line as the sun was appearing behind the clouds. It was a strange moment because I remember thinking it looked like the heavens had opened. I think that's when our little baby left this earthly world.

Upon arrival, with my husband by my side, a quick ultrasound showed my fears. I noticed his little heart had stopped beating. It was like a still photo.

I said to the doctor, 'His heart?'

He asked me to cough and nothing changed. He looked at me and said, 'I'm sorry. Your baby is dead.'

I pleaded with them to do something but they told me it was too late. It was confirmed our baby had died. I remember everyone's faces looking over me – another still image in my head. Adam and I were left in the room alone, just hugging. I could hear them arguing with the doctors from the other hospital saying I should have been here that morning.

When the doctor came back into the room, they explained that I was bleeding internally, causing the pain and causing my tummy to be so big. I was thirty-two weeks pregnant but measured to be around thirty-seven weeks. I *was* too big. I pleaded to have a caesarean as I wanted all this to be over, but they said it was all too risky and I had to be induced for a natural labour. I had to wait.

As I was left to be induced my husband and I were left to take in what had happened. This was when our lives changed. We were caught in this time warp where we were dealing with death and birth, the apparent start in life, fused together. We were now proud parents of a dead baby and not a living one. Here we were living what should never be lived. Only a few know all too well this isolated feeling.

The next day my waters were broken. I remember just before they were doing it someone came into the room and said the blood was ready for a transfusion. When my waters broke it was just amniotic fluid. No blood. I wasn't bleeding internally. I did however have an abnormal amount of amniotic fluid.

After a quick labour on the 27th of September our stillborn son Byron Terrence was delivered. He was so beautiful, just like his father, but we could not bring him home. We left in a state of helplessness and numbness, empty-handed and weak after a near full-term pregnancy.

Byron was so perfect. I remember how soft his skin was. He had these incredible bright, sky-blue eyes and dark-brown curly hair. We got hand- and footprints, we bathed him, we clothed him in a white wishing-star suit, we held him and we told him all the things that we were meant to have a lifetime to tell him. I sang him all the songs I was going to sing to him. He was just so perfect.

I was struck down after the birth with a severe uterine infection which caused temperature and blood pressure to rise to dangerous levels. I wasn't allowed to move too much. Due to the fact I am allergic to penicillin they tried me on amoxycillin, which I also had a severe reaction to. My chest tightened up and I couldn't breathe. I remember thinking, Adam has lost Byron and now he is losing me. I had images at the time of being resuscitated on a table, a real life-flashing-before-my-eyes experience. I was so exhausted and ill I was worried I wasn't going to get out in time for Byron's funeral on Friday. The infection ended up lasting seven weeks and I was constantly in and out of hospital.

Leaving the hospital on the Thursday after having Byron with us for just over two days is no doubt the hardest thing I have had to do in my life. To get up and do what feels like turning your back on your baby or abandoning your baby, and then walk out past the postnatal ward where all these mothers with their crying babies are oblivious to the fact that I, Erin Nugent, am now a mother and our baby existed, was just heartwrenching. Never would I wish anyone to ever have to experience that.

The funeral came and went. I don't think I had any feeling then. I remember it clearly, but the days were just flying past and the state of shock remained still deeply imbedded into us. We miss him so much!

We had to wait six weeks to find out why our little one died. When we got the results of Byron's pathology (we didn't have an autopsy) from our new doctor, it was explained Byron's death was caused by the following conditons:

My placenta had stopped growing at some point after the eighteen-week ultrasound. But it did, however, remain feeding Byron properly as he was the perfect size for a thirty-two week old baby. Most of these cases end with small babies.

Minimal bleeding behind the placenta (placental abruption), which was causing the severe pains I was getting. This was not a cause of death either but a contributing factor.

Byron's side of the placenta had thrombosis (clots). They believe the thrombosis was in his throat or stomach, causing a blockage to occur. This caused the next contributing cause . . .

Polyhydraminous, meaning the amniotic fluid was not being

271

processed and was building up around the baby. The reason I got so big: I *was* blowing out.

They found an overgrowth of the virus group B streptococcus in my uterus, which was the infection I was also battling at the time.

The first hospital told me they did not find it necessary to test for group B strep even though it is found in thirty per cent of women, and the most severe cases are stillbirth or death after birth. It can be treated by antibiotics during labour.

They believe all of the above were contributing factors and individually should not have been the cause of death. The placenta was still feeding Byron to help him grow normally. The minimal bleeding was not a cause. The thrombosis could have been corrected by surgery, a risky procedure but a possible one at that. The group B streptococcus is treatable by an intravenous antibiotic, which I should have received at the first hospital had I been properly tested for it. Unfortunatly the polyhydraminous caused too much stress on little Byron. If the polyhydraminous was detected earlier Byron could have been delivered before it caused too much stress. But the fact he was not well with the above caused him to stress really easily. Unfortunately it was all too much for Byron. I was told he would have just fallen asleep.

As time went on and reality and the world started to turn again, life was now to us a desperate attempt for us to have Byron recognised as having existed. No-one but a few saw our beautiful son. We found people finding it difficult to grasp the fact that we had a baby. We were showing people photos but I don't think it was truly computing. It was not their fault; it was just how it was. We are also currently living in a society where we either talk about our babies who have passed away or maintain the attitude of society many years ago when we do not talk about them as 'it is easier'. No-one gets over their baby's death. Our choice is to live life with Byron as a huge part of our family.

So soon do people move on, leaving you behind with your depression and grief. I found great comfort in the support offered to me through specialist organistaions. I was part of a group doing a memories book on our special babies so their lives can be remembered. That's right, they lived! It may have been for a short time but the loving movements of our son in my tummy and his reaction to music or his father's touch very much made him living. And real!

It has been two and a bit long exhausting years for our family as the realisation that the pain of losing Byron does not go away. We have learned to live with the pain; it has now become a part of us. It is who we are now. Our Byron's photos hang proudly on our wall and we talk about him every day. Byron is our firstborn and became an older brother to Lachlan Peter in November 2006. We are also now anticipating the arrival of our third baby, another child who will be proud of her firstborn brother.

Our lives have changed again as parents – not as first-time parents but to being the proud parents of our two children leading two very different existences: one is in the stars to watch over his little brother, and one to hopefully live life to the fullest being the proud younger brother. Byron has made a huge imprint on our lives – he was stillborn, but to us he was still born.

Postscript: Keira Val Nugent was born happy and healthy, March 2008.

Erin Nugent

God's Lent Children

Our first two babies, both girls, were born healthy in 1965 and 1967. Then in 1969 I had a stillborn baby girl at twenty-six weeks, born in the breech position. My legs and feet had swollen badly during the pregnancy and I spent some time in hospital prior to having her, as things did not appear to be going too well. I had an x-ray at some point after being admitted and the baby was born soon after this. I soon learned that it was stillborn although I can't remember how. The hospital, believing I would be upset at being with mothers whose babies had survived, moved me into a room of my own. This isolation made me feel as though I was being punished. When I came out of hospital, I went to the cemetery where my baby was buried in the public sector. We paid a fee for the burial but there was no sign that a funeral had taken place. In fact, I was disturbed to notice that rubbish had been thrown on the site from over the fence. I went to the cemetery office to complain and I believe the woman said that this sometimes happened. I was very distressed for about a year following her birth and was not able to put any of it out of my mind.

Nobody mentioned the birth to me except for one unfortunate woman who saw me wheeling my youngest live daughter in a pram and made a dive at me, saying, 'Let me see the baby.' I explained to her about the little girl being stillborn and I think I was as embarrassed as she was because of her mistake. I felt as though I had leprosy with people avoiding me and saying nothing.

When a fourth pregnancy in 1970 also resulted in a stillborn daughter at thirty-two weeks, I could not understand why the doctor said nothing to me at the birth, so I asked him if the baby had been born. He replied, 'Yes, but not live.' I was again placed in a single room and as a result I asked to go home straightaway, which I did, on the second day. My memories of the previous burial prevented me asking about burial proceedings. I often wondered where the baby was buried, particularly over the next months, but was never told.

These two stillbirths had made me appreciate my two lovely living girls and I realised that it was really a privilege to have a live baby, where once I'd taken it for granted. My arms yearned to hold an infant and I spoke to a very caring doctor at the hospital about adoption, perhaps of a baby with some disability, since adoption was becoming very difficult. He was very supportive and said he would help me. He made the point that I shouldn't have to take a baby with a disability after having two stillbirths. We did not follow through with this idea and put it on hold for the time being.

I was pregnant again in 1971 and booked in at another hospital for the birth, but unfortunately this baby, a boy, was stillborn, at full term. Although I was very uncertain about the progress throughout the pregnancy, the hospital had not given me to understand there was anything wrong.

However, in time I knew that there was a problem and took myself into the emergency department. I was still not told that it was going to be another stillbirth, although I was almost certain it was. He was a big baby and I was very aware of his birth. I guess the hospital had not wanted to alarm me when they knew I had to give birth to him. Like my other babies he was born spontaneously. The hospital was full, so I was found a bed in the cancer ward. I was obviously unhappy with my situation. However, placing me in this ward proved to be something of a godsend, as I was forced to think about other people's misfortunes. It was almost Christmas and the Salvation Army came around with small gifts. The hospital spoke to me about the little boy's burial so this time I did not have any doubts as to where he had been interred. No-one mentioned the other births or pregnancies to me; all this was regarded as not happening. The only person who seemed to remember was me!

I decided not to put myself through any more misery and had further tests at the hospital. I eventually discovered that, as well as Rhesus antibodies, I had a rare antibody known as Kell, which my husband carried. (I read in a newspaper some time ago of the death of the obstetric researcher named Kell, after whom this antibody was presumably named.) I was told that I had a 50–50 chance of having a baby with my blood group. Following my second child, I had been immunised for Rhesus antibodies. After each successive birth 50–50 sounded like a reasonable gamble to undertake but of course 'it ain't necessarily so'.

However my next baby, born in 1974, was a lovely little girl with the right blood group, which made up for all the worrying I had done throughout the pregnancy.

Still hoping for a boy baby, I was advised that I was expecting twins in 1977. It was another worrying time when I discovered that both babies were affected with the haemolytic disease that had doomed my other three babies. The hospital performed amniocentesis tests which only served to worry me more, especially since I observed blood in the needle as it was withdrawn. A second amniocentesis was even more distressing. The doctor expressed that his ideal plan would be to bring one twin into the world and leave the other in the uterus. This was politically unpopular at that time. It was decided that the babies' blood was to be totally transfused with the right blood group once they were born.

During my six weeks as an in-patient, I made a soft toy for the babies and a mosaic clown which I still have at home. As I had been in hospital for some time, I was granted weekend leave so went home. Arriving back at the hospital, my waters broke and a varicosity in the birth area broke, so I was taken to the labour ward, where I remained for two days. Although I had no contractions, the doctor insisted on the twins being born naturally, so eventually they were delivered with forceps, although there was a team standing by to perform a caesarean. There was also staff waiting to do the babies' transfusions.

I lost consciousness after the first twin, a girl, was born. When I regained consciousness, I glanced up to see her with blood dripping down, all over her. In my mind, I resigned myself to two girls. I can't remember anything else until someone told me the second twin was a boy. I was too tired to show much enthusiasm. I also had some hours to wait, as the nurses were insisting there could be a third child. It was some time before they decided they were wrong, when the placenta presented.

As I drifted off to sleep, I was woken to be told that they were halfway through transfusing the girl baby. This was done through the baby's umbilicus. I was also told when they'd completed her transfusion. Two other messages were delivered regarding the boy's transfusion. Although I was exhausted by this time, I have to say that they did a wonderful job. They had originally determined to send me to another hospital when the babies were born but they must have changed their minds.

I had a picture of my two and a half year old on my bedside table and the doctor remarked on her being a lovely little girl. The doctor was from the Indian culture, and told my son's fortune, saying that he would be an executive because he had been born with his nose in the air. He was a thumb-sucker from birth and she had ideas of preventing him from doing this. Later, we would tease him saying he would be sucking his thumb when his executive phones were ringing!

This was an exciting time after all the previous disappointments. The twins were a month premature but still five and six pounds in weight. So it wasn't long before I was able to take the girl home, leaving her brother to stay in for a bit longer, being fed through a tube. I came in to bring milk to feed my little boy.

Since this time, my family have grown and we now have seven grandchildren.

Sadly, our beautiful twin boy Paul died aged twenty-six. We the family love and miss him every day. The name we had chosen for him, I did not give to my previous son as I knew I could never use it again. Although the name I chose for the first son was also a good name, I always felt rather guilty about not giving him our first choice.

When Paul died, I wanted to memorialise all four of my children and I set about trying to find where the second of the stillborn infants was buried. All of my efforts proved futile. I tried the Registry of Births and Deaths, as well as several undertakers. I was told by one funeral parlour that there was a funeral strike in 1970 and babies were buried interstate. However, I could not find any further information about this, despite contacting the two major political parties. I feel as though I will have to resign myself to not knowing where my second stillborn girl is buried. I noticed that undertakers tended to bury infant children, in those days, as 'Baby' followed by the family surname.

I miss all my departed children and particularly my grown son. We need to tell them of our love continually and to appreciate them while they are still here.

Christine Gamble

My Three Beautiful Babies

❧

RJ – 21 June 2003 – eleven weeks
Piper Jane – 6 January 2005 – sixteen weeks
Aiden – 20 March 2005 – seven weeks

It has taken me a year and half to put pen to paper. The pain has been just too enormous to deal with. I think I'm ready now to tell my story. Reading other people's stories has helped me enormously over the past year and a half. It's sad to know that there are many other people out there that have had to deal with the worst kind of sadness. It's heartening to know that there are people you can talk to and, more importantly, people that will listen!

RJ

I have three living children: Jordan eight, Keane seven, and Tayla four months. I found out I was pregnant a little over three years ago with what was meant to be our third child. This baby was a surprise, much like my two older children. I was stunned but happy. Unfortunately my husband was not. We argued for a couple of weeks about the financial problems another baby would cause. I went off to work, as usual.

One day at lunchtime I had severe cramping. I called my husband to say that I needed him to take me to the hospital. He was too busy so I took myself off to hospital. The next day I was sent home to see my doctor. He ordered the usual blood tests and rest. Sitting alone each day for two weeks thinking about whether this baby would live or not was extremely draining. At about eleven weeks the baby was born at home. I didn't know what to do with the foetus. I was confused and ended up flushing it down the toilet. I wish I had known what it was and I would have kept it to be tested for abnormalities. I called our baby RJ; my initials and my husband's. I was devastated. My husband was less than supportive. He eventually saw my pain for what it was, and we discussed having a planned pregnancy. We decided to wait a year before we tried.

Piper Jane

After planning for pregnancy eighteen months later, I found out I was pregnant again virtually straightaway! We were over the moon. I had the nuchal scan at eleven weeks and four days. She wriggled so much that the scan took a lot longer than it should have. She was such an active little thing. At around fourteen weeks my baby kicked for the first time. I was elated! For the next two weeks I didn't feel my baby kick at all. My stomach seemed to stop developing. Every night I lay in bed waiting for that elusive kick. I poked and prodded my abdomen looking for a sign. I had my four-month check-up just after the new year. I had been feeling off and decided to leave work early to get some rest. I saw my nurse and she attempted to find the baby's heartbeat. She couldn't. She reassured me that my doctor would probably find it straightaway. My heart began to sink. My doctor couldn't find a heartbeat either. He took me into his office to have a mini ultrasound. I took one look at my baby and knew immediately that she had died. She was curled up in the foetal position and there was no bleep for the heartbeat. His comment was, 'I'm sending you to radiology. Their equipment is better than mine. I hope I'm wrong.' I felt numb. The radiographer confirmed that my baby girl had died. She died around Christmas Day; this would have been the time I felt her kick for the first and last time. I felt alone and an overwhelming feeling of sadness came over me that has never left me.

My doctor gave me the option of going straight to hospital or waiting it out. I found out at 4.00 pm that she had died. I desperately wanted to see my baby so I opted to go straight to the hospital. I was in hospital two hours later discussing funerals and autopsies. The hospital staff were compassionate and kind. One midwife in particular was extremely kind to me. She stayed behind an extra three hours to make sure that I was okay. Meanwhile my husband went out driving to think and left his mother to talk to me. It was the last thing I needed. I asked that she not come, but she insisted. I needed my husband. My water broke at 5.30 am. I was so delirious that I didn't realise what had happened. I fell back to sleep until 6.30 am. I got out of bed to go to the bathroom and she was born without a whimper or a whisper. I stood at the side of my bed looking at my husband who had returned and fallen asleep on the couch. I contemplated waking him. I decided against it and rang the bell for the midwife instead. My husband eventually woke up with all the commotion. He couldn't look at her at first. All he could do was cry.

I asked the midwife what sex she was. The midwife initially thought that she was a boy. I called her Aiden John.

She was so tiny I could hold her in the palm of my hand. A perfectly formed little life! I spent five hours holding her, touching her and looking into her beautiful blue eyes. I held her tiny hand between my fingers. I watched her deteriorate before my eyes. I told the midwife to take her away so the doctors had a good chance of finding out why she died. What a thing to have to think about.

The naming of Piper

The day I was told that Piper had died my husband was supposed to drive interstate with his dad to buy a boat. I suggested that we should still go. The fact that Piper had died changed nothing, so off we went. While I was away in Queensland I found out that during the autopsy the mortician found her uterus, therefore my little boy was actually a little girl. I immediately called her Piper Jane. Piper because it's a name I couldn't get out of my head the whole time I was pregnant with her. Jane is my middle name. I figured that I was the only one that had real connection with her.

While interstate trying to mourn the loss of my baby I was told of a complaint from a family member regarding the name of our baby. Apparently her name was already 'reserved' unknown to me, and causing tension.

After all the arguments and yelling, my older children don't feel comfortable talking about their sister. I think this is really sad. My husband tried to convince me to change the name from Piper to Ashlee to try and keep the peace. I reluctantly agreed. When I collected my baby's ashes from the mortuary the paperwork and coffin had 'Piper', and still have. She was meant to be called Piper.

I made the arrangements for the cremation, collection and burial of my daughter. On the morning of the funeral I went to a little shop where they sell trinkets, fairy wings and the like. I found a lovely pink glass candle and a beautiful butterfly made out of coloured stockings and wire. I took my items to the counter to pay. The lady who served me asked if they were for my older daughter that was with me. I told her what they were for; she waved me away not wanting to take my money. I will never forget her unselfish act of kindness.

The day of the funeral was dry and hot. Only a small handful of very close friends and family were in attendance. I requested that everyone who attended wear bright, colourful clothes – no black allowed! We released brightly coloured balloons and I read out a letter to my beautiful baby girl. My kids put some sand on her tiny white coffin. It was one of the most painful weeks of my entire life. It was compounded by uncaring family members.

Aiden

A couple of months later I fell pregnant again. This time the baby didn't last very long at all. I called this baby Aiden. I was still numb from my previous experience. When I found out I was pregnant I had a feeling that there was a problem. I think we tried too soon to fall pregnant and my body just wasn't ready. My husband and I went off to the doctor for the umpteenth time. He suggested some genetic testing.

Tayla Jane Ashleigh

While we were waiting for the results of the genetic blood tests I fell pregnant again. I don't seem to have any trouble conceiving. It was an anxious nine months. I took myself off to the hospital many times because I was scared my baby had died. The staff knew me quite well by the time my baby was ready to be born. I had been in and out of the hospital for three years. They all knew my history and understood my nervousness. On 2 February 2006 I had a healthy baby girl. I called her Tayla Jane Ashleigh.

I spent five days in hospital. The nurse knew something was wrong when I didn't want to go home. She queried me for a while and found out that I was scared of going home. I was worried that I would lose this baby too. I felt safe at the hospital. I was scared of loving this child just in case something bad happened. I was trying to protect myself from more pain. I decided to go to the cemetery where Piper was buried to make peace with my feelings. I realised that it was okay to love Tayla. It didn't mean that I didn't love Piper any less. I have allowed myself to fall in love with my baby. I cry sometimes for the babies I have lost and I cry because I love the babies I have. I have three beautiful children that I love very much, and I have three beautiful babies that watch over their siblings.

When Tayla was born I wanted to call her Ashleigh. I thought that I could change the spelling and it would be okay. I felt like a part of Piper had come back to me. My daughter and my husband said that I couldn't call her Ashleigh because it might upset the family member.

I am blessed with three beautiful children. I have been so busy racing around being a career woman that I lost sight of what is important. My kids are my life. They are my legacy. They are worthwhile. I now want to devote my time to my family. I have learned some very difficult lessons: not to squander the opportunity life has given me, and to love my family and appreciate the time I have with them. I won't be making that mistake ever again. If my husband agrees I want to have a house full of healthy happy children.

Rebecca Graeber

Mary and Josephine:
Fifty-five Years Later

❧

November 1952: Pregnant? Confirmed!

April 1953: 'Your BP is up a bit. Do you have anyone you prefer to see? I think it would be good to get a specialist check, to be on the safe side.'

My army husband was stationed in New South Wales, but my family lived in Melbourne. It seemed the simplest answer was for me to go to my parents', and seek expert advice among our medical friends.

I was advised to rest as much as possible, and avoid stress. This was agreeable as by now I was the recipient of remarks about beached whales and though I tried to laugh, for me it was not funny. I was tired and lethargic and was told to stay in bed. My brother (MD) came to see me and contacted the specialist who came to check me out. Pre-eclampsia was mentioned, but not decisive. My booking for the hospital was checked, and possible early admission noted.

On 29 May 1953 an ambulance took me to the hospital. I was not very aware of the trip, but I do remember I asked them to turn off the siren, as I felt hugely embarrassed by this. On arrival the remark I remember to this day was 'she's on the nest', which I considered most demeaning. There was no severe pain, just a feeling of unreality.

After the birth of a stillborn baby it was discovered there were twins. It was only the sound of a feeble cry that alerted the staff, and of course everything was done to save the tiny second baby. As they had arrived nearly three months early, the chances of survival were impossible in 1953, and after two hours the twins were together again and all hope was gone. A wonderful nun had asked me if I would like to have the babies christened, so the first one was named Josephine (St Joseph being the patron saint of little children) and the second was named Mary (after Mary the mother of Jesus). This has been a lasting comfort to me, even now when I am over eighty years old. I am eternally grateful to this wonderful nun, who showed such insight and compassion.

After leaving hospital, apart from feeling bereft and stunned, as well as physically in limbo, I was unbelievably embarrassed by the change in my bust measurement: previously thirty-four inches, now a whopping forty-four inches, as well as being very painful. I had no preparation for this, nor any advice as to the way to deal with it. The result was trying to hide it with tight bandages and keeping out of sight. I did not want even my parents to see me as I was so ashamed. There was a visit by a government nurse from some department who asked questions about the babies but did not seem to have time to talk. It was a brief visit of interest in statistics only, and so I did not get the chance to ask her about my ballooning bosom. Literally, I went into hiding and gradually this improved, though in later years some discomfort would recur: probably cysts or whatever.

Eventually I went to the cemetery to visit the grave. To my shocked disbelief I found the twins were with other babies who had not lived, and the best I could do was to leave the flowers not just for our twins but 'for all the little ones resting here'. It was a comfort to mentally gather them all together, and give them all my love. Such was my state of mind, I would gladly have stayed there forever.

Eventually I returned to New South Wales. A whole new

set of problems: everyone being careful, and avoiding questions, while trying to help. I felt a total failure and tried to 'get over it', attempting to act as if life was as before. Of course this was impossible, and it was easier to avoid people than to meet them. I took refuge in volunteering to do night duty at the local bush nursing hospital, which gave the excuse that I was sleeping during the daytime. The mental vacuum was beyond description, but magically a solution arrived.

My husband was sent to a course in Sydney and I had the option of staying where I was, or taking over the care of someone who had been discharged from hospital after a stroke. His wife was nervous about trying to look after him, and I was glad to be asked to help. For nearly three months my mind and concern was for these two people, who treated me kindly and with generosity, being with them at all times, as if I were a friend, while taking care of my charge.

While there I took the opportunity to check my situation regarding the pre-eclampsia, for any future pregnancy. I was advised it was possibly the twin pregnancy which may have been the trigger. We decided to wait a while, at least a year as my blood pressure was still up a bit, before we thought about it again.

Life regained some semblance of normality, though I felt a smouldering sense of resentment that my brother and sister both had familes, and they were younger! And my husband was an only child, which made me feel I had let the side down badly.

Late 1954: Pregnant! This time nothing would go wrong. All the signs were good. At three months my blood pressure was slightly higher than normal. This was put down to my being over-anxious. We were back home, and feeling pleased and confident, but I had a queasy feeling which bothered me. I decided to take no chances, and bullied my husband into getting leave to take me to Sydney to see the super-specialist. I was admitted to hospital for observation and it was discovered, to my dismay, that it was an ectopic pregnancy and early surgery was the only answer.

After surgery we were told it was unlikely we would have a successful pregnancy, as apart from my blood pressure going haywire again, we were of incompatible blood groups and a 'D factor problem' is involved. This was never fully explained, and we were advised to consider adoption.

Knowing how much my husband and his mother wanted a son and heir, I offered my husband a divorce. I was also getting thoroughly disenchanted with this marriage business, and was quite prepared to join a convent, or resume my single life. To my great surprise and relief he was upset, and declared it would be worth a thought to help some unfortunate children, as he did not want a divorce in any case, and we could do what we could in that way.

To go quickly to our resolution: we did adopt two boys, and later a baby girl. They filled the vacuum for us and gave our lives meaning and a goal, as well as the joys and sorrows every family has as the years go by. We are proud of their achievements, and now have the joy of seeing *their* children blossom to adulthood.

It is when we care for others we discover true happiness, and our horizons expand beyond our wildest dreams. I am sure Josephine and Mary will agree.

Margaret May